Contemporary Issues and Insights of the Anthropology of North East India

Contemporary Issues and Insights of the Anthropology of North East India

Editors

Haobijam Vokendro
Milonjyoti Borgohain

KALPAZ

First Published, 2020
Published by

Kalpaz Publications
C-30, Satyawati Nagar,
Delhi – 110052
Ph.: 011-47034999, 9811692060
www.kalpazpublications.com
E-mail: kalpaz@hotmail.com

Printed at: Gyan Press, Delhi

Cataloging in Publication Data—DK
Courtesy: D.K. Agencies (P) Ltd. <docinfo@dkagencies.com>

Contemporary issues and insights of the anthropology of North East India / editors, Dr. Haobijam Vokendro, Milonjyoti Borgohain.
pages cm
Contributed articles.
ISBN 9789353242947

1. Ethnology—India, Northeastern. 2. India, Northeastern—Ethnic relations. 3. India, Northeastern—Social life and customs. I. Vokendro, Haobijam, editor. II. Borgohain, Milonjyoti, 1985- editor.

LCC GN635.I4C66 2020 | DDC 306.09541 23

Contents

Foreword

It gives me immense pleasure to write the foreword of the Book edited by Professor Haobijam Vokendro and Milonjyoti Borgohain. As is suggested by the title *Contemporary Issues and Insights of Anthropology of North East India*, the present edited book by Professor Haobijam Vokendro and Milonjyoti Borgohain is a compendium of contemporary cultures of North East India. Scholars from various parts of North East region presented their research findings on various ethnographic accounts of different ethnic groups of the region particularly, Assam, Arunachal and Manipur. Contemporary issues of topics on birth, marriage, death, dress and ornaments, indigenous issues, gender, media and e-learning methods are all encompassed in the book. I sincerely appreciate all the contributors and thankful to the editors for their motivation particularly to talented budding scholars. The pains and hard efforts of the editors in making such a volume come into this final stage is really worth to encourage and appreciate. I strongly believe that the book will fill up certain gaps on the study of anthropology of north east. I congratulate the editors for their dedication for the publication of this volume.

Prof. Kh. Narendra Singh
Prof and Head
Department of Anthropology
Assam University (A Central University), Diphu Campus
Diphu--782462
Assam

Editorial

The North East India comprising eight states is located in the easternmost part of India bordering to Bhutan, China, Nepal, Bangladesh and Myanmar and is home to different variegated tribes, flora and fauna. Each tribe has its own unique culture, history and identity. Despite of such heterogeneous nature of these tribes, there are similarities in the overall culture of these tribes. That's why one may paradoxically described the tribes in North East India as 'homogenous yet heterogeneous'.

Because of such homogenous-heterogeneous paradox, different socio-cultural issues are similar in broad but different if one looks into minutely. Insurgency problems for instance, if look up from historical perspective, the rivals of the indigenous people against the British forces during colonial period before India got independence and insurgency in post-independence in some states like Manipur, Nagaland and Assam show similar history of inclusion into the Indian dominion. Likewise, food, drink, fairs and festivals, dance and music, indigenous knowledge such as ethno medicinal practices, magico-religious beliefs and practices and folklores, conversion into Christianity and so many such aspects of the tribes of North East India show similarity. However, if one minutely examines, there are so many other aspects of dissimilarities. For instance, the Meitei of Manipur which is not included in the scheduled tribe list of the North East India has a very highly rich culture, history and indigenous scripts unlike any other tribes of North East India. Unlike the tribes of the whole North East India, from 18th century, these group of people, the Meiteis were converted into Hinduism with the then royal patronage of the king. Therefore, the paradox homogenous-heterogeneous on the culture and history of the people of North East India which started from past history still show the similarity at present. That's why we can say that the contemporary problems, issues and challenges of the people of the

North East India shows homogenous-heterogeneous paradox. It is in this backdrop, the volume attempts to discern different socio-cultural practices of the ethnic people of North East India with special focus to ethnic people of Assam.

The papers contributed in this volume by different scholars of the region consist of different themes of papers from general ethnographical perspectives of different cultural practices. In her paper on marital customs and tradition of ex tea garden community of Kanjikhowa tea state, Dibrugarh in Assam, Panna Garg describes different marital practices of mate choices viz., Christian and Hindu marriage. This paper is followed by the paper of Nabajit Kumar and Dhanmani who pick up a segment of Karbi women in order to find out their status in society by examining demographic status and participation in decision making. In the next paper, Nilmani describes the roles of members and the rules to follow of different office bearers of different village organizations of Bhogpur Karbi village in Kamrup district of Assam. The next paper describes the *rites de passage* of Sonowal Kachari women during pregnancy and at birth. Purabi also describes different rituals at different stages of the crises rites. The next paper on sustainable traditional pest management technique of Sonowal Kachari farmers by Ripunjoy and *et. al* documents ten different sustainable traditional pest management practices. On the similar theme on indigenous knowledge, Franky Boro, shows and documented the rich cultural heritage of hand woven traditional dress types, patterns and designs and their uses in different socio-cultural practices.

Dritiman and Antoni describes the important socio-cultural functions of bead in Adi society. They mention the significance of bead as ornamentation and symbol of status and identity, source of compensation and fines, in ritual and as therapy, in marriage and as property of inheritance and as barter and an alternative to money. The same tribe but in different issues, Kasimang Moyong attempt to throw light on the changing socio-cultural lives of the Adis.

In their paper 'The folklore of the Kom Tribe of Manipur with special reference to their music, dance and festivals' Romio and Sunita describe in detail the indigenous music, dance and festivals of one of the tribes of Manipur, the 'Kom tribe'.

A unique paper of different theme of Ratna Tayeng attempts to examine on the inter-state boundary dispute between Assam and

Arunachal which is still an unsettling issue despite many attempts to solve. The paper tries to locate the issue in its historical context and seeks to highlight the nature and extent of the territorial problems of the Assam-Arunachal border basing on historical and empirical observations.

Padi Hana, in his paper 'Urbanization and its Implication in Tribal Society of Apatani' looks into the different factors of urbanization vis a vis modernization in different socio economic and cultural lives of the people Sotechand and B.P. Sharma endevour to examine the homestay tourism in the picturesque Ziro valley in Arunachal Pradesh. The scholars find out the reasons of preferences of homestay by the tourist, their experiences, problems and suggestive measures to improve for such tourism.

Chayantika in her paper 'Growth and development of adult women among the Ahom of Dhemaji district, Assam describes the growth and development profiles of Ahom adult women by measuring ten anthropometric parameters. She also measures blood pressure of the women and categorized into different findings.

The next paper on cephalic index and head shape of the Deoris of Dhemaji, Assam, Milon and vokendro randomly pick up a sample of 100, 50 males and 50 females in the age group 18-50 years and analyzed and classified into different head types

The paper 'Virtual Accelerator: A Review of Current Issues' presents the key aspects of virtual accelerator and its role in entrepreneurship education. Gautam and Sunil attempt to examine the role of virtual accelerator in catering service to diverse potential entrepreneurs especially those living in remote and isolated state of Arunachal Pradesh. They also discussed the best practices of pedagogical approaches in local and global virtual accelerators.

Rabikanta in his paper 'Religious Experiences within the Meitei context of Manipur towards Sustainability of Plant Resources' mentions some of the significant plants used by the Meiteis of Manipur for their socio-religious beliefs and practices. He also mentions the different plants associated with the seven clans of the Meiteis. A comparison of the number of plants used in crisis rites of the Meitei indigenous worshippers and Meitei hindus is also mentioned.

Binarani in her paper on 'Economic culture, entrepreneurship and women empowerment: Manipur chapter' discusses the role of Manipuri women in agricultural sector, in handlooms and handicraft sectors, in Ima Market and small scale entrepreneurship. She mentions the significant contribution of Manipuri women in such sectors. She opines that for empowering women it's not only to make a better law to help women for empowerment but to support from all sections of people in society.

Premchandra attempts a field based research work on the Kidana people of Tripura in his paper, 'Koratpa: The 'First Death' Ritual of Meitei Kritanias (Kidna) of Tripura'. He interprets the matrix of death ritual from structural and functionalistic perspective and tries to locate the performance of ritual from different theoretical explanations.

Benny and Sotechand attempts a paper on e-learning in Arunachal Pradesh during Covid 19 lockdown period so as to examine the challenges associated with the adoption of e-learning, the extent and attitudes of learners and learned. They also suggested some practical measures to improve the learning and teaching strategy on such critical period of lockdown.

Yaipharemba in his paper on Covid 19 looks into the impact of the pandemic among the north easterners working in different parts of India. He addresses different issues on the security of lives of these migrants.

Sunil and Gautam in a joint paper on the theme of changing media education frown at the mushrooming of media institutions. The scholars stress on their importance of designing a pedagogical approach based on ground reality and context instead of 'a size fit all approach'.

Tiatemjen Tzudir in a unique paper of traditional and indigenous knowledge on iron smelting of the early Konyak and Khiamniungan Nagas attempts to show different metallurgical technologies of professional iron smelters. The scholar strongly feels that the cultural practice of iron smelting and stone clay mold casting are on the verge of extinction among the Konyak and Khiamniungan Naga regions of Nagaland.

The volume will serve useful resources for general reader, students, scholars and researchers in North East Studies. The contents and opinions of the papers are solely answerable by the respective author(s) of the paper.

List of Contributors

Panna Garg: Former Guest assistant professor Rajiv Gandhi University

Nabajit Kumar Das: Regional Medical Research Center, ICMR, Dibrugarh, Assam.

Dhanmani Medhi: Guest Lecturer, Department of Anthropology, Gauhati University, Assam. Correspondence to: Dhanmani Medhi, Email: medhi.dhanmoni900@gmail.com

Nilamani Das: Ex-student, Department of Anthropology Gauhati University

Purabi Gogoi: Research Scholar Department of Anthropology, Assam University, Diphu Campus.

Dr. Ripunjoy Sonowal: Independent Researcher (Alumnus, Dept. of Anthropology, Dibrugarh University), Dibrugarh - 786003, Assam, E-mail: ripunjoy.anth@gmail.com

Somnath Sonowal: Research Scholars, Department of Anthropology, Dibrugarh University, Dibrugarh - 786004, Assam, E-mail: somsz1314@gmail.com

Nilutpal Sonowal: Research Scholars, Department of Anthropology, Dibrugarh University, Dibrugarh - 786004, Assam, E-mail: nilutpalsonowal555@gmail.com

Mayurtrishna Hazarika: Research Scholars, Department of Anthropology, Dibrugarh University, Dibrugarh - 786004, Assam, E-mail: mayurtrishna89@gmail.com

Franky Boro: Department of Anthropology, North Eastern Hill University, Shillong Email: franky.boro@gmail.com

Dhritiman Sarma: Asst Professor Department of Anthropology Rajiv Gandhi University Arunachal Pradesh

Antoni Perme: Research Scholar Department of Anthropology Rajiv Gandhi University Arunachal Pradesh

Kasimang Moyong: Asst. Guest Prof, Dept of Sociology RGU Arunachal Pradesh

Dr. L. Romeo Singh: Asst. Prof. Dept. of Anthropology, Moreh College, Moreh

Ksh. Sunita Devi: Asst. Prof. Dept. of Anthropology, Thambal Marik College, Oinam

Dr. Ratna Tayeng: Assistant Professor, Department of Anthropology, Dera Natung Government College, Itanagar Email: ratnatayeng@dngc.ac.in

Dr. Padi Hana: Guest Asst Prof Dept of Sociology, RGU

Dr. K. Sotechand: Asst. Professor, RGU

Mr. B.P. Sarma Barua: Asst Professor, RGU

Chayanika Hazarika: Department of Anthropology Gogamukh College, Assam

Milonjyoti Borgohain: Assistant Professor, Moridhal College, Dhemaji Assam Anthropology Department

Prof. H. Vokendro S.: HoD, Anthropology Rajiv Gandhi University Arunachal Pradesh

Gautam Huidrom: Assistant Professor, *Department* of Management Rajiv Gandhi University Rono Hills, Doimukh Arunachal Pradesh -791112 Email: ghuidrom@gmail.com

Sunil Koijam: Assistant Professor Department of Mass Communication Rajiv Gandhi University Email: skoijam@gmail.com

Thiyam Rabikanta Singh: Associate Professor, D.M. College of Science, Imphal, trabikanta123@gmail.com

Dr. Th. Binarani Devi: Principal, Ideal Girls' College, Imphal, Manipur State Email-thokchom2009@gmail.com

Kshetrimayum Premchandra: Assistant Professor Department of English Tripura University Suryamaninagar – 799022, Tripura Email-kshetrisingh@tripurauniv.in

Mr. Benny Sebastian: Research Scholar, Department of Management, RGU,

Dr. K. Sotechand: Asst Professor, Department of Management RGU

Dr Ingudam Yaipharemba Singh: Assistant Professor Department of National Security Studies

Sunil Koijam: Assistant Professor Department of Mass Communication Rajiv Gandhi University, Arunachal Pradesh Email: skoijam@gmail.com

Gautam Huidrom: Assistant Professor Department of Management Rajiv Gandhi University, Arunachal Pradesh Email: ghuidrom@gmail.com

Tiatemjen Tzudir: PhD Scholar, Dept of History and Archaeology, Kohima, Meriema campus, Nagaland University

1

Marital customs and traditions: Ex tea garden community of Kanjikhowa tea estate, Chabua, Dibrugarh district, Assam

— *Panna Garg*

Introduction

From the second half of 19th centuries with the opening of tea gardens in many parts of Assam people of various tribal groups like Munda, Ho, Kharia, Gond, Santhal, Savara, Oraon of Bihar, Orissa, Madhya Pradesh etc. migrated into Assam to work in the tea gardens. Most of these tribes are Australoid in origin. They are mainly found in the district of Darang, Sonitpur, Nagaon, Jorhat, Golaghat, Dibrugarh, Kachar, Hailakandi, Karimganj, Tinsukia and almost all the districts of Assam. In this paper an attempt is made to throw light on a part of the socio-cultural aspect of the Ex Tea Garden Labour Community of Kanjikhowa Tea Estate of Bishmile, Chabua of Dibrugarh District, Assam. The community is heterogeneous showing existence of both Christian and Hindu people. It is seen that with the increased influence of factors like modernisation, westernisation, urbanisation, etc. social institutions are changing rapidly. Here, emphasis is made on the institution of marriage of the particular study area.

Objectives

The main objectives of the paper are to-

(I) Find out marital practices prevalent in the society
(II) Make a comparison of the Christian and Hindu marital practices
(III) Find out the existence of culture survival

Methodology

As it is not possible for oneself to be restricted within only one particular method or technique during the data collection, various techniques were simultaneously applied depending on the nature of enquiry. Methods and techniques implied in the field were observation, interview (structured and unstructured), collective of concrete cases and informal discussion. Basing on the nature of data, some relevant persons and sources were selected. The key informants were the line headman, pastor of the church, and some newly married couples. The doubtful data were cross-checked.

The description and interpretation have been done depending upon the etic and emic nature of data.

Findings and analysis

The institution of marriage has widely been studied in the context of different societies. But here, the population which is studied is heterogeneous in itself. So a kind of intra group variation in the practices is actually noticed. Marital practices of the area were analysed from a comparative angle as the area was inhabited by both Christian and Hindu people. Some of the practices were however common among them.

Marriage customs of Christians in the studied area

Among the Christians, the girls' age at marriage is usually18-20 years and boys' age at marriage is 22-30 years. They practise tribe endogamy and at the same time clan exogamy is also found.

At first the groom's family goes to the bride's house to see her and after some days the groom's family proceeds and gives positive message

to the bride's house. Thus the marriage is finalised. Thereafter in a specific day both the family meets and perform a ceremony called '*pindhan*'. Here, the groom's family gives saree (a single piece cloth worn by Indian woman), blouse (upper garment worn by Indian woman), and other important clothes to the bride. Then both the family take bride (in full make up) and groom to the church. In the presence of the public of the village, they perform a ritual called '*lotapani*'. Here, mango leaves are kept in a bell metal pot filled by water and the pot is kept on a bell metal disc. This lotapani is known as their first marriage. They keep mango leaves in the pot as a sign of longitivity of the marriage bond as mango leaves are seen throughout the whole year. At first the girl takes the disc and comes three steps towards the groom and gives the disc to him. By this she admits that the marriage is not done forcefully. She walks forward as a sign of willingness. Then again she comes three steps back. Now the groom walks three steps towards the bride and pass the disc to her showing that he is also agree for the relationship. The same is done three times. After this public decide to marry them. Boy's family serves local sweets like '*Muriladu*', '*Bundiyaladu*' etc to the people.

Again there is a ceremony performed by them as '*Jurooni*'. Here, grooms family gives the girl all the cloths, ornaments and cosmetics that are to be worn by her in the day of marriage. Marriage is done by among them in the month of January. They don't perform marriage ceremony before Christmas as the father does not give blessings before 25th December. Again schools and other organisations remain close in the month of January. So, for the convenience of the local people, they perform marriage in January.

But three week before marriage, bride and groom have to go to the church in Tinsukia for 15 days. There both will be trained by nun and pastors about the ways of living. The aspects of the training are - how to respect and pray God, how to respect each other, how to rare child and how to maintain family. Two- three days are taken to discuss per aspect. The training is done from 8 a.m. to 3 p.m. in the Tinsukia church.

Thereafter, in the month of January, in the presence of the relatives and village people, bride and groom accept each other as husband and wife. The father conducts the marriage. In the day before marriage the bride and groom do not take meal and in the day of marriage both take bath in the church. Bride wears their traditional or white saari or gown, crown in head, silver Christ chain in the neck and no cosmetic is used by her. Groom wears white pant, shirt, coat and white or red rose in the pocket. They both take oath in front of the father, pastor and the public and signs in the marriage paper. The parents or the pastor also sign as witness. Then the groom puts vermillion on the bride's forehead. They are Christians. But their root was Hindu. So, they kept the custom of putting vermillion in girl's forehead. Here we noticed cultural survival. The bride also puts vermillion on the groom's forehead as a sign of acceptance.

After the marriage is conducted, boy's family cleans the house with bucket of water and bride and groom enter the house. While entering, aged lady of the house takes '*aarti*' of the couple with a bell metal disc taking rice as a sign of inviting Lakshmi, incense stick and earthen lamp as a sign of fertilisation. Then bride and groom's feet are washed with water kept in bell metal pot, the remaining water is thrown in the roof of the house. Thereafter, the elder brother of the groom takes the bride and enters the household. But after that very day, they maintain avoidance relation. A pandal is made on the same day and in the presence of public and father of the church all the relatives and newly married couple prays. There, the bride's brother gives his sister's hand in the groom's hand. In the evening, the couple with relatives and other village people perform dance, song, etc. They perform *jhumoor* dance (their traditional dance) and *sadri* songs (their traditional songs), *madol* and *nagada* are the musical instruments. After these the couple can live together. After 9 days the couple goes to bride's mother's house for food. They also bring sweets, *roti*, etc to the bride's family. They stay there for one or more nights.

Widow/ widower remarriage is found among these people but one cannot marry if the counterpart is alive. In case of extra marital affair, public informs the father of the church. Father held meeting for the solution of the issue. If the accused deny obeying the public's decision, he will be excluded from the Christian society. Dowry and bride price is absent among them. They give everything to the couple like a gift. Consanguineous marriage is punishable among them. If it happens they exclude the couple from Christian society.

Usually patrilocal residence was found in them. But existence of matrilocal residence was also found there.

In their society, if marriage is done by mutual consent which is enacted by elopement, the parents first try to know whether the two are of the same tribe/caste or not. Again they try to enquire whether the clan/gotra exogamy is maintained or not. If not, they exclude the girl or the boy from their society. But if the relationship is acceptable to them, then the two families arrange their marriage and thus the couple become socially approved.

Hindu marriage customs and rituals in the studied area

Caste endogamy and gotra exogamy is found in their society. At first the groom's family goes to the bride's family in search of her. They may also be helped by a middleman. After some days groom's family pass the positive message to the bride's family via the middleman or by themselves. After that bride's family comes to boy's house and finalise marriage in the presence of priest. The priest deals with calendar (panjika) and finalise the dates and times (mahurat) of marriage ceremonies. Thereafter, in a specific day, boy's family goes to bride's house to give her saree and other important ornaments, cosmetics, etc. thus they arrange the marriage. After this function called 'jurooni' no other boy's family can see the girl for marriage.

As these people are Hindu and they worship Shiva, so they do not perform marriage ceremony before *Shivratri* i.e. in falgun. They believe that if they marry after the marriage of Shiva- Parvati, they will live happily. So particularly in the Assamese month of *Sot* and *Bohag*, i.e. March and April respectively, marriages are held among them. As decided earlier by the priest, on a specific day ring ceremony as well as marriage is done. Seven days before the marriage water is brought in earthen pot. In the day of marriage the bride and groom are taken to "Charıalı". They have to seat their on a banana leaf. Five old women will put rice, battle nut, mango leaf, basal leaf on the bride/groom's head and pour the water on them. Bride and groom cannot take their meal for 2-3 days before marriage. In the evening time, ring ceremony is done in the presence of village people. This ring is of silver. They do not use gold ornaments. After this, a pit is dug by the people and water is poured on it. In the mud both the rings are hidden by the relatives.

The couple have to find out the rings, they believe that one who wins will rule in the house. At 12 o' clock at night, the marriage rituals starts and it goes on till 2 o' clock. Girl's family has to pay priest's fees. Bride and groom's father and mother serve *hariya* (local drink) to the aged people. They perform *hoom (firing)*, *saatphere* (seven time move), *mangalsutra* (sacred chain), *sindur* (vermillion), etc. After the rituals are done, both bride and groom break their fast. After the marriage is done, the bride-groom along with their relatives and village people dance and song "*Jhumur*". They use instrument like "*madol*". While entering the house the younger brother of the groom takes the bride and enters. After 2-3 days the couple couple goes to the girl's home. They stay there for one or more day.

In case of marriage by elopement, if the tribe endogamy is found and clan exogamy is found the family arrange marriage of the couple. If not, they are excluded from the society.

Widow/ widower remarriage is found among these people but one cannot marry if the counterpart is alive.

Conclusion

Thus the studied group shows a kind of intra group variation of practices regarding the institution of marriage. This heterogeneity is actually a product of co-habitation of both tribe and caste people as well as both Hindu and Christian people.

Bibliography

A Committee of Royal Anthropological Institute of Great Britain and Ireland, 1954 (Reprint), *Notes and Queries on Anthropology*, Routledge and Kegan Paul Ltd., London.

Harlalka, S.S., (1975), *Tea Garden Labourers in Assam*, Dhubri People's Publishing House.

Kar, R.K., (1975), Unity in Diversity: A note on the Adaptation of a Tribe in a Tea Industry, *Bulletin, Department of Anthropology, Dibrugarh University, and Vol.4:11*-15.

Kothari, C.R., 2009, *Research Methodology: Methods and Techniques* (second revised edition), New Age International Pvt. Ltd., New Delhi

Minna, H., 2012, *Adivasi Duniya*, National Book Trust, New Delhi.

Sengupta Sarthak, 2009, *The Tea Labourers of North East India*, Mittal Publication, New Delhi (India)

2

Role of Karbi Women in Decision Making: A Study from Dimoria Block

— *Nabajit Kumar Das, Dhanmani Medhi*

Introduction

Women empowerment may be the key slogan for every government since independence, but the findings of a government report show women still lag way behind men in having a say in decision making and in their participation in economic activity. In most societies, women have a low social status and low level of autonomy, so they have considerably a small role in decision making at household level. Several reports show a positive relation between autonomy of women and their role in decision making at household level. Women decision making authority was clearly related to the context in which they live, as urban women had more roles in decision making at household level but women lived in rural setting were not having active role in decision making.[1]

The Universal Declaration of Human Rights states that everyone has the right to take part in the Government of his/her country.[2] The empowerment and autonomy of women and the improvement of women's social, economic and political status is essential for the achievement of both transparent and accountable government and administration and sustainable development in all areas of life. The power relations that prevent women from leading fulfilling lives operate at many levels of society, from the most personal to the highly public. Achieving the goal of equal participation of women and men in decision-making will provide a balance that more accurately reflects the composition of society and is needed in order to strengthen democracy and promote its proper functioning. Equality in political decision-making performs a leverage function without which it is highly unlikely that a real integration of the equality dimension in government policy-making is feasible. In this respect, women's equal participation in political life plays a pivotal role in the general process of the advancement of women. Women's equal participation in decision-making is not only a demand for simple justice or democracy but can also be seen as a necessary condition for women's interests to be taken into account.

Objective

Keeping this view, the present study is an attempt to explore the women's role in decision-making at household level among the Karbi women of Dimoria Block in Assam.

Methodology

For the present study, data have been collected from the women of Dimoria block in Assam. Altogether, 250 women were selected by using purposive sampling procedure. Data on various socio-demographic condition of the household, present age of the women, educational status, occupational, status, monthly income, marital status, age at marriage, role of decision making in different household activities were collected personally by the researcher with the help of detailed structured schedule. Data were subsequently entered into computer by using Microsoft excel. Results were analyzed by using percentage distribution.

Results and discussion

Education is the key that helps in empowering women. Education also undoubtedly contributes to development. It is universally accepted that female literacy rates have a positive impact on health and other social issues such as maternal, newborn and child health, mean age of marriage, awareness of right etc. It raises income, improvements and also enhances the level and magnitude of women participation in various development activities. In the present study literacy rate is found to be 82.8% which is higher as compared to state and national level. In state level, Kerala holds the first rank in the country in female literacy with 91.98%. Rajasthan (52.66%) has recorded the lowest femaleliteracy rate preceded by Bihar (53.33%). In Assam, female literacy is found to be 67.27, which is higher than the national average (65.46%). While, the states and Union territories with female literacy rate below the

Table: 2.1 Socio-economic demographic profile of respondent

Variables	*No (n=259)*	*%*
Educational status		
Illiterate	43	17.20
Primary	63	25.20
Secondary	90	36.00
Higher Secondary	47	18.80
Graduate	7	2.80
Age at Marriage		
Less than 30 years	64	25.60
30- 39 years	140	56.00
40 years & above	46	18.40
Occupational Status		
Govt. Service	5	2.00
Pvt. Service	10	4.00
Business	67	26.80
Homemaker	135	54.00
Labour	33	13.20
Monthly income		
Less than Rs 6000	55	22.00
Rs 6000-Rs 12000	92	36.80
Rs 12000-Rs 18000	75	30.00
Rs 18000 & above	28	11.20
Marital status		
Married	225	90.00
Divorces/ Separated	5	2.00
Widow	20	8.00
Age at marriage		
Less than 18 years	27	10.80
18-25 years	112	44.80
25 years & above	111	44.40

national average (64.46%) are Orissa, Chhattishgarh, Madhya Pradesh, Andhra Pradesh, Arunachal Pradesh, Uttar Pradesh, Jammu and Kashmir, Jharkhand, Bihar and Rajasthan. Most of the women in the study area are found in the age group of 30-39 years (56.00%), followed by 40 years & above (18.40%) and less than 30 years (25.60%). Most of the women are homemaker (54.00%), they do not earn but they support the earners to earn properly. The comparatively dominant occupation is business (26.80%), followed by labour (13.20%) mostly engaged in unorganized sector which is ranging from household workers to construction side workers. Service profession is found to be very less among the study group. Only 4.00% women have engaged in Pvt. sector service while a very least proportion women i.e. 2.00% have govt. job. Regarding wage of working women, the highest (36.80%) is found in Rs 6000-Rs 12000 income group category. The income group of Rs 12000-Rs 18000 share of working women is 30.00 % whereas 22.00% and 11.22% occupied by Less than Rs. 6000 and Rs 18000 & above respectively. Out of 250 respondents, 90.00% women are married, 8.00% women are widow and 2.00% women are either divorced or separated. Regarding the age of marriage of the respondent most of the women fall in the age group of 18-25 years (44.80%) followed by 25 years & above (44.40%) and less than 18 years (10.80%).

NFHS-3 gives data related to whether women have any money of their own and whether they own a bank or savings account which they can alone decide how to use[4]. In India, 45% of women have some money that they can decide how to use. Only 15% of women have a bank or savings account that they themselves use. In the present study, 36.00% of women can decide how to use their money in their household activities, which is found lower than national average and higher than state average (27%).More than one fourth (26%) of women in the present study have their saving account in the bank which is also higher than state (12%) and national (15%) average.

The study reveals that the percentage of the women(69.0%) under study who participated in all the four decisions like 'decision about own health care', 'major household purchases', 'visiting relatives or friends' and 'making purchases for daily household needs' are much better as compared to Assam (60.5%) and national level (36.7%). In the four categories of decision making at household level, it could be seen that the percentage of women is higher than national average but lower than the state average (Figure 2.1).

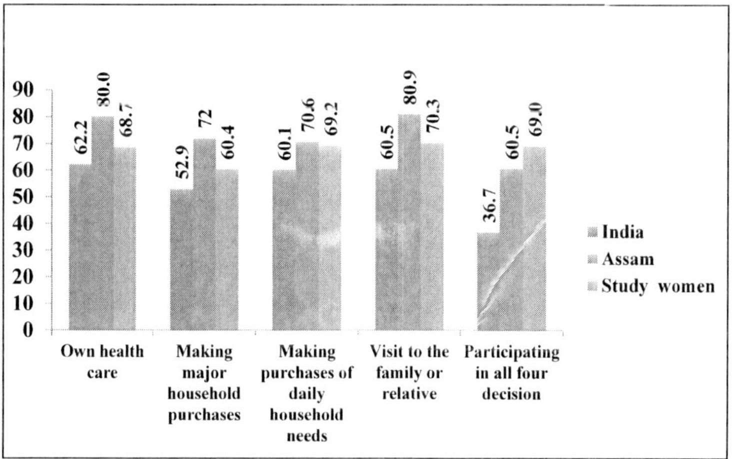

Figure 2.1: Showing the percentage of women take part in four decision making (in %)

Conclusion

Women empowerment may be the key slogan for every government since independence, but the findings of a government report show women still lag way behind men in having a say in decision making and in their participation in economic activity. Women participation in decision making process is required for the betterment of their human right condition. If democracy has to be sustained, the women have to be incorporated at different levels and different processes of decision making. Around the globe, it is seen that women now have more influence over the decisions that affect their lives. Even in the most conservative societies, feminists and gender advocates have been able to forward more equitable policies and outcomes.

In the present study it is seen that literacy rate among the Karbi women is found to be higher than the state and national level. Similarly, the proportion of women taking part in all four household decision making activities is found to be higher than the state and national level.

Percentage of women in decision making in how to use the money is found more than Assam but lower than national level. Percentage of women who have bank accounts is more than Assam and India. Most of the Women in the study are now receiving subsidy from Govt. in purchase of LPG so they need a bank account for deposition of subsidy. This could be the reason of the higher percentage in having their bank accounts. Again, recent initiation of Govt. scheme viz. "Jan Dhan Yojana" by the Govt. Of India also contributed towards opening a bank account particularly by rural women as on in zero balance so that they can open an account. Therefore, Govt. initiatives could be consider as one of the reasons of their empowerment. The impact of Self Help Group (SHG) has also made the women less dependent on others. Thus, self-employment and economic upliftment has played an important role in their empowerment. Government schemes are also contributing factor in the empowerment of women of the study area.

Bibliography

1. Archarya Dev R, et al., Women's autonomy in household decision-making: a demographic study in Nepal, Reproductive Health, 2010; 7: 15.
2. The United Nations Fourth World Conference on Women, United Nation, 1995, Available from http://www.un.org/womenwatch/daw/beijing/platform/decision.htm
3. Government of India, Census of India, Office of the Registrar General and Census Commissioner, India, 2001.
4. National Family Health Survey, India, http://rchiips.org/nfhs.

3

Village organization of the Karbis: a case study on Bhogpur village, Kamrup district, Assam

— *Nilamani Das*

Introduction

Social organizations would consist of the inter-relations between particular types of groups, viz., those groups that make social life possible. The family, school (if any), dormitory, clan and men's club are example of such groups. Groups of people engaged in economic pursuits comprise the economic organization of a tribe; and groups like the Panchayat constitute its political organization. The former sustains, and the latter controls and regulates the social organization. The inter-relation between the three would present the total pattern of tribal organization. Religion and religious groups are both social as well as regulative organization.

North-east India in the context of India occupies a distinctive place due primarily to its geographical, historical, social, cultural, and political features (Ali and Das, 2003). North East India is the Homeland of a large number of ethnic groups who came from different directions at different historical times. These groups are belonging to different racial stocks, speak different languages and have varied socio-cultural traditions. This region of India is a thought provoking example of diversity well reflected in the matrix of socio-cultural traits, which are followed by myriads of distinct aboriginal tribal communities inhabiting in this region. The Karbis, mentioned as the Mikirs in the constitution order, Government of India, constitute an important ethnic group in the hilly areas of present Assam. At present, they are found to inhabit in Karbi Anglong district but some small pockets of Karbis are also found in the North Cachar hills, Kamrup, Pragjyotispur, Nagaon and Sonitpur Districts of Assam. Racially the Karbis belong to the Mongoloid group and linguistically they belong to the Tibeto-Burman group. Agriculture is the Primary occupation of the Karbis. They are patrilineal and patilocal. Animism is the pristine religion of the Karbis.

Area of Study

The area of present study is Bhogpur village of Kamrup Districts, Assam. The village is situated in Khetry area and it is about 2 k.m from NH 37. Karbi People solely inhabit the village.

Methodology

The primary data for the present paper is collected from Bhogpur village situated in Khetry area of Kamrup District Assam. The data is collected by applying various anthropological methods such as Observation, Interview, and Case study as well. Moreover, help of some secondary sources like books, journals, etc. is also undertaken.

Objectives

(a) To study the prevalent village organization of Karbis inhabited in Bhogpur village.

(b) To find out how these village organizations contribute to the society for smooth running and its development.

Result and Discussion

In every society, we found some of village organization that regulates individual personality to run the society well. In North – East India various ethnic groups inhabited in its different parts along with diversified culture. All of these tribes have different types of social organization in the forms of village council, youth dormitories, the family, clan organization, school, religious centre etc. which moulds individual personality to run the society smoothly. All these social organizations prescribe some forms of rules and regulation and various degree of punishment for their violation.

Village officials of Bhogpur village

The village office is head by six persons. Bhogpur village consists of five hamlets. These are Bhodaikuchi, Sitalpur, Deolguri, Pachimkili and Habirgoan. There are five main persons to run each hamlet. But, whole Bhogpur village is administered by one official village Headman (Goan Burha) appointed by Government.

The village headman (*goan burha*)

The whole Bhogpur village is administered under the single 'Headman' or '*Goan Burha*'. *Goan burha* is considered the most powerful person in the village administrative machinery. He is the supreme authority in the village.

Government with the support of villagers appoints the goan burha. For the post of Village Headman S.D.O. of Dimoria sends recommendations to the D.C of Kamrup district, he then appoints the headman. The minimum educational qualification for the post of Goan Burha is H.S.L.C and he can serve the post at the age of adulthood up to the age of his working capacity.

A headman is appointed by hereditary process in this village. If in case, there is no male child of the previous headman or the son of the headman is accused of any criminal case, then the post goes to another person based on eligibility and educational qualification.

He has the power to call a meeting in any instances. His authority is the final one regarding the matters of judgment. It is according to his consent only an accused person is punished. If he wishes, he can also rescue a person found to be guilty.

The village headman who is appointed by government gets Rs 1900 per month as his salary and gets other facilities from the government.

Functions of the village Headman

(1) The village headman is the main person who is responsible for maintaining peace in the village.

(2) In case of sudden instance, which may arise in the village, the village headman has given the authority to inform the police and to take hold of the whole situation.

(3) The village headman helps the Maujadar to get the annual tax from the people.

(4) The village headman helps the Mondal in measurement of the land and if any problem arises in accurate measurement on the land then the village headman helps to solved out the problems.

(5) The village headman acts as the mediator between the government and the village people and helps them to receive the schemes given by the government.

Bangthe

The Bhogpur Village is administered by one official village headman appointed by Government. As mentioned earlier there are five hamlets in Bhogpur village. To run each Hamlet more than one Banghte is appointed by the villagers. Right after the village headman, the 'Bangthe' occupies the second post to be the chief person in the village. The Bangthe plays the main role in maintaining proper rules and regulations and peace in the village.

For the post of the Bangthe, no educational qualification is required instead, he is appointed on hereditary basis.

Functions of the Bangthe

1. Just after the village headman, the Bangthe plays an important role in maintaining peace and serenity in the Hamlet.
2. The Bangthe plays an important role in solving out the problems that arises among the people of the hamlet into which he is appointed.

Reso-bangthe

Another important person in the village is Reso-Bangthe who is appointed just after the post of Bangthe. He can also be termed as the assistant of Bangthe. In case of the absence of the Bangthe, the Reso-Bangthe handles and performs all his duties. The villagers appoint Reso-Bangthe on hereditary basis.

Bisar

Bisar is another important village official of Bhogpur village. His duty is to solve out the problem that may arise in the hamlet or among its people. He punishes the guilty individuals and announces fines regarding ones guilty.

The post of Bisar is also appointed based on heredity.

Kathar

Another post of the village is the Kathar, who acts as a religious persons and helps in performing all the religious rituals of the hamlet. He is appointed on hereditary basis.

Kurkun

Another post of the village is Kurkun. This post is just after the Kathar. His duty is to help the Kathar in performing his religious rituals. He is also appointed on hereditary basis.

Tamuli

This is also an important status among village officials. The function of Tamuli is to distribute betel nut and other items to the invitees during their meetings and social functions.

Rules and regulation of the Bhogpur village and nature of punishment

Social control is the means or method by which behavior pattern of the members can be regulated or controlled. In a society if everyone can do whatever they like then it will be a chaotic and in this way a society cannot run smoothly. Therefore, in every society there are various rules and regulations and also various degree of punishment for their violation.

In Bhogpur village, there are some rules and regulation, which is followed by every person in the village. Marriage between same clan is strictly prohibited. Females are not allowed to enter inside the youth dormitory club. In the community feast, the women are not allowed to take food along with men. They are to partake food separately. Brewing of the rice-beer '*hor*' required in the family is the primary responsibility of the women. All the male members of the village should be present in the ceremonial work of the village.

In Bhogpur village the punishment is mainly concerned with fines. The fine is a pig or money in cash. If a person refuses to pay the fine he is expelled from the village. If anyone marries between the same clan, he would have to pay 9 pigs as a fine. Concern to other guilt like, thief, murder, dacoit etc the people of village take help of nearby police station.

Different organization in the village

Progatihil attmo hahayak goot

One of the important organizations found in Bhogpur village is Progotihil Attmo Hahayak Goot. This is a self-help group mainly confined to women. It was established in the year 2002. The total members of this group are ten (10), including president (one) and Secretary (one) selected by the members of the group. The main aim to organize this self-help group to empower women as well as to fulfill the needs of money in every possible trouble. They organized one meeting in every month; a sum of money is fixed for every member to deposit in the hands of secretary. Some rules and regulation are also associated with this group, which is strictly followed by its members. To take a loan from this group a rate of interest 3% is fixed for the members of the group and for outsiders they take 10% of interest. For the members it is duty to return the loan in time with interest. The member of the group had taken a loan of 50,000 from the government in the year 2006, and they got subsidy of Rs 10,000 from the government. In now days they utilized this money by giving loan to the poor woman with a minimum interest of 2% for rearing broiler, duck, fish pig and also for weaving which give the poor woman in economic support. The members of this group also involve in various kinds of works like cultivation, farming, and domestication of animals. They performed this work based on groups not individually and they share their profit equally among themselves.

Goan-rakhi-bahini (Village Defense Party)

For maintenance of peace and serenity in the village, Goan Rakhi Bahini (V.D.P.) has been formed one of the important organization of the village. In order to save the village from any possible trouble the members of the village unitedly organized this party. The V.D.P. party of Bhogpur village was established in 2010. In order to run this group, they organized a committee. The committee consists of president, and secretary and one member is selected from the young people or the youth. This post is known as 'Nayak'. The Nayak decided the duty of every member from each house to guard the village at night. Each person of this party has their turns after alternate days. The main motive of forming this group is to save the village from any possible trouble like thief, dacoit, terrorist etc. in night they do not give permission to the outsiders to enter in the village without proper identity. The V.D.P. has also connection with the police so that at the time of trouble they may seek help from the police. This party also gets government concerned and facilities. They are provided with some materials, such as Torch light for night duty and blanket, (winter season) jacket etc. Moreover, the government provided financial help to them.

Deka chang (youth dormitory)

Another group of Bhogpur is Dekachang. It is also known as 'Tarang ahem' in Karbi language. Tarang means judgment and ahem means 'house'. In the real meaning of the term, 'Dekachang' is the main office of the village. The number of meeting, religious, calculating of the annual funds etc. all is done in this office under the supervision of the youths and the elder persons. The president of the Dekachang is Bang the and general secretary is Reso-Bangthe. In Dekachang, there are certain rules and regulations, which should be strictly followed by the villagers. Anyone going against these rules, he will be punished severely.

In the Dekachang the entrance of the women folk is not allowed. The Dekachang performs all the duties of the village, including birth and death of a person, apart from these it lays its emphasis on the marriage ceremony, yearly festival such as *deohal*, *kachari puja* etc. It helps to bring unity among the people of the village.

Lower primary school (anganvadi)

The school management committee is composed of eight (8) members. The headmistress of the school herself is the president of L.P. school committees. The two members of the committee have to perform the duties of the school committee. One is called the '*karmi*' and the other one is the helper. They have to call the general meeting and have to discuss the problems of the students with their guardians. They have to look after the school building and the whole surrounding of the school. School consists of 15 students as a whole. Each hamlet of the village has at least one primary school for the children.

The teachers get salary from the government and also get other facilities. The functions of the teachers are to learn drawing, singing, dancing and other necessary subject.

The Anganvadi Kendra receives rice for mid-day refreshment tiffin among the children. Every year, they get medicine, black board, pencil etc. These are given by the I.C.D.S. office.

Summary and conclusion

From collected data in several aspect of the Karbi community of Bhogpur village, we get a clear picture of social, economic etc. and about at all the socio-political system prevalent among them. The above discussion provides a fully elaborate description mainly about village social and political organization in the Bhogpur, inhabiting by Karbi people.

The villagers are very simple, honest, friendly, co-operative, law addicting people. Most of the people of the village are illiterate. They are enslaved by the chains of tradition and primitive ways of thought and action.

Urbanization of city of Guwahati touches very much the village. Since the food habits, dress and ornaments are totally changed. They use modern dress and ornaments. Road and path, water supply facilities are too backward.

My special topic is village organization. I have discussed about the leaders of the village as Goan Burha, Bangthe, Reso-Bangthe, Bisar, Kathar, Kurkun, who is in the special administrative rule over the village. They solve the problems of the village based on thief, illicit, sex relationship, fight among the villagers etc.

They also help the villagers doing their welfare activities inside the village. Their contribution to run the administration inside the village is very important.

There are some other institutions and organizations inside the village, which play an important role to run smoothly the administration of the village. These institutions are as Dekachang, V.D.P. etc. highly related with the development work of the village.

The women of the village established the 'Progotihil Attmo hahayak Goot' in 2002. Among a few days, they have done many welfare deals inside the village.

Thus, studying over all such condition of the village has concluded that the originality of Karbi customs and traditions are not maintained in the true sense of the term. The impact of urbanization as in every society now a day's, can be found in every aspects of their culture in this village.

Bibliography

Ali Irshad, A.N.M. and I. Das: *Tribal Situation in North-East India*, 2003

Basu Roy, Indrani: *Anthropology the Study of Man*, 2003, S. Chand & Company ltd, Ram Nagar, New Delhi.

Barua, Birinchi Kumar: *Asomor Loka Sanskriti,* 2005, Bina Library, Guwahati.

Bordoloi, B. N.; G. C. Sharma Thakur; M. C. Saikia: *Tribes of Assam, Part-I*, 1987 Tribal Research Institute, Guwahati.

Bordoloi, B. N.; G. C. Sharma Thakur; M. C. Saikia: *Tribes of Assam, Part-II*, 1988 Tribal Research Institute, Guwahati.

Majumdar, D. N. & T. N. Madan: *An Introduction to Social Anthropology*, 1986, Mayoor Paperbacks, Noida.

Rao, Ratna N.: *Social Organisation in an Indian Slum: Study of a Caste Slum*, 1st ed. 1990, Mittal Publications, New Delhi, India.

4

Crises Rites Special Refinance to Birth, among the Sonowal Kachari of Dainijan Villagc of Dibrugrah District, Assam

— *Purabi Gogoi*

Introduction

Human life is a complex process encompassing some vital events and changes in its course. Each and every living being has pass through certain definite stages in its life time starting from birth to death. The life cycle of a person is divided in to three stages, birth, marriage and death. This three stages, which a person passes through his life time and rituals mean the code of ceremonies of rites which human beings possessed or performed.

Birth

Every society possess what might be referred to as social organization of the life crises which the birth of new member constitute. This includes a series of accepted behavior both for the mother and her kin which observes rituals to the birth itself and to the new born baby. A well-known example for the extant of male participation in the birth is the CAUVADE which refer to the rituals observance by the father of the rest when his wife gives birth of child. Commonly both father and mother of the new born baby must observe certain avoidance relating to food physical activities and contact with potentially magically dangerous substances in other to protect the child from harm. In majority of traditional societies, most of the rituals observance surrounding birth of babies are comparatively private in nature and are restricted to the protection of the mother and child against harmful influence or diseases. In many of these societies, however, the image of birth is central in other rituals concerning the individual lifecycle or the ceremonial / religious life of the group as a whole.

A women's takes a new dimension when she starts a family and becomes a mother. Motherhood completes the life of a woman. Human being has the longest gestation period of all the members of the order primates to which he belongs. Similarly a mother needs constant care during the pregnancy period for giving birth to a healthy baby.

Objective of the Study

1. to understand the socio-economic and religious life of Sonowal Kachari population of Assam;
2. to assess the knowledge of the Sonowal Kachari woman regarding various reproductive health issues;
3. to understand the vital elements of Sonowal Kachari women's life, food habits and behaviour of the pregnant women.
4. to understanding the knowledge of various rites and rituals related to birth performed by the Sonowal Kachari population of Assam.

Materials and Methods

Assam is one of the smallest state with 2.8% of the total area of the Indian union and 2.7 percent of its population. It is located between 90°-96° East longitude and 22° - 26° North latitude. The present study was carried out in the Dainijan village of Dibrugarh District Assam. The village is located about 11 km away from Dibrugarh town. The individual of Dainijan village are belonging to the Sonowal Kachari tribal population. The Sonowal Kachari belong to Mongoloid racial stock of the Sino - Tibetan linguistic family. They have migrated to alluvial plains of the Brahmaputra valley from the Northern plateau along the sub–Himalayan water channels like Brahmaputra 2000 B.C.

The characteristics features of Sonowal Kachari people are short to medium stature people with generally built body. The colour of the body is dark to light brown, the face is broad and flat. Nose is medium and among some of them epicanthic fold is also present. The people use Assamese as their mother tongue. Many of them also speak Hindi, English etc.

The Sonowal Kachari are one of the aboriginal tribes of Assam. The common view that the Sonowal Kachari belongs to the great Bodo group of Indo Mongoloid Tibeto - Burman stock. Dr. B.M Das, a renowned Anthropologist of Assam divided the Bodo group into two, viz., the eastern and western and brought the Sonowal, Thengal, Dimasa, and Jharua in to the eastern group and the Rava mech Garo etc in to the western group. Although Sonowal Kachari refers as schedule tribe (Plain) of Assam. Traditionally, Sonowals economy is based on agriculture and religion. Agriculture is the primary source of their economy. They also maintain their own beliefs and traditions.

Methods of Data Collection

At first extensive literature and intranet search were carried out to review and assess the exiting information on the rituals of birth performed by Sonowal Kachari tribal population and several other adjacent tribe and ethnic population on baseline for the present study. The primary data from the present study is carried out intensive field work from Dainijan village, Dibrugarh District Assam (Figure 4.1). Information were gathered using interview, case study and group discussion method.

Result and Discussion

A few birth rituals of Sonowal Kachari are described as follows:

Rituals Related to Pregnant Women

The Sonowal Kachari performed numbers of rites and rituals related to pregnant women. Both the parents observed certain restrictions during pregnancy period. Husband is not allowed to kill or harm any kind of bird and animal. Pregnant woman should not move particularly during night and sunset because they believe that this is an auspicious time

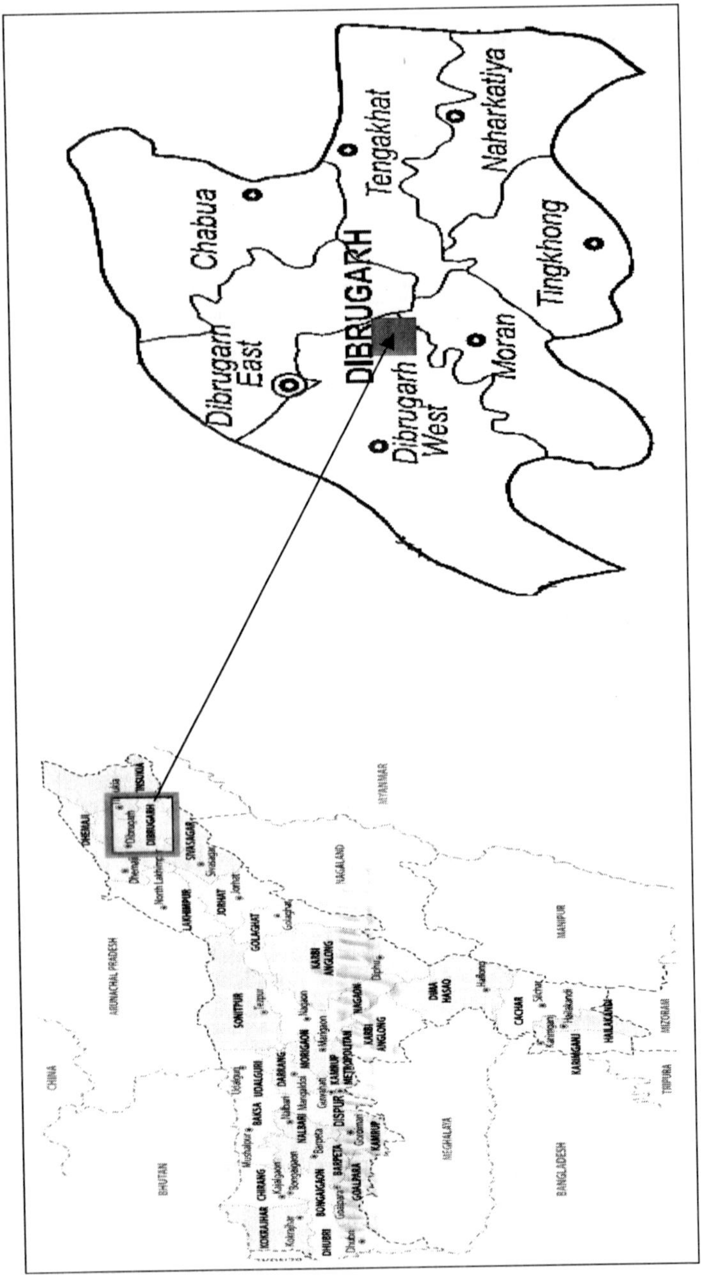

Figure 4.1: The location of the study area of Dibrugarh District of Assam.

and hours. She also avoid from listening to the news of accident, death, bad news etc.

The Sonowal Kachari women are very active. Pregnant women continue to work till the time of her delivery.

Birth related Rituals

After birth of a child, the umbilical cord mainly cut by the expert lady (Dhai) with the help the bamboo piece. But sometimes also use a new blade instead of a bamboo. The cut cord after dried up, is kept by the mother of the baby kept it in a small box, in their society. There is a strong believe that this would save the baby from any kind of disease.

Kachur Jal Ceremony

After the birth of a child the Sonowal Kachari people performed one kind of ritual which is known as *kachurjal* ceremony. On this occasions a special kind of food prepared like chicken *jal* (a hot spicy chicken curry) *kachurjal* (arum leaf *jal*) this curry is mainly prepared by the mother in law and other elder women of the house. On this day one drop of curry is given to the tongue of the baby with help of finger.

Bajuliwa Ceremony

When the umbilical cord falls male devotees and *gupines* are invited and offered "Mah Prasad". The devotees and *gupines* shower blessings to both the baby and mother for their healthy life.

Sudhi Ceremony

The sudhi ceremonial ritual is mainly held after 20 days in case of male baby and in case of female baby, this ceremony held in 30 days. On this occasion of "Sudhi", few devotees are invited to worship God which is known as Namkritan. The devotees' blessing and wishing for both baby and mother.

Bhaat Mukhot Diya or Annaprasana Ceremony

The term *Annaprasana*, *anna* means rice and *prasana* means to enter. So *Annaprasana* means introduction solid food for the first time. This ceremony is also known as first rice eating ceremony. This ceremony is mainly performed when the child is between six and seven month old. On this occasion, the Sonowal Kachari people invite a priest to conduct the ceremony and he recites religious rites and prayers on this day.

Conclusion

The present paper studies the characteristics, ways of behavior, and value of rites and rituals of Sonowal Kachari community. Sonowal Kachari becoming modern in every aspect but they have a strong belief that the birth and death of a person is mainly controlled by God. So they thought that a baby is a beautiful gift of God. Sonowal Kacharis are depended on agriculture, weaving, rearing animal for their livelihood. As a result of acculturation, now a days they were too become the followers of Assamese society and culture. Therefore, it is proved that Sonowal Kachari are the aboriginals of Assam.

Acknowledgement

The author gratefully acknowledge to the help and co-operation of local people of Dainijan village and specially village head man who help for successful completion of the present paper.

References

A Committee of the Royal Anthropological Institute of Great Britain and Ireland, 1954 (Reprint), Notes and Queries or Anthropology, London, Routledge and Kegen Poul Ltd.

Anderson, Janathan, Berry H. Durston and Millicent Poole, 1992, Thesis and Assignment Writing, New Delhi, Wiley Eastern Limited.

Beals, R.L, H. Hoizer and A.R. Beals, 2007 (Reprint). An Introduction to Anthropology, New York, Macmillan Publishing Co.Inc

Beattic, John, 1999 (Reprint), Other Cultures:- Aim Methods and Achievement in Social Anthropology, New Delhi, Replika Press, Pvt.Ltd.

Bordoloi, B.N., G.C. Sharma Thakur and M.C. Saikia, 1988, Tribes of Aaasm – Part –I Guwahati, Tribal Research Institute.

Ember, Carol R., Melvin Ember and Pater N., Peregrine, 2003 (Reprint) Anthropology (Tenth Edition), New Delhi, Pearson Edition (Singapore) Pvt. Ltd.

Herskovits, Milville J., 1974 (Reprint). Cultural Anthropology, New Delhi, Oxford and JBH Publishing Co. Pvt. Ltd.

Kothari, C.R.2009 (Reprint) Research Methodology Methods and Techniques, New Delhi, Wiley Eastern Limited.

Mair, Lucy, 1998 (Reprint) – An Introduction to Social Anthropology (Second Edition) Delhi, Oxford University Press.

Majumder, D.N and T.N Madan, 2005 (Reprint) An Introduction to Social Anthropology, Noida, Mayoor Paper backs.

Mead, Margaret, 1961, Coming of Age in Samoa, (3rd Edition) New Delhi York Morrow Mead, Marget, 1931, Growing Up in New guinea, London, rout ledge and Kegen Paul.

5

Sustainable Traditional Pest Management Techniques Applied by the Sonowal Kachari Farmers: Some Anthropological Observations

— *Dr. Ripunjoy Sonowal, Somnath Sonowal, Nilutpal Sonowal and Mayurtrishna Hazarika*

Introduction

The 21st century has created an ever greater need for research based information and practical utilization of anthropological skills. Globalization, economic and political strife, indigenous peoples varied issues, industrial development and its impact upon nature and traditional cultural values, global attention on sustainable ecological resource management, environmental protection, climate change, poverty, food security, health, violence, militarism, human rights, demographic shifts, etc. have created new work contexts and challenging opportunities for applied anthropologists in multiple settings.

Exploration, systematic documentation and scientific evaluation of Traditional Knowledge (TK) or Indigenous Technical Knowledge (ITK) of the tribal communities worldwide has become a significant emerging area of anthropological research. ITK refers to the complex bodies and systems of knowledge, specific skills and technologies, intangible traditions, beliefs, practices and representation maintained and developed by indigenous people around the world, drawing on a wealth of experience and interaction with the natural environment. ITK is the holistic sum of facts that are known or learned from experiences or acquired through careful observations, and trial-and-error experiments and transmitted from one generation to the next by word of mouth and cultural practices. ITK covers a wide range of topics - crop production, natural resource management, livestock rearing, food preparation, healthcare, agricultural pest management, and many other areas.

For centuries, tribal/indigenous farmers have adjusted farming systems to local agro-climatic conditions, and evolved location-specific TK gained through close interaction within natural and physical environments and cultural adaptation, which are now recognized to be more eco-friendly and sustainable (Kumar, 2010). The use of chemical pesticides and insecticides for higher farm yield has been viewed as an integral part of modern agriculture. However, most of these chemicals affect non-target organisms and contaminate soil and water. In recent years, there has been a growing concern that chemical pesticides/ insecticides constitute a potential risk to ecology and ecological resources including man. Hence, traditional pest management practices, an important component of sustainable agriculture, are being promoted as alternative to chemical pesticides. It incorporates the simultaneous management and integration of tactics, the regular monitoring of pests, the use of thresholds for decisions, and spans methods from pesticide product management/substitution to whole agro-ecosystem redesign (Pretty and Bharucha, 2015). In India, studies by Mohaptra et al. (2009), Chanu et al. (2010), and Firake et al. (2013) are some of the significant reports on ITK based practices of sustainable pest management among different tribal communities.

Anthropological studies often in collaboration with other scientific disciplines have elucidated significant aspects of traditional farmers' agricultural decision making and their unique ITK practices, which have become important topics for agro-biodiversity research. In North East India, the traditional farmers are using ITK based pest management measures – both on and off the field. These methods are the output of the people's empirical experience with nature and the close link maintained between man and environment. In this backdrop, the present brief study is an attempt –

1. To explore and document the different sustainable traditional pest management techniques applied by the Sonowal Kachari farmers.
2. To ascertain the scientific basis of action of the traditional pest control measures.

Methodology

The study is qualitative in nature; an exploratory research design was adopted. 03 Sonowal Kachari villages' viz. *Boiragimath Kachari gaon* and *Paroliguri* in Dibrugarh district; and *Dangori* in Tinsukia district, Assam were purposively selected for the study. Standard anthropological methods of data collection - extensive personal interview, in-depth discussion and observation were used to document and assess the traditional pest management techniques. The collected data was systematically analyzed and presented in convenient form. All the local plant species documented are provided with their scientific, family, and English names.

Results and discussion

The Sonowal Kachari farmers have been using several biological products that are locally available and easily accessible to keep different kinds of pests infesting rice, vegetables and stored grains under the threshold levels. The traditional pest management techniques based on bio-products, as well as the eco-friendly and culture-friendly practices are being described as follows –

1. Leaves of *Bon dhopat* (*Nicotiana plumbaginifolia* Viv.; Solanaceae; Wild tobacco) and *Borpatdhopat* (*Nicotiana tabacum* Linn.; Solanaceae; Common tobacco) are grind to powder and mixed thoroughly in water; the thick solution is sprayed over the infested vegetable crop plants, which acts as an effective insecticide. The dry leaves are also burned; the smoke and pungent smell are good insect repellent.
2. Leaves and branches of *Posotia* (*Vitex negundo* Linn.; Verbenaceae; Chaste tree) are effectively used against insect

pests of paddy. The aromatic leaves are boiled and the filtrate liquid is sprayed over the affected crop plants; also, the leaves and branches are put in the paddy fields when the rice seedlings are in the submerged stage. The dried leaves and branches are burned near the standing vegetable plants so that the smoke repels the insect pests.

3. Peels of *Sokola tenga* (*Citrusaurantium* Linn.; Rutaceae; Sour orange) are placed near grain and vegetable storage. The citrus peels have insect repellent properties.
4. Leaves of *Moha neem* (*Azadirachtaindica* A. Juss.; Meliaceae; Margosa tree) are kept in the granary as well as over stored rice grains. *Neem* leaves are natural pest repellent that effectively repels stored grain pests.
5. Leaves and fruits of *Ou tenga* (*Dilleniaindica* Linn.; Dilleniaceae; Elephant fruit); and *Tezpat* (*Cinnamomum tamala* Ness and Aberm.; Lauraceae; Indian cassia) leaves are kept along with stored rice grains. The strong aroma of the used plant parts are good repellents of storage grain pests.
6. Leaf decoction of *Tita bahek* (*Adhatoda vessica* Ness.; Acanthaceae; Basaka), *Lota mahudi* (*Croton caudatus* Geisel.; Euphorbiaceae) and *Pothorua bihlongoni* (*Polygonum hydropiper* Linn.; Polygonaceae; Water pepper) is used as insect pest repellent of paddy and vegetable crops. Fresh leaves of these medicinal plants when boiled release insect repellent substances or molecules which inhibit the pests.
7. Ash from the traditional fire place and from burning rice husks, fire wood, etc. is regularly sprinkled over and around the different vegetable plants like pumpkin, bottle gourd, brinjal, cabbage, cucumber, tomato, etc. in the kitchen garden and is very effective against insect pests viz. beetles and leaf defoliating insects (*Muwa puk*). The deposition of thin film of ash coat prevents these chewing and sucking type of insects from chewing the plant parts. Ash also acts as a nutrient when it gets washed due to rain.
8. Cow dung, which has always been a good source of bio-fertilizer, is effectively used to control insect-pests in vegetable gardens, particularly for cabbage and green vegetables like

leaf mustard and spinach cultivation. Cow dung heaped in selected places of the vegetable garden is allowed to dry; thereafter, it is mixed with soil, the seeds during sowing get conditioned in dry cow dung + soil mixture. In addition, raw cow dung is also spread in the paddy field water as well as a suspended solution of raw cow dung + water is sprayed over the standing young rice plants. The strong odor of the cow dung repels the insect pests; also, rice worms are not able to survive in the cow dung mixed water.

9. The water in which fish are washed is applied over and at the base of citrus (*Nemootenga*) and chilli plants in order to repel *gundhi* bug. In addition, the pungent smelling water with fish scales and intestinal parts attracts the red tree ant which is a predator of worm pests that fest on the leaves and stems of citrus plants. Fish wash water also effectively restricts the proliferation of pest and pathogens.
10. Bamboo sticks smeared with latex of *Kothal* (*Artocarpus heterophyllus* Lam; Moraceae; Jackfruit) are fixed in vegetable gardens and home plantations to control *gundhi* bugs. When the bugs come to feed on the crop plants, they get stuck to the sticky portion of the bamboo sticks.

Importance of traditional pest management measures

Although the swiftness and knock down effect of the traditional pest management measures are sometimes slower in comparison to the chemical pesticides and insecticides, they do have certain advantages.

1. They are simple, innovative, technically viable, easy to prepare and apply, cheap and effective methods that use local raw materials which are eco-friendly and devoid of any side effect.
2. The uniqueness of the traditional practices is their suitability to the existing farming system and effective in all agricultural seasons; thus, ensures better growth of the crop plants and enhances productivity.
3. The traditional pest management measures are very effective due to their collective action. As different practices are used for the same purpose at the same time, one practice

complements another, resulting in less pest damage to the crops.

4. The traditional measures minimize the harmful and expensive synthetic chemical pesticides and insecticides. Since, the possibilities of developing resistance by pests towards a culturally influenced control are very low, it is expected to provide a long-term solution for agricultural pest management.
5. Efforts made towards production of the ITK based products on cottage scale can be an economically viable option for sustainable development of eco-friendly pesticides and insecticides.

Conclusion

ITK continues to be an invaluable resource that benefits all of mankind. The use of non-chemical methods of pest control and crop protection is fast gaining importance, because they have strong foundations in well-established biological and ecological principles. Hence, there is a need to utilize the potential of traditional bio-products and eco-friendly practices of pest control, as they are safe and bio-degradable as compared to the chemical pesticides. Further scientific studies are required to identify, isolate and analyze the active molecules of the traditional bio-products for a better insight into their insecticidal properties and for developing better agricultural pest management strategies in the future.

Acknowledgement

The authors are thankful to the Sonowal Kachari farmers of the micro-field for sharing their innovative and traditional pest management practices, and for extending necessary help and facilities during the field work.

References

Chanu, L. Bidyalakshmi., Chhetry, G.K.N. and Sharma, G.D. 2010. Sustainable indigenous practices for the management of pest and diseases of upland rice in Manipur, North East India. *Assam University Journal of Science & Technology*, 5(1): 58-62.

Firake, D.M., Lytan, D., Thubru, D.P., Behere, G.T., Firake, P.D. and Azad Thakur, N.S. 2013. Traditional pest management practices and beliefs of different ethnic tribes of Meghalaya, North Eastern Himalaya. *Indian Journal of Hill Farming*,26(1): 58-61.

Kumar, K. Anil. 2010. Local knowledge and agricultural sustainability: A case study of Pradhan tribe in Adilabad district. *Centre for Economic and Social Studies*, Hyderabad, Working Paper No. 81.

Mohapatra, P., Ponnurasan, N. and Narayanasamy, P. 2009. Tribal pest control practices of Tamil Nadu for sustainable agriculture. *Indian Journal of Traditional Knowledge*, 8(2): 218-224.

Pretty, J. and Bharucha, Z.P. 2015. Integrated pest management for sustainable intensification of agriculture in Asia and Africa. *Insects*, 6(1): 152–182.

Murdock, G.P. 1969 Social Structure, New York, The Free Press.

Sengupta, Sarthak (ed.) The Sonowal Kachari ; Some aspects of their life, Kalyan Baruah, page no. 120 -121-126 gyan publishing house New Delhi 2012.

Symour – Smith, Charlotee, 1990 (Reprint), Macmilan Dictionary of Anthropology, London the Maclillan Press Ltd.

Sinha, K.S (ed), 2003, People of India: Assam, Vol –XV, Part One, Calcutta, Sengul Books Young, P.V. 2001 (Reprint), Scientific Social Survey and Research New Delhi, Prentice – Hell of India.

6

A Study on Traditional Dress Pattern of Bodos

— *Franky Boro*

Introduction

Dress and ornaments is known as an integral part of material culture which can be regarded as a symbol of identity and distinctive feature of a particular community. In this civilized world, there are various types of dresses and ornaments worn by the people in different parts of the globe. It symbolizes the existence of different culture and traditions of different community and society on the basis of their geographical location and natural conditions. The material culture of people is closely dependent on the availability of natural resources in the local area and the scope of its utility.

Regarding material culture Prown (1982) wrote, "Material culture as a study is based upon the obvious fact that the existence of a man-made object is concrete evidence of the presence of a human intelligence operating at the time of fabrication." Again he wrote, "The underlying premise is that objects made or modified by man reflect, consciously or unconsciously, directly or indirectly, the beliefs of individuals who made, commissioned, purchased or used them, and by extension the beliefs of the larger society to which they belonged. The term material culture thus refers quite directly and efficiently, if not elegantly, both to the subject matter of the study, material and to its purpose, the understanding of culture."

On the other hand in the article "Material of culture, fabric of identity", Jarman (1998) wrote, "Tradition is used to signify the historical and unchanging basis for their status and customs, traditional practices are assumed to have greater validity than non-traditional practices, and tradition is assumed to bestow rights and obligations."

By analysing various author's opinion regarding dress, Eicher (2000) stated that, "Throughout the writings, the concept of holism is paramount; dress is analyzed, as part of a larger configuration of human behaviour of a specific people in a specified time and place. The culture of specific people in relation to their habits of dress is also analyzed, with cultural diversity in dress from group to group becoming readily apparent."

The Bodos are the largest community among the tribal populations of Assam. They have a rich and beautiful culture in regards of dresses. Dresses and ornaments of the Bodos are the symbol of their traditional art and culture. It reflects their artistic mind and creative nature. They have the tradition of weaving and most of the dresses are hand woven with unique style and attractiveness.

Objectives of the study

The main objectives of the present study are

(i) To study the Bodo weaving culture and its significance in Bodo folk life.

(ii) To study the traditional dress pattern, its designs and use of various raw materials.

(iii) To focus on the various dresses worn by the people in different occasions and festivals.

Area of study

The area of study was Majgaon village of Darrang district in Assam. The village is situated about 7 km far from Mangaldai town of Darrang district. The village is mainly inhabited by the traditional Bodo-Kachari people.

Methodology

The present paper has been prepared through both primary and secondary data. Appropriate anthropological research methods were applied to collect primary data. An intensive fieldwork was conducted among the people of the village.

Participant observation was done to know about their weaving culture and its relation to the folk life of the studied people. Some individual and professional handlooms were visited and interview method was applied among the people to know about their traditional dress pattern, its design and use of different raw materials in weaving. Case studies method was also applied and open structured interviews were also taken from the key informants and concerned people to get detailed information regarding the studied issue.

Results and discussion

Weaving as folk culture and folk industry: Weaving is one of the great folk cultures of the Bodo which plays a significant role in their socio-economic and village folk life. There were two types of weaving culture found in this particular village. One is the individual handloom in the household and the other is professional handloom for business purpose. Weaving is a kind of folk industry for the village people which supports in their economic life.

Women make their own traditional attire *dokhona* in their handlooms. Besides *dokhona,* they have also weaved *gamsha, jwngra, aronai, shawl* etc. The tools and implements of weaving consist of yarns (acrylic, cotton or silk), spindle, spinning machine, warp drum, or pegs and a loom. Most of these tools are made of bamboo and sometimes wood. The people of the village considered weaving as their part and parcel of the society and most of the houses have their own loom. Though agriculture is their main occupation, however, women mostly fond of weaving and it reflects their higher socio-economic status and artistic and creative skill as well. They believed that their courtyard is incomplete without a loom. The complete loom consists of weaving area and poles for the frames and weaving. Regarding the loom, S. Endle (1975) stated that, "The loom is usually set up on a shady side of the dwelling house, or where that is impracticable, a rude structure of thatch and bamboo work is provided to shield the weaver from the sun."

Traditional dress, its design and raw materials

Dokhona: *Dokhona* is the main traditional dress of Bodo woman which is of length 2.5 m and width 1.5 m and it is wore to cover the whole body from chest to ankle by tying one round at a time in the waist. According to Siiger (2015), "It is a garment of red silk mixed with yellow, pink and mauve. Along the sides, there are ribbons of brocade pattern woven in brown on yellow or red. The cloth is woven in coarse yellow silk in stripes (silk or cotton) of red, orange, yellow and nuances of red woven in two warps with red, green patterns along some of the ribbons. The garb ends in fringes. The weaving technique is very complicated, perhaps brocade. Length 241 cm., width 121 cm." Different *agor* (design or flower) and colours are weaved for *dokhona. Dokhona thaosi* (pure dokhona) is generally used as bridal attire, *bwirathi* (woman receptionist of Bride and bridegroom in marriage) or during the festivals or other ceremonies. *Dokhona* without *agor* is popular among the Bodo people and used to wear in worshipping God. Yellow is the popular colour among them. Besides yellow, they used to weave *dokhona* in a variety of colours like green, red, blue etc.

The different *agors* which Bodo people used to weave *dokhona* are-

(i) Agor gubwi
(ii) Parraw megon
(iii) Makri agor
(iv) Taigir bibar
(v) Maoji agan
(vi) Dokan agor
(vii) Laosung agor etc.

Jwngra: *Jwmgra* is an upper garment used by women in yellow silk or cotton interwoven with ribbons in red, green, orange and blue. The length of *jwmgra* is about 264 cm. and breadth 107 cm. The cloth is used as shawl or scarf with *dokhona*. The *jwmgra* is woven of red, yellow and white with minor patterns of orange and black. The main pattern is goose eye but some of the vertical stripes are just the red and white thread left open for about 8 threads. The red thread is silk, while the yellow and other colours seem to be cotton.

Aronai: *Aronai* (small scarf) is the most beautiful cloth woven by the Bodo women. It is the sign of their tradition and it is used for various purposes such as to felicitate people with honour and also in all Bodo dances. The Bodo girls used to present *aronai* as a token of love and affection to their loved ones. *Aronai* is their traditional symbol of love and respect. The women make it with various designs of *agor* (design or flower) in different colours like red, green, yellow etc.

Gamsha: *Gamsa* is the male garment which is worn as household attire and in dance as well. The length of *gamsha* is of 1.5 m and width is 1.2 m. It is used to cover the portion from waist to knee by tying it in the waist. The *gamsha* is weaved of different colours like green, yellow, and sometimes mixture of different colours like white and white and green, white and blue etc. specially the *gamsha* of green colour is used as wedding dress of the concerned people.

Besides these traditional clothings, another piece of cloth, the locally woven shawl is of white cotton with interwoven thin lines of black and yellow is also used by the people of the village. The shawl has fringes at the ends. It is used by both men and women for covering the shoulders for keeping warm.

Raw materials: Since time immemorial, the indigenous people of this village were accustomed with the production of clothes from the tread of *Eri* and *Muga*. The *eri* cloth is of dub colour and is durable. The women of this village are expert in rearing the *Endi Emphow* (Eri worm) and *muga latha* (muga worm) and find out the threads from them. For the raw materials the women of the village have been practiced sericulture such as harvesting of leaves, rearing of silkworm, spinning or reeling of silk yarn etc.

Regarding the *eri* silk culture of Bodos, in the "The Kachari" Endle (1975) wrote, "One of the chief industries, a very profitable one among the kacharis, is that of the culture of the silk-worm known as *eri,* and the manufacture of *eri* cloth."

He again said, "The loom employed for weaving the *eri* silk is of very simple construction, and most, if not all, the material needed for the purpose can be provided by the villagers themselves from local resources."

Significance of various dresses in different occasion

The people of this village used to wear different dresses in different occasions and festivals. For example, the *dokhona thaosi* is worn in wedding ceremony and especially it is regarded as the bridal attire. It is known as the pure *dokhona* among them. Likewise in any religious ceremony or during the time of worshipping God or ancestor they preferred to wear plain *dokhona* or *dokhona* without *agor* or design. In religious activities they usually wear white cloth and they do not prefer colourful dresses in this time.

During the festival of *Bwisagu* or other seasonal festival, they like to wear colourful *dokhona* with colourful and designable *jwmgra.* In their traditional dress *bagrumba,* the dancer girls use *aronai* also along with the *jwmgra.*

The male also preferred to wear their traditional dress *gamsha* in various traditional festivals of the community though now- a- days they used to wear modern pant shirt, coat, pyjama etc. Simple *gamsha* (without design or colour combination) is generally used as household attire and sometimes it is used as bathing towel as well. In wedding ceremony, they usually wear *gamsha* of green or yellow colour. The *aronai* is also used which is woven with different designs and motifs. The groom has to tie an *aronai* around on his head and another one has to hang on his neck or shoulder. This is the traditional attire of marriage ceremony.

Depending on the occasion, *aronai*is being worn in different ways- in dancing, it is hanged on one side of shoulders and tie both the edge through another *aronai* in the waist and in the felicitation, it is simply hanged on neck.

Conclusion

From the above discussion we have found that the Bodo Kachari women of this village are expert weaver and they show their talent and artistic nature through their weaving skill. They are expert in rearing silkworm as well and it helps in their economic development of the entire family and community of this particular village. Though in present context, they used to purchase clothes from the market or they like to wear modern clothes, still they have been continuing their traditional costumes and they are not willing to give up their traditional weaving culture which reflects their rich and remarkable folk culture and age old folk life as the aboriginal ethnic group of north east India.

To conclude, we can say that the Bodo-Kacharis of this particular village have different multifaceted and distinctive cultures of their own including the beautiful and skilful weaving culture and traditional dress pattern which make them unique and special among the various communities of the said region.

References

Eicher, Joanne B. 2000. The Anthropology of Dress. *Dress, 2000,* Vol. 27 p. 59-70.

Endle, S. 1975 *The Kachari,* Delhi, Cosmo Publication.

Miller, D. [Eds.] 1998. *Material Culture, Why Something Matter,* London. UCL Press. http://www.researchgate.net/publication/27483231 p. 121-145 accessed on 3/11/2017

Narzi, B. 2009 *Boro Kacharir Samaj Aru Sanskriti* (Boro Kacharis's Society and Culture) Ghy, Bina Library [Assamese]

Prown, J.D. 1982 Mind in Matter: An Introduction to Material Culture Theory and Method, *Winter Portfolio,* Vol. 17 No. 1 p. 1-19.

Siiger, H. 2015. *The Bodos of Assam.* [Edited by B. Peter Anderson and S.K. Soren] Denmark, NIAS Press. www.niaspress.dk accessed on 3/11/2017.

Website: www.craftmark.org accessed on 4/11/2017.

7

Adi Beads in Adi Society and Culture

— *Dhritiman Sarma and Antoni Perme*

Introduction

The *Adi* are hill people who constitute a major tribe in Arunachal Pradesh. They are spread in a considerable part of the state in East Siang, West Siang and Upper Siang districts, in eastern part they spread as far as Lower Dibang Valley and Lohit districts and rich in folklore, traditional articles and ornamentation. Among the *Adi* any kind of necklace or garments that a person wears in his or her neck is called *Lunggu*, but the word *Tadok* is specifically used for bead which is the most precious among the necklaces of *Adi*. The *Adi* people have its distinctive way of body ornamentation, although some variations are noticeable in the personal decoration and ornamentation from area to area but there ornaments are all common.

Among the ornamentation bead is regard as one of the most precious and multifarious object which is commonly known for body ornamentation not only important for beautification rather associated with festivals, rituals, marriage, economic and other aspects of society. As per belief system of *Adi* bead is not a produced of human it was made by *Misummyang* (mother of bead) when even human was not came into existence. The importance and utility of beads lies in the belief system that people have on the beads. To them there is a soul or we can say supremacy that given by *Donyi Polo* which possess a capability of healing and overcome the evil eye and harm.

Bead: Importance and functions

Bead as ornamentation and symbol of status and identity

Beautification seems to be the important function of beads. *Adi* women and girls wear a mass of beads of various sizes and colors for enhancing their beauty which goes neck to waist these are *Dokpun, Dogar, Doksor, Liiro, Seliing* etc. Men also wear various strings of beads that go round the neck and neck to belly. Such types of beads are *Podat, Kuro, Kuli, Tagee* and *Dudap* etc. Generally, beads are worn on special occasions such as festivals, *Kebang* and while performing traditional dances and songs for beautification and fortune.

Besides, bead is the sign of identity and status. Wearing of bead identify which culture and group the person belongs to, further it enhances the person's status in the society. Within central Arunachal, however, beads are the only items of material culture that mark both wealth and cultural identity. Other objects, such as Tibetan bells and plats, and now cars, are also expensive, but they are not displayed as markers of identity and wealth.[1] Wearing of beads in such socio-cultural occasions or in public gathering enhances the wearer's value in the society and displays his or her wealth and status in the society.

Bead as source of compensation and fines

In *Adi* society valuable beads and metal of various qualities are used to pay penalties or fine for various crimes or guilt like murder, theft and adultery etc. that committed and established for any crime is usually compensated with a fine. The compensation for any crime is demanded generally in the form of valuable beads, metals as these are considered wealth.[2] If anybody found committing adultery and taken away other's wife he has to pay female beads called *Nero Abii* as compensation. He has to pay to husband of the women the following in addition to above: (a) *Tipil* – spear for his deprivation from use of his wife's clitoris. (b) *Tilong* – a sword for the pubic bones. (c) *Timit* – a bear skin for pubic hairs and d) *Lisik Pure* – set of beads for fireplace.[3]

Besides, it is used to compensate beads. If anyone breaks beads of others knowingly or unknowingly he/she must compensate a bead of same color, shape size and quality if he could not afford his family or any clan members near or residing at any corner of *Adi* areas should bear the penalties by paying same quality bead.

Beads in ritual and as therapy

In *Adi* society beads are used in rituals related to birth, death, sickness etc. Wearing of beads is the greatest weapon of being protected and to overcome the devils and considers as best therapy.

Firstly, it is the chief weapon for priest while carrying out various rituals for curing sickness caused by the evil spirit and in exorcisms priest used to wear or bound with beads on his leg or hand to overcome the evils. An *Ipak Miri* wears special type of beads called *Rogum* in his hair, he also decks himself in an ornaments called *Lakjin*; it is a string of two to five beads worn round the wrist or on the butt-end of the *Yoksha* [4]. As *Adi Aabang* describes – *Kuro nammare toktik nako, kuli namkire tiktak nako*, which means, smell of beads petrify and scare the evil spirit. In order to perform such rituals the priest has to be compensated by giving some valuable pieces of beads.

In case of sickness, attack and possession by evil spirit one distant *Akii* (maternal uncle) binds some pieces of beads in a string and tie it to the sick person for getting well and good growth. Whenever men hunt animals like lion, tiger, elephant and bear and by mistake a man the maternal used to bind some pieces or strings of beads to hunter so that the spirit of men and animals he killed would not caused any harm to him. This process of binding beads is called *Likee* or *Emul. Kodang Ginpak* is another way of use of beads as therapeutic item. When a new baby is born a few pieces of beads in a string is tied to his or her wrist, waist or neck by parents, maternal and relatives so as to protect from diseases, evil eye and harm.

Dorung, is a ritual that last for ten days. For instance, if one does not give birth to male child he would perform a ritual called *Dorung* where relatives, priest are called and animals sacrificed is done. Here some pieces of male beads are bound to female child by performing rituals with hope to see a male child in the next or vice versa.

Beads in marriage and as property of inheritance

In marriage also beads serves important function, it is used as a item in the bride price along with *Apong*, mithun, meats and squirrel etc. Every girl is considered an asset to the family which she belongs. So, depriving a family of a girl by taking her away in marriage has to be compensated by payments, commensurate with the status of the family and the personal belongings of the girl, such as *Tadok*. This payment of bride price is known as *Aree*.[4]

Besides, bead is an important property of inheritance in the society. *Adi* society as a whole is a patriarchal where their descendents are traced through the father and properties are inherited by the sons. The youngest son looks after the old parent and performs the last rite. Thus, he inherits the beads if it is in less quantity if not share equally by brothers. In absence of son the nearest clan member has the right. But the one who inherits the beads has no ultimate power on it, he cannot sell or misplace it without prior consent from his brothers and clan members, as the beads has been preserved and passed down from generations to generation since time immemorial by their forefathers for their pride and status. Preservation of beads gives prestige to the family and makes them feel the presence of their departed forefathers. As per customary law female does not have the inheritance right but in case of beads she can inherit her mother's property. Thus bead preservation has been maintained by both male and female in the society.

Beads as source of barter and an alternative to money

Since time immemorial beads have been used as medium of exchange for material objects both living and non living. Thus, people used to exchange their beads with cattle, food grains, cloths and agricultural plots, cash money etc. In the early days their common transaction in trade was only through barter, since they did not know the use of coins nor had a common medium of exchange. They however, used some of their articles as money like big brass, bowls, old dishes, sword and beads.[5] In present day also beads are used as alternative to money. Persons having beads exchange their beads with money specially when there is crisis or situation that demands money in a family. The exchange of goods and services is done because of requirements of particular unavailable commodity or services; sometimes a situation compels a man even to sell his valuable property. For example, a part or the whole of the agricultural field is exchanged for some valuable beads such as *Kuli,Kuro, Dokpun* [Opcit].

Conclusion

Since long the *Adi* are preserving and practices the age old established beads culture in different spheres of life as per condition and needs which resulted into scarcity of beads. Since last few decades with the rapid growing population and the human wants and capability of formulate new tools and objects has generated new era beads or replica which later altered the perception of beads culture.

With time and space the long established tradition of beads has undergone changed, people hardly used beads where it is associated. The main reason behind may be the unavailability and preciousness of original beads which curtails its utility in every aspects of life. Besides, modern medical and economic system has great influence on bead culture. For instance, instead of performing rituals and to get bound with pieces of beads people now wish to have scientific treatment, importance of money makes them to sell their valuable beads.

In state of crisis people now do not used beads as therapy and in many rituals related to sick, birth, death etc. It is obvious that still people used to wear beads in different or same way as ornamentation and symbol of identity in various festive occasions but only few haves original one and the rest used replicas. The contemporary reality is, the common people are seller and white colour people are the buyer as such the beads has become in possession of rich people. The long established bead culture has become a tale for the new generation today. But it is obvious that *Adi* still use beads in various socio-cultural aspects of life and will preserve it in days to come also.

Bibliography

1. Blackburn, Stuart, *Memories of migration*, European bulletin of Himalayan research, 2004.
2. Lego, K, *The exchange and distribution system in Adi*, in Mibang and Behera (eds) *Tribal villages in Arunachal Pradesh,* Abhijeet Publication, Delhi, 2004.

3. Nath, J, *Cultural heritage of tribal societies-the Adis* (vol. 1), Omson Publication, New Delhi, 2000.
4. Roy, Sachin, *Aspects of Padam Minyong culture*, Directorate of Research Govt. of Arunachal Pradesh, Itanagar, 1960.
5. Nyori, T, *History and culture of Adis*, Omson Publication, New Delhi, 1993.

8

Culture and change among the Adis of Arunachal Pradesh

— *Kasimang Moyong*

Introduction

This paper is an attempt to depict the processes of change with regards to the account of change and continuity. Generally, a cultural change can be associated with innovation, invention and acculturation while it can also be defined as any kind of modification in the life of the people be it material or non-material culture. According to contemporary sociological research, culture is describing everything from elite artistic activities (Becker 1982) to the values, styles, and ideology of day-today conduct (Swidler 1986). Beside with art and everyday conduct, included among the "mixed bag" of research that takes place under the auspices of the sociology of culture is work in science (Latour 1987; Star 1989). However, the concept of culture also refers to the patterns of social organization, belief system and economy which are being learned and shared among the social group. Further, culture is a traditional knowledge that is passed down from one generation to next generation.

Prior to the arrival of the British and Christian missionaries in state like, Arunachal Pradesh, the Adis lived a simple life. The Adis of the present study is one of the major tribes of the Arunachal Pradesh and are exclusively concentrated in Siang Valley of East Siang, Siang,

Upper Siang, West Siang, Lower Dibang Valley and some parts of Lohit districts. Originally the Adis are of Mongoloid origin and they have their own rich traditions, culture, myths, legends, tales and folk-lore's. However, the entry of British administration after the Anglo-Abor war in 1911-12, established head quarter at Pasighat, the foothills of Abor areas. Moreover, it also brought along the Christian missionaries later. Eventually the British Administration in the Adi (Abor) introduced new changes in term of: political institution and in the subsistence activities of the people; changes in the indigenous religious beliefs and practices and many other aspects of their life. After Independence in 1947, with the modern and formal education initiated for the tribal people embarked, drastic changes in transforming the traditional structure of the Adi society. Hence, the objective of the present paper is to understand the process of cultural change among the Adis of Arunachal Pradesh and the study also seeks to limit itself to some aspects of the material and non-material culture. The present study is based on field work which is conducted in a purposively selected village under East Siang district. Participant observation and informal interviews were also employed.

Material Culture

1. Food and drinks

The staple food of the Adis is rice. Rice was used both for eating and for making drinks. Apong (Rice beer) was used by every household for making a special drink especially during festivals. But, nowadays especially the converted Christians have given up as from the time of their conversion, they have been taught not to drink rice beer. Although, only those who follow the traditional religion brew rice beer (Apong) and make drinks for themselves but at present they have realized the negative effects of excessive drinking. Therefore, they have minimized to drink occasionally. Thus Apong has been replaced by tea and green tea.

Meat is highly relished and was considered a luxury. They used to preserved meat especially for guests. They hardly kill animals except at the time of sacrifices or when giving a feast and during festivals. Though, today the consumption of meat is as high as meats are available in the market. Unlike in the past the present generation food habits have changed, earlier the cooking method was very simple, it mostly done with boiling vegetables and meats. Today they have learnt the art of cooking various dishes including frying, boiling, steaming with all sorts of modem accessories for cooking. Besides, today they have also come to know the art of making fruit juices, jams and other modern recipes by various medium of platform especially through mass media.

2. Dress and Ornament

Regarding dress and ornament one can notice many changes and today most of the Adis, be it men or women dressed in full traditional attires are hardly seen. On the other hand, they are more comfortable and used to, with the modern outfit and dressing lifestyle. No doubt, they wear traditional dress and ornaments during festivals and cultural programmes or during important social gatherings. Therefore, today one will hardly find a modern man or woman dressed in full traditional attires except few aged people in the village. From most of the respondents, it have been found that they prefer wearing modern dressing because unlike traditional the modern clothes are more comfortable to wear. Besides, there are various dresses for various seasons and weather conditions. Another factors based on the social living standard, which demand for changes and the influence of westernization especially by the students.

3. Economy

Adi society traditionally base on agriculture for its survival. Therefore follow agro-based economy. Although at present many changes have taken place in agriculture but still there are some elements of continuity that prevailed. Rice is the main occupation besides; vegetables, fruits, etc., for their daily needs. With the advent of modern and formal education which provides job opportunities the present generation is slowly extricating themselves from agricultural works. Consequently, today we hardly see young generation indulging themselves in the field of agriculture. However, some of the positive outcome is the advancement in science and technology; many new things have been introduced even in the field of agriculture like various kinds of insecticides, pesticides, fertilizers, and good yielding seedlings supplied by the government through agriculture department. This has increase the surplus production in the society.

In the present generation both men and women folks hardly take interest in their traditional arts like weaving and crafting. The traditional skills is being fading away gradually as today, it is observed that only few women weave as most of the villages wear clothes bought from the nearby towns. In the Adi society, weaving is done by the women. It is also being noted that with the advent of education, many women do not know the art of weaving. Only few girls know the art of weaving. In the past weaving of clothes was for domestic consumption, but today it is more for commercial purposes. Along with all sorts of dresses, they modify it with traditional patterns and designs and colours to make it more vibrant and unique. These have created avenues for some women especially illiterate and unemployed women take up weaving as a profession because there is a market demand. Even the government gives grant in aid and schemes from time to time providing them raw materials and assisting them by providing loans for the needy. On the other hand men folks, the Adi society still are very much attached with their traditional form of basketry. Therefore, till today, basketry is a very important means and source of their economy. However, only old people are expert in these works. While few younger generations have learnt the art of basketry but majority of them hardly know the art of making even simple basketry works.

Non-material Culture

1. Family

Adis follow a Patrilocal and Neolocal type of residence after marriage. The nature of Adi family system is patrilineal. They trace their descent through the men line exclusively; this makes the Adi society as patrilineal in character. Through the ages, still the basic family structure of the Adis remains unchanged. The Adi family, being patriarchal, the father assumes the headship of the family even today. The father continues to carry the greatest authority and any decision relating to family matters. In past the duty and responsibility of a father was to look after the family members, He also voluntary help his wife in the time of need hours like; agriculture work, splitting firewood, fetching water and even cooking sometimes. While the role of the mother is to play an important part in the household works, child care, agriculture and animal husbandry. However, the main occupation is agriculture and the mother is the one who does most of the agricultural work. The mother has the authority over the disposal and consumption of the agricultural products and also equal rights in utilization of their fruits of labour together.

Nevertheless, with the passes of time, today the duty and role of both the father and mother towards their children has taken a new direction and responsibilities. Education has engulfed the society. Henceforth, every modern family has geared their interest and priority towards education as a new value and aspirations for their children unlike the traditional culture which emphasized on Agricultural and households activities training to their children. Most of the respondents emphasized on education that how important it is especially for the society like the Adis. This new wave of thoughts clearly indicates that how the modern families view education and takes up new challenges and responsibilities for their children knowing the value of education.

Even the children, at present have changed to a great extent. They gives priority to education so, they are not able to help their parent in field. However, during their vacation they try to assist and help their parent in the field. In the Adi society the work pattern is divided according to gender roles or to say there is a division of labour accordingly. Therefore, a son is expected to help his father and brothers in their works, likewise a daughter are expected to assist her mother in her household chores works respectively. The traditional socio-religio-political institution like the Mushup (male) and Raseng (female) which is known as the boys and girls' dormitories has perished due to the foundation of education. Regarding inheritance, as a tradition till today, the eldest son gets the most of the share from the ancestral property such as land, terrace fields, forest etc. And after his father expires he is considered to be the head of the family, his final decision will be taken by the members of the family. The youngest son is entitled to inherit his parent's house and to take care his parents when they become old as per the Adi customary law.

2. Marriage

The modern form of socialization has made it easier for a boy and a girl to know each other. These mediums of socialization takes place through schools, college, universities, students activities, youth activities, church activities, birthday parties, clubs, work places, etc. Hence today, the mode of acquiring spouse in compares to past become more accessible and informal. In the past, selection of spouse was based on: qualities and abilities of a person; and hardworking and strength and particularly weaving was expected to know and adhere by a woman. But, today, the criteria and standard that people use are different. Education, wealth, beauty, chastity etc., are more emphasized by the modern people. Further, educated people prefer government job holder as their partner and also feel that one should first be financially stable before getting married and thereby plan accordingly. The Adis prefer monogamy practice of marriage and still strongly follow clan exogamy.

The system of marriage ceremonies are changing at the present scenario. With the coming of education and modernization traditional forms of marriage are almost dying out. Most of the working people so called 'Adi middle class' who are engaged in governmental sector at present conduct and practice abstentious kind of marriage ceremony by spending huge amount of money for luxurious items and decorations. Further, the Adi society is also witnessing marriage gift systems which are becoming common and conventionally practiced in the Adi society.

3. The Advent of Christianity in the Adi belt

In Arunachal Pradesh, the role of Christian missionaries increased after independence, evidenced by growth of many Christian missionary schools in the society, like the Catholic and Baptist Christian Missionaries. The Missionaries contributes lots of effort and support to the tribal of Arunachal Pradesh in motivating them towards education. Beside educational policy, on the other hand, they also equally educated the tribals in their religious reformation, by preaching them about the truth and importance of Christianity. Further they also taught about the notion of hell and heaven, good and bad, and the concept of eternity after death. As an outcome, for the first time in the history of Adi society, conversion of religion took place by replacing their indigenous religion, which is known as Donyi-Polo (the sun and the moon), among the Adis of Arunachal Pradesh. This led to the change of mind set amongst the Adi society. Thereafter, when any one gets sick instead of performing the sacrifices they prefer to visit the doctors. And the Christians they invite the pastor to pray for them. This major change is the outcome of the Christianity and modern sciences which manage to eradicate the old traditional superstitions of the sicknesses being caused by evil spirits.

However, in the contemporary Adi society the conversion process is further, transforming into a new cult base on religious cultural identity disputes and emotional sentiments among the traditional Adis. Here I would like to code, most of the converted Christian respondents explained that the main reason for embracing Christianity was because of sickness and rigorous sacrifice rituals of practices.

4. Conclusion

The change in Adi culture has come about as a result of British Administration and post-independence. The influencing factors such as; Christianity, Education and Modernization have contributed for the massive transformation of Adi society at present. Changes in both material and non-material culture have taken place. Conversely, in aspects of non-material culture, change is not very tangible, whereas in material culture changes are more apparent. Therefore, in conclusion, we can say that the culture of Adis shows the dynamics of the society and the capacity of adaptation to a new way of life. Hence, these culture changes are the resultant of its cultural contact with the outer society in the form of acculturation and assimilation. New ideas have begun to sweep the Adi society and particularly their material culture is affected. Nonetheless, these cultural changes have made life more comfortable and good for the Adis in general and particularly the man, woman, children and overall as an individual in the society.

Reference

1. Becker, Howard S. (1982). *Art Worlds*. Berkeley, University of California Press.
2. Bose, N. K. (1961). *Cultural Anthropology*. Bombay, Asia Publishing House.
3. Choudhury, S. Dutta. (1994). *Gazetteer of India Arunachal Pradesh; East and West Siang District*. DIPR, Govt. of Arunachal Pradesh, Itanagar.

4. Elwin, Verrier. A Philosophy for NEFA, Shillong: The Advisor to the Governor of Assam, 1957.
5. Elwin, Verrier. *The Art of NEFA*, Shillong: North-East Frontier Agency, 1959.
6. Erring, O. (1970). *Religio-cultural trend in NEFA*. NEFA information, 5(3).
7. Latour, Bruno (1987) *Science in Action: How to Follow Scientists and Engineers through Society*. Cambridge, Mass.: Harvard University Press.
8. Nyori, T. (1993). *History and culture of the Adis*. Omsons Publication, Oxford University Press, New Delhi.
9. Rondo, J. (2010). *Transformation of Socio-Cultural and Political Life of the Adis of Arunachal Pradesh*. Himalayan Publishers, New Delhi.
10. Roy, S. (1960, 1966, 1997). *Aspects of Padam-Minyong Culture, North East Frontier Agency*, Govt. of Arunachal Pradesh, Shillong.
11. Star, Susan Leigh (1989).*Regions of the Mind: Brain Research and the Quest for Scientific Certainty*. Stanford, Calif.: Stanford University Press.
12. Swidler, Ann (1986).*Culture in Action.* American Sociological Review 51: 273–286.

9

The folklore of the Kom Tribe of Manipur with special reference to their music, dance and festivals

— Dr. L. Romeo Singh, Ksh. Sunita Devi

The Kom tribe is one of the 33 scheduled tribes of Manipur under the Constitution (Scheduled tribes) order 1950 Article 342 Clause (I) of India. Their habitations are found in both the hills and the plains of Manipur.

Few reports on Kom tribe of Manipur have been made earlier by the British administrators (Grierson 1904, Brown 1873, Shakespear 1912, McCullock 1859) and recently by some Kom writers such as Teba Karong -1976, Benjamin Kom- 1990, Mangpu Kilong- 2000 etc. Although, these reports have provided some important information related with their origin, and aspects of their social organization.

The present data is a compilation from the following informants collected during the period of 2000 – 2001 from five different locations of the two districts- Churachandpur and Imphal East districts.

The informants consists of Sinkhuplin Serto, Chief of the Village, Sagang Khopui; S. Songkhupthang, Village elder, Sagang Khopui; Mr. Achon Kom, Cultural Leader, Khoirentak Khopui, K. Korpu, Village elder, Khoirentak Khopui; M. Lenkhomang, Chief and President of Kom-Rem Chief Welfare Organisation, Harmontlang;

T. Hensing Kom, Information Secy., Kom-Rem Union, Manipur from Churachandpur district and Serkhopao Kom, Village elder, Maramhunsong Telen, Editor of Kom Rem Dictionary, & Kom Folk tales, and Lalkhomang Karung, President, Kom-Rem Union, Manipur from Imphal East District.

Etymologically, the 'Kom' means 'cave', meaning thereby the cave man. Their traditional songs refer that their ancestors lived in the caves. The folk song is recorded as follows:

Kan hong sok e, khurpui a khan, hong shok a (2)
Kan lengsial le Kholei eng e;
Kan lak pon leh kholei eng e;
Kan shak long leh kho lei eng e;
Kan chim shi leh kho lei eng e;

Free Translation:

We came out from the cave or route;
With our mithuns and clothes;
Our physique well built;
Out necklace as decoration;
With the pointed thorns of porcupine;
Which beautified the world.

Their tradition refers that the Kom tribe of Manipur, is originated from the East Asia. The site Khojengpui, now at China, is believed to be their first home land.

Due to enmity and frequent feuds, they were compelled to shift to different places. They had to pass through a cave (*khur*) known as Kom-Khongram from which the nomenclature of the tribe 'Kom' had derived. All the folklore of the community were based on this cave. According to this folklore, inside the cave, there was a tiger, which kills any passerby. Unlike other tigers known as *Khumpui* and *Kamkeis*, the *Samang Lampuis* was the one which involved the act of killings. On hearing the news, one person known as Sahumpa wearing the cloth known as *Ponthre* or *Leiponpin* (woven and embroidered by a woman named Chongnu, while at Khothoutpui) came to meet the tiger and sang with two songs in front of the tiger. Still, these songs are known to the village elders. The meaning of the folk lore is as follows:

> *We are the brothers, see this cloth and its patterns and compare it with your own body colour. As your desire, God has provided it on your skin, and for us, we got it as cloth according to our desire. Of these similarities of patterns, we are brothers, so don't kill me as well as my followers, they are all our brothers and sisters. In case of you kill anybody, your teeth may break or if we kill you and eat, our throat may swell. The tiger was tamed. Sahumpa left for Chongkhupui – a place situated at the border of China and Burma now as Myanmar. Many people followed him. After sometime the tiger again started killing the people as usual. It provoked anger to the survivors. Two brothers of the group firmly decided to kill the tiger and thus proposed a plan, as while the elder brother talking with the tiger, the younger brother was to kill the tiger with poisoned with bow and arrow. Thus, the plan was carried out accordingly. The tiger was dead. Everyone –young and old enjoyed the victory with feast and dances, from the incidents of the killing of the tiger, the clans of the tribe have been formed (Songkhupthang Serto.* Thus the traditions of merrymaking in the form of dance and music and festivities with the tune of the seasons are reported to have started.
>
> Dance and music:

A. Dance

All young and old, boys and girls know their traditional songs and dances. In the annual festivals, they performed various dances. In their earlier dormitory life, each young boys and girls learned such arts.

It is claimed that the Kom had eight types of folk dances, which are listed below:

1. *Berlam*
2. *Buntak lam*
3. *Thlang lam (Khorpui lam)*
4. *Vai-khong lam*
5. *Khorron lam*
6. *Reilam*
7. *Heilam*
8. *Lamkut lam*

The cultural dance of the Kom may be classified into two – (i) Group dance (*Mipui lam*) and (ii) Duet dance (*Sang lam*). Both these cultural dances are performed accompanied with musical instruments, clapping their hands, and wrapping with pieces of wood upon horn of Mithun. Men and women sing and dance jointly. However, their favourite songs are duets. In a group dance, the artists consists of the drummers (*Khongpu),* dancers (*Lamkeipa* and *lam keinu*), singers (*Hlapu* and *Hlapi*) and musicians (*seampu* and *Darpu*).

(i) Group dance (*Mipui lam):*

Dancing in group is very common among the Kom. This kind of group dance is derived from the *Berphun*, which is the greatest customary feast of the Kom. The various kind of group dances which includes are *Hennyalam* (Opening dance), *Vokolok lam*, *Secherahmei lam*, *Ronghoi lam*, *Phaison lam*, *Vaikhong lam*, *Bechap lam* and *Dairet lam* etc.

Almost all these group dances are performed in circle, and the style of dancing consists of well defined steps and leaps with the little variation of average slow and jerky motion.

(ii) Duet dance *(Sang lam):*

The duet dance is performed by a pair which consists of one man and a woman. However, sometimes the number of pair may increase. Most of the Kom cultural dances are performed in the traditional festivals which are held seasonally. As for instance, *Lam-kut* is generally held during the month of August or September, and *Pase-lampak* is held during the month of February.

The Kom cultural dances were named after the names of the customary feasts. The customary feasts of the Kom such as *Lam-kut*, *Silingphun*, *Pase-lampak,Nuhmei-lampak*, *Reithak* deserve special mention.

B. Music

The musical instruments specially accompanied in the dances consists of the following:

(i) *Khong* (Drum, Fig. 9.1)
(ii) *Sumpui/Shum* (Gong, Fig. 9.2)
(iii) *Dar* (small gong)
(iv) *Russem* (Trumpet, Fig. 9.3)

(v) *Sarangdar /Sananda* (a type of violin, Fig. 9.4)

(vi) *Seiching* (String bow, Fig. 9.5)

(vii) *Bunglir* (Flute)

(i) Shung (a short cane use as beating handle for mithun horn, Fig. 9.7)

(viii) *Seraki* (Mithun horn, Fig. 9.6)

(x) *Feifit* (a small bamboo split instrument)

(xi) *Bingboi* (a kind of whistle made of bamboo)

Russem is basically a sizable dry gourd, in which at least 6 pipes of reed stem are imbibed from the top. A shooting sound is produced when it is blown through the upper end of the gourd.

Different notes are produced by the varying lengths of the pipes. It is a very common wind instrument among the tribes of Manipur. *Sarangdar* or *sananda* is a stringed instrument hollowed out from a single piece of wood with a curious shape. The upper part of this hollowed out from a single piece of wood with a curious shape. The upper part of this hollow is left open. Another simple instrument is *Sarki* which is made from the mithun horn. The *Shum* or the gong is a metal drum, as used with a beating stick. Drum is made of *wang* (a kind of tree), the inner part of which is scooped out. At both ends, it is covered with hide preferably of deer. The pieces of the hide at both ends are kept in position and stretched at the same time by means of narrow strips of hide passed through the perforations on their borders. The drum is generally kept hung up within the house and brought out only on festive occasions.

Some musical instruments as used by the Kom

Fig. 9.1: Khong
(Drum)

Fig. 9.2: Shumpui/Shum
(Gong)

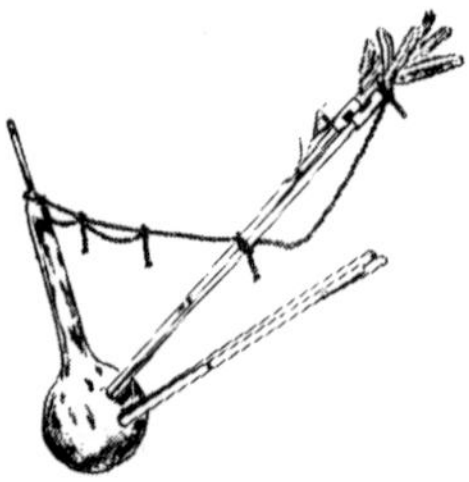

Fig. 9.3: Russem
(Trumpet)

Fig. 9.4: Sarangdar/Sananda
(A type of violin)

Fig. 9.5: Seiching
(String bow)

Fig. 9.6: Seraki
(Mithun horn)

Fig. 9.7: Shung
(A short cane (use as beating handle for mithun horn)

Festival

The Kom are said to have many festivals. Some of the earlier Kom festivals are described below:

(i) Seiram: It is regarded as the festival of origin for the Kom tribes. It is celebrated with the mithun (*Sitak*) at the centre of the courtyard or a ground all young and old, boys and girls enjoys with singing and dancing with feasting for two to three days. it is usually celebrated when the annual harvesting is over, around November and December. In this festival, the song of their origin is usually sung.

(ii) Romjin: It is celebrated in which a wealthy person who is fond of festivity may be proposed during the harvesting season. Those youth boys and girls helped in the procurement of paddy in the field from morn till evening, enjoys this celebration killing with a big size pig normally measuring 5 palms. They dance and sing right from the evening throughout the night and the following day and then concludes by the evening. Thus, the festival takes two days.

(iii) **Nuhmei lampak:** It is a festival in remembrance of the dead women of the family and relatives. It was their belief that if they celebrate such festival, the dead women would comfort in the heaven.

(iv) **Lampak/Latlal or Kakphut:** It is festival of merry making, anyone who is fond of festivity may arrange such celebration gathering with all boys and girls. Like that of *Seiram*, it is usually celebrated when the annual harvesting season is over.

(v) **Kut:** It is also a post harvesting festival. There is a belief that if the harvest is ended with warm and happily, the next season also will be more productive. In the festival, the boys and girls will jointly participate in the harvesting. The crops will be brought using their clothes. When they arrive home, the celebration will start with killing a big pig for pork. All the young and old enjoys throughout night with singing and dancing, till the next morning.

(vi) **Berphun:** It is one of the most important cultural group dances of the Kom/this kind of group dance is derived from the *Berphun,* which is the greatest customary feast of the Kom. '*Ber*' is a bird like thing made of plank, also called *Berva* which is meant *Berbird*, and it is suspended over the top of a very high bamboo post fixed at the enclosure of the courtyard of the host's (feaster). Expert archers would compete shooting on the seventh day of *Berphun* when the festival is concluded with a grand feast. That during the function, feasting and drinking, besides dancing and singing are the order of the days.

(vi) **Partha:** It is also a festival of flowers. All the youths, boys and girls will collect various flowers from the hill and they will gather at the evening with their bunches of beautiful flowers. When all are gathered, they will sing songs around a mithun (tied with a rope on the neck). While dancing, they will move around the mithun for three cycles. When the cycle is over, the mithun will be killed with indigenous methods. After dead, they will proceed with dancing and singing. After the dinner again, they will continue with dancing till the next evening.

(vii) **Sarulang:** It is a hunter encouragement celebration. When someone or a team of hunters killed a wild animal, a man of generous would arrange such a rejoice and encouraged celebration with the offering of dog meat. Usually, dance is performed by a couple. The dance will take standing over a short legged stool with holding the horn of the hunted animal either with one hand or two hands. The celebration starts in the evening and may proceed till the next day.

(ix) **Waikhing Lang:** It is a celebration in which four or five pairs of boys and girls dance with the rhythm of beating three drums. They cook the meat of the mithun and thus enjoy by all.

(x) **Sakhong lam:** It is dancing of a pair of young man and a girl in the centre accompanied with songs and music.

(xi) **Jorlam:** Two men and two girls would be dancing in the centre according to the music instruments and songs.

But nowadays, their cultural festivities are not common. They are retaining only a few group dances mainly for the purpose of cultural shows.

At present, the Kom as a whole are found to be converted into Christians. As a result, they have abandoned most of those traditional believes and practices.

References

Benjamin, Kom 1990. *The Kom-Rem People,* Mrs. T. Yangpi Kom, Lower Keirap, Loktak Project, Manipur.

Brown, R. 1873. *Statistical Account of Manipur,* Delhi Sankaran Prashak.

Das, Rajat Kanti 1985 .*Manipur Tribal Scene,* M.C. Mittal. Inter India Publications. W.Z-96V, Raja Garden, New Delhi-02.

Grierson, G.A. 1904. *Lingustic Survey of India*, Delhi, Motilal Banarsidass.

Mangpu Kilong 2000 *A short history of Indegenous communities of Kangleipak,* (ed) The League of the Fourth World People, Kangleipak, 1st floor WEDA, Building, Keishamthong Keithel, Imphal Kangleipak, Manipur.

McCulloch, Major, W. 1859. *Account of the Valley of Manipur and the hill tribes: with a comparative vocabulary of the Manipore and other languages*, selections from the Records of the Govt. of India (for Dept), 27.

Shakespear, J. 1912 *The Lushai Kuki Clans*, Central Building House, Delhi.

Teba K. Christian 1977 *8th Thousand Years of Koms.* Komlane, Imphal.

Teba Karong 1976 The Koms, in An *introduction to tribal language and culture of Manipur (7tribes), (*ed) Manipur State Kala Akademy. Imphal.

10

Boundary dispute between Arunachal Pradesh and Assam: An intractable problem

— *Dr. Ratna Tayeng*

The Making of the Assam-Arunachal Border

Assam and Arunachal border is an administrative interstate border dividing the two states of a single nation. Put differently, it is a boundary that divides hill and plain set up by the colonial rulers. However, with the passing of time the political influence of dividing line has grown stronger. It ultimately helps in developing "a sense of distinctiveness among the people and a sense of imaginative communion –'Arunachali' and has been promoting inter-ethnic integration among a large number of ethnoses in Arunachal Pradesh" (Acharya 1988, p. 1073 emphases added). Borders are binary constructs. Borders divide and create dichotomies (Konrad et al., 2019). Consequently, there exists a strong sense of differentiation like "us-hill people" and "they-plain people" among the people. According to Wouter (2012, p. 59) "The categories hill and plain do not just refer to a natural division of space but are also a reflection of socially constructed images and perceptions". The reason why people maintain such mental boundary is because it gives them a sense of distinctiveness, security and freedom. Donnan and Wilson (1999, p. 24) noted "these boundaries are constructed by people in their interactions with others from whom they wish to distinguish themselves. These are reflected by the fear and hatred of the other". Danda (1991, p. 51) argues that "an individual or a group can possess several identities, hidden or visible, simultaneously and project one that according to the self-assessment of individuals or groups may appear appropriate in specific context. Which particular identity the person will project at the given point of time would depend on his strategy adopted for the specificsituation".

Baruah (1989, p. 2089) noted "Since the formation of Arunachal Pradesh as a distinct state, tribal leader in power have sought to continue and even strengthen the exclusionary rules". In similar line, Blackburn (2003) noted "Benefit of the isolation policy implemented by Elwin and Nehru after Independence; protecting indigenous tribal cultures has apparently insulated them from the worst elements of post-Independence politics in the northeast". Sharma (2017, p. 9) "Rather than facilitating a harmonious relationship between the plains and the hills, the foothills have become the focal point of antagonism and conflict between the two". Zhoto and Wouters (2016, p. 9). "The inhabitants of different Northeastern states are unable to make connections intellectually and emotionally also exists in its reverse as a certain community in one state might profess kinship, intimacy, and belonging to a community in a neighbouring state while maintaining more antagonistic relations with ethnic groups within their own state". It is worth mentioning that Roy Burman (1989, p. 693) noted "Ethnic consciousness is to be considered as a dimension of interaction between society and state as well as of social organization of production and culturally determined pattern of consumption, it also relates to man's quest for belonging".

Barth (1969, p. 9) noted "Ethnic distinctions do not depend on an absence of social interaction and acceptance, but are quite to the contrary often the very foundations on which embracing social systems are built. Even if people cross their own community, and get contact with other community, social process of boundary maintenance will continue to persist". Categorizations like 'us' and 'they' are found all over, although the size and composition of such categories vary from culture to culture and society to society. By and large, there is a sense of assumed homogeneity in either of these categories. The problem with this distinction is that it presumes that there is a unified 'plains' culture and similarly a unified 'hill' culture, or even unified Arunachali culture (Tayeng, 2018). It may not be fair, therefore, to blame the indigenous people for their increasing ethno-political consciousness over the issue of outsiders, for they fear that rapid demographic transformations would perhaps outnumber them. Roy Burman (1989, p. 693) noted "Ethnic consciousness is to be considered as a dimension of interaction between society and state as well as of social organization of production and culturally determined pattern of consumption, it also relates to man's quest for 'belonging'. Baud and Schendel (1997, p. 242) noted "Whatever may be their real impact, borders become part of the perception and mental map of border landers. The paradox of how borders simultaneously separate and unite is the direct consequences of this mental map-making. Borders divide people living on both sides, who may have had a long history of cultural and social contact, but at the same time it unites them in the experience of closeness to the border and (partial) dependence onit".

These borders – legal and emotional borders, as well as inner-lines – cannot be found on conventional maps, and may also not always be clearly etched into the landscape but nevertheless divide and relate territories in ways similar to political and physical borders" (Zhoto & Wouters, 2016, p. 7). Today, the people of the state argue that peace and demography of the state lie in this border. According to Heyman (2004, p. 306) "Borders are no longer thought to have a block age function but a labelling one, filtering out of stigmatize dent rants while facilitating the travel of privileged entrants". At the crux of this issue is the larger question of the territorial identities plains vs hills. Assam claims all the plain territories of Arunachal as their own, Arunachal on the other hand, claims many of their plain areas were transferred to Assam in 1951 (Tayeng & Sonam, 2014). As divisions between plain/hill and tribal/non-tribal have hardened, Arunachal is re-imagined as a tribal state, with a tribal population, governed by tribal customary law. According to Daphne (1999), "borders are artifacts of history and are subject to change over time. When borders shift, lands and peoples are subjected to change". After closely analyzing, it appears that this inner-line boundary resembles closer an international boundary than a state boundary as its crossing is subject to identification and a pass akin to a visa. According to Kikon (2008) these borders operate like international borders, restricting mobility of people and goods as well. While these borders appear as mere lines on a map, they are best understood as sites that are continually shaped, altered, undermined and re-inscribed by numerous social actors. Some of these are, of course, local border landers –people who happen to live in the vicinity of borders –but many others actors also impinge directly or indirectly on border related process.

Sharma (2017, p. 6) noted "The colonial policies had a disjunctive effect on the traditional hills–plains relationship". He further noted "During precolonial times, the foothills as fluid boundaries served as critical sites of hills–plains interaction under the aegis of the medieval state formations in the Assam valley. The colonial regime stifled this system of interaction by turning the foothills into hard boundaries and an instrument for controlling the hills" (Ibid). The bond of friendship between the hills tribes and the Ahom plains dates back to the days of Sukapha (Bezbaruah, 1958, p. 102). According to Bhuyan (as cited in Hazarika, 1958, p. 55) "The Ahom kings never desired to occupy the hill territories and bring the people under their full control: for they knew it perfectly well that if they would do that, then the hills people would recede to the more interior areas of the hills and in that case they would derive no other material gains". Nonetheless, according to Choudhury (1982, p. 78) "the Ahom rulers were always ready to exploit any opportunity that presented itself to extend their sovereignty over the neighboring hill tribes. The Ahoms, however, did not always have an easy time". The tribes strongly resented the loss of their traditional rights and privileges in the foothills villages and made frequent raids to Ahom, therefore, developed a policy of conciliation by assigning to each tribe a certain number of paiks (tax-paying settlements) and giving it the right to realize from them a certain quantity of cereals, cloth, iron and salt, called Posa (Rahul, 1970, p. 47). There is no doubt that for centuries since then, people of this borderland have always maintained economic and cultural linkages.

During the Ahom period the main concern of the rulers, was to contain them within their hills and forests as they disturbed peace in the foothills. The Ahom kingdom thus created boundaries throughout the foothill regions which were vastly different from modern boundaries. The garhs formed defenses against raids, but their most important feature was the buffer zone. Unlike hard boundaries that are carefully delineated, the buffer zones were soft boundaries; parties across such boundaries had shared rights and obligations (Sharma, 2017, p. 5). However, with the advent of British colonialism in the 1820s led to a large-scale transformation of the conventional political systems of the region.

Hence, the history of the Assam-Arunachal border began with the expansion of the British Empire in the region. The history of border making has been dynamic and complex and it has impinged on life in Northeast India in many subtle ways. Various stages of colonial incorporation produced fluctuating borders and contested borderlands (Pachuau & Schendel, 2016, p. 1). Sharma (2017, p. 2) noted that "the foothills, as natural borders between the plains and the hills, occupy a crucial position in the socio-political and economic landscape of northeast India. The nomadic semi-savage tribes inhabiting hills were the trouble maker for Ahom. Hence, Ahom, made settlement with them through *posa* system and secure immunity from attack". When the British took over control of Assam from Purandar Singh, they found that the warlike tribes of the frontier had become even more aggressive. With the object of pacifying the hill tribes the British also follow the same tactic to keep hill tribes at bay (Administrative Reforms Commission Report, 1968, p. 195). But frequent raids in the valley threaten the peace and security to British administration. Alexander Mackenzie noted "From the beginning of our occupation of Assam the Duphlas gave much trouble to the local officers, and many fruitless efforts were made to induce them" (as cited in Elwin, 1959, p. 167).

Hence, with no choice left, the government began to set up chain of outposts along routes of the tribal movements to check the attack of the tribes. The posts were held by the armed police and military guards. By 1870s, to guard against the Daflas guard posts were set up at Kariapara, Behali, Singlijan, Ghera, Gohpur, Katori, Barpathar, Ooahat, Sellonibari and at Joyhing. To guard against the Aborsand Mish misguard posts were setup at Dimoh, Poba, Sesei, Dibong, Dikrang, Disoi, Difoo and at Sonpura (Bose, 1979, p. 147). Apparently, the gradual establishment of British rule over these tribal belts in the teeth of stiff resistance (Chakravorty, 1964, p. I). There were regular conflicts over the jurisdiction of their administration; hundreds of such territorial disputes have been reported on the historical text.

Frictions continue to arise time to time. The British considered it absolutely necessary that something should be done. Hence, on March 7, 1873, the Inner Line Regulation was passed. The Regulation is in force even today. Bhattacharya (1995, p. 203) noted "The British interest in this part of borderland was primarily commercial, the development of the tea industry and, later, the exploitation of oil, mineral and forest resources". However, the promulgation of the Inner Line Regulation was insufficient for maintaining relations with the tribals, was realized by Government with the passage of time. It was, therefore, decided to appoint a whole time officer of tract to take up the work of cultivating better relations with the tribal people (Administrative Reforms Commission Report, 1968, p. 196). Accordingly, Government of India defined and notified the internal boundaries for loose administration which came to known as Outer Line- external territorial frontier or the limits of the British territory. This was demarcated in 1875 as far as the river Burai and beyond which the boundary followed a readily recognizable line along the foot of the hills as far as Nizamghat to be throughout well recognized by usuage. Beyond Nizamghat, evidently, there was no Outer Line (Barpujari, 1981, p. 118). "The areas beyond this boundary were declared off-limits for land transfers to non-tribal outsiders" (Karlsson, 2011, p. 270). Their concern with the hillmen was that they should not come in the way of acquisition of land and forest areas required for establishing tea gardens (Reid, 1942). This borderland "ceded to the East India Company in 1938 and have given the land peace and prosperity ever since" (Dunbar, 1984, p. 75). But the hill tribes were never reconcile to the British rule (Johri, 1962, p. 4). Historically, inner-lines were imposed to provide a territorial frame to British capital (Kar 2009, p. 51). More deeply, it was to "demarcate 'the hills' from 'the plains', the nomadic from the sedentary, the jungle from the arable – in short 'the tribal areas' from 'Assam proper'" (ibid.: p. 52).

After the delineation of the North-East Frontier external boundaries popularly known as McMahon Line in 1914, the Government of India took effective measures to exercise control over the area. Hence, in September 1914, a fresh division of the areas was made under a new administrative area named North-East Frontier Tract (Bezbaruah, 2010, p.61). In 1937, the aforesaid areas came to be known collectively as the "*Excluded Areas of the Province of Assam*" under the provision of Section 91 (1) of the Government of India Act, 1935. These excluded areas came under the direct charge of the Governor of Assam who administered them in his discretion through the political officers and Deputy Commissioner of Lakhimpur District (Bezbaruah, 2010, p. 213). According to Kumar (2013) in a significant historical development, on June 30, 1947, The North East Frontier (Assam) Tribal and Excluded Area Sub Committee (popularly known as Bordoloi Committee) was constituted under the leadership of Gopinath Bordoloi and assisted by Mr. Justice Bijan Kumar Medhi. The Committee was asked to prepare a report on the future pattern of the administration of North East Frontier Tracts and submit it to the President of India before August 25, 1950.

The Commission submitted its report on August 22, 1950, to the President of India. The committee recommended that Govt. of Assam to take over the administration of NEFT. However, this recommendation was overlooked and centre continued to administer North East Frontier Tracts as "excluded area" through the governor of Assam. Their recommendation of transferring of certain plain areas of the North East Frontier Tracts to Assam on the ground that the people of these plain areas should not be denied the advantages of the franchise and regular administration was accepted (Administrative Reforms Commission Report, 1968, p. 203).

This report was accepted by the Minority Sub Committee of the Constituent Assembly presided over by Late Sardar Ballabh Bhai Patel in 1950. And once the presidential assent was obtained, Assam, having the authority, formally notified the report on 23.02.1951 that demarcated the 716 kms boundary of the then NEFT and Assam (Ibid). This 1951 notification is the present day boundary of Assam and Arunachal which runs from the tri-junction of Assam, Arunachal and Bhutan at Bhairabkundo on the west bank of the Dhansiri River to the tri-junction of Assam, Nagaland, and Arunachal on the Tiok River on the east. It has a length of about 716 kilometers. The repercussions of this step are being felt even today, and will be discussed in next head.

The Notification excluding these areas from the North East Frontier Tracts was issued on 23-02-1951. In the Notification, the plain portions of these tracts, (Balipara Frontier Tract, Tirap Frontier Tract, Abor Hills district and Mishimi Hills district) were transferred to the Assam state government and the rest became one of the Tribal Areas in Assam state. Considering the difficulty in governing the North East Frontier Tract with special features of its own, the governance of this area has been entrusted for the time being to the President acting through the Governor of Assam (States Reorganization Commission, 1955, p. 193). NEFA as a political entity formally came into existence in 1954 as a result of the promulgation of the North East Frontier Areas (Administration) Regulation, 1954 (Administrative Reforms Commission Report, 1968, p. 197). Again on 1st December 1957, the Naga tribal areas also called as Tuensang Frontier Division was transferred to Nagaland and merged with the present Nagaland state. It was transfer to Naga Hills on special consideration owing to the activities of the extremist elements. It was decided that unless the entire area is brought under the regular administration the situation of the law and problems cannot be effectively dealt with (States Reorganization Commission, 1955, p. 193). The remaining frontier areas now together form the present day Arunachal Pradesh.

The Demarcation of Assam-Arunachal Boundary

"The first proposal to demarcate the boundary on the ground was initiated in 1952 and some survey work was done in demarcating the boundary, but in 1962 due to certain representations from either side against such a survey work, the work was discontinued. Then on 08-01-1969 again, the question about the demarcation of the boundary was reviewed and it was decided that the Survey of India demarcate the boundary" (Bhattacharyya, 1995).

Accordingly, in 1971 the ground demarcation of Assam-Arunachal boundary was started. The Survey of India carried out the groundwork of demarcation. The fixation of the boundary pillar was given to Assam PWD. Till 1979, out of 716 kilometers, a total length of 396 kilometers was demarcated (Ibid). "The first sector, which is from Dhansiri River to the Panchoi River, was completed in 1971; the second sector that begins from the Panchoi River to Bharali River was completed in 1972.

However, the fixation of boundary pillar in this sector was not materialized due to the objection raised by the people of Arunachal. The third sector from the Bharali River to Borgang River was completed in 1972 and fixation of the boundary pillar was completed in 1973 without any opposition. The fourth sector from the Borgang River to Burio River, which is Tarasso area, was not carried out, owing to the opposition from the Arunachal sides. The length of this boundary is 27 kilometers. The fifth sector beginning from Burio River to Mornadi was done in 1973 but fixation of the boundary pillar was not done. From Mornadi to Dikrong River, which is Banderdewa, the area was completed in 1972, but no boundary pillar was fixed due to the opposition from Assam. The sector from the Dikrong River to Subansiri River was completed in 1974 and boundary pillar was also fixed in this sector. However, subsequent demarcation could not be continued due to problems arose in some portions of the un-demarcated areas and in portions of the demarcated boundary" (Government of Arunachal Pradesh, 2007).

Again, "on 12-04-1979, the proposal for demarcating the remaining portion from Subansiri River upto the tri-junction of Assam, Nagaland, and Arunachal on the Tiok River was decided and a High Powered Tripartite Committee was constituted for that purpose to carry out the demarcation of the boundary between Assam and Arunachal Pradesh. A preliminary mapping works were proposed to take further steps for the survey on the ground for demarcation. Regrettably, owing to the difference in the opinion, the mapping work was not materialized and whole dialogue for demarcating remaining portion perishes" (Ibid).

The Assam-Arunachal Boundary Dispute

The basic cause of territorial boundary disputes is the superimposition of the boundary on the cultural or physical landscape and some boundary disputes arise because of incomplete boundary evolution" (Prescott, 1987, p. 115). Misra (2011) noted most of the uncertainty of boundary demarcation in Indian subcontinents lies in the fact that states or sub-state authorities never consider border landers views on the forefront rather believe in territorial supremacy and it percolated to every region between the neighboring nation-state and between interstate. In similar line, Khamrang (2015) noted, "Territories in

Northeast India are demarcated by contradictory superimposed boundaries—modern state boundaries over traditional boundaries. Historically, traditional boundaries coincide with the ethnic mapping. Such ethnic territorial identity has been blatantly ignored during the reorganization of states in the post independence. Territorial politics, revolving around these two entities —modern and traditional boundaries, compound regional conflict with many ethnic groups asserted to restore the traditional boundaries". Nagaraju (2007, p. 12) noted, "Growing research about border disputes in the Northeast shows that much of the blame for these disputes is laid at the door of colonialism and the policies followed in that period. Colonial forms of knowledge of India, it is now established in no uncertain terms, have transformed the fuzzy borders between communities into rigid ones. Colonial authorities, seeking information in terms of 'hard facts' about people and land, introduced enumeration or census and mapping, which though useful, had other implications for communities with strong perceptions of their land, identity and the production of them in their knowledge and their social relations. With displacements and mutations caused to the communities during the colonial period, these communities developed a perception of threat. In the postcolonial nation-states, this has become a source of conflict and violence". Similarly Gellner (2013, p. 7) noted, "It is quite disheartening that the post-colonial state has become more of a problem than a blessing in most of Northeast India. They are 'pre-modern' in the sense that in practice - whatever the spurious precision of the lines drawn or claimed in treaties and maps - they are fuzzy and contested, and also because in many places along the borders the local populations have strong ties across them and often carry on daily life in disregard or even (in the past) in ignorance of them. The question that begs for an answer is whether a borderless Northeast as a replacement for the multiplicity of unviable states that currently dot the Northeast landscape will necessarily make a positive meaning to the long-suffering people. Unfortunately, ruling elites of the region are merely paying lip-service to the idea of regional integration and peaceful solving of problems".

Every day, there are reports on the newspapers about border conflicts of Assam and Arunachal, Assam and Meghalaya, Assam and Nagaland, Manipur and Nagaland and of course between Bangladesh and Meghalaya, Tripura and Assam and so on. Some of these disputes are decades old, and now they are assuming more and more violent forms (Gohain, 2007). Unfortunately, no serious work have been undertaken to understand the border problems over years. A book written by Bhattacharyya (1995) entitled "The Troubled Border" is perhaps only work pertaining to Interstate borders problem of North East India. The book, though sketchy, makes an attempt to provide some detail especially government notifications, notes, records and document about the inter-state boundary problems between Assam and Nagaland, Assam and Arunachal Pradesh, Assam and Meghalaya and Assam and Mizoram. Apart from this book, Hiren Gohain also published an important article in Economic & Political Weekly, entitled "Violent Borders: Killings in Nagaland-Assam" (2007) which touch upon the inter-state border problems of the Nagaland-Assam border. Other than these two, there is no literature that talks about the inter-state border problems of north east India. What is interesting is that both the writers favor Assam without understanding and not knowing the in-depth cause of such a violent border clash accused all the other Northeastern state of encroaching Assam land.

The current dispute between Assam and Arunachal is becoming more prominent over the years. The changing demographic landscape of the foothills coupled with the emerging resource use patterns among communities living there have turned foothill borders into a seriously contested space in recent times (Sharma, 2017, p. 2). Both states accused each other of playing faulty and illegally occupying other's territories. However, the first major border clashes with Assam and Arunachal Pradesh border were reported on 5th July 2005 where during an eviction drives by the Assam government, some 100 houses in three villages of Bhalukpong circle of the West Kameng district of Arunachal Pradesh were allegedly set ablaze by Assam Police and forest officials. The news stirred widespread anger and unease in Arunachal Pradesh. The All Arunachal Pradesh Students' Union (AAPSU) ordered: "Assamese migrants to vacate Arunachal territory". Since then intermittent clashes have taken place making the border tenses and the latest being occurred on January 29, 2014 at Behali where 11 persons were killed.

But this does not mean that there were no border disputes in the region before, in fact, during the times of British also there were disputes over the boundary and jurisdiction of "Inner Line" from hillmen time to time. Hundreds of such territorial disputes have been reported on the historical text of Dalton (1879), Mackenzie (1884), Allen (1906), Gait (1906), Shakespear (1914), Dunbar (1932), Reid (1942), among others. And every time the hillmen raided the British territory punitive expedition was followed to suppress through numerous expeditions. The expeditions to Daflas in 1874-75, Akas in 1883-84 and 1897, Abor clans five times between 1858 and 1894 and against the Mishmis in 1885 and 1899-1900 (Chakravarti, 1971, p. 37). The British accounts of these confrontations are at best one-sided as we have no means of knowing today how the tribesmen themselves viewed these clashes, as they left no written accounts (Choudhury 1982, p. VIII). Whatever was the rationale behind frequent attack of plain, the fact was the hillmen were zealous of their independence and possession of their lands. Infact, the hillmen considered the lowland contiguous to hills as their rightful preserves (Ibid). Just after independence also numbers of boundary problems of NEFA and Assam have been reported from Likabali and Jonai areas of the then Siang district of NEFA, Rupa in Kameng district, Kimin in Subansiri district and Sonpura in Lohit District of NEFA.

An Atmosphere of Fear and Mistrust

"It was about 11:00 am, on 9th January 2014, when most of the villagers left for the agricultural field, Assam forest Official led by DFO Biswanath Charali and Borgang Ranger with huge numbers of gun-toting armed forces proceed to tear down my house. Altogether, four houses were demolished before my eyes. Then they chop down our orchards that we grew with our sweat torch. We didn't even resist" noted Nabam Tado (name changed), a resident of Sango village. This is the incident in a Sango village under Taraso circle of Arunachal Pradesh on 9th January 2014, two weeks before the Behali incident. Sango village falls under Taraso Circle of Papumpare district of Arunachal Pradesh. The Sango village has total 26 families residing. All the families belong to Nyishi tribe. It is bounded by Behali Reserve forest in the south, the village Dipik in the east, the Shgungso village in the west. The village is said to be 100 years old.

After the incident, on 29th January 2014, ten persons were killed and eight others received bullet injuries near Sango village under Behali

Reserve Forest area of Sonitpur and Papumpare District border areas. According to Assam Tribune report (2014)[2] "Around 100 miscreants, armed with guns and other lethal weapon attacked the villagers, who have been camping there to protect those areas from further encroachment". It is by far the most violent dispute along Assam Arunachal boundary in post independence. Among 10 dead identified, 6 are Nepalis, 2 Munda Adivasi and 2 Rajbongsi. None were remotely present in Arunachal or even in Sonitpur in the past. This Behali reserved forest was declared a forest reserve by the British colonial government in 1917 without the knowledge of the people. This reserved forest areas were initially inhabited by Nyishi. However, the area under the reserve is shrinking due to encroachment and the reserve itself has become a site of conflict between Assam and Arunachal Pradesh. Gradually, during the 1980s, more people from the Assam began to settle in the area, encroaching on forestland. Most of the forest areas were encroached and inhabited by Miyas, Adivasis and Nepalis. About 3,375, ha area of Behali Reserve Forest is encroached by various groups of people namely Nepali, Karbi, Bodo and Tea-tribes (Borah et al., 2018, p. 182). After the events, the central security forces were stationed in the area and so far the culprit involve in killing is yet to be book. A few days later after the incident again the Assam Forest officials started to construct a forest camp inside Arunachal territory at Radhaso. Following which Mr. Ajay Kanoujia, The Director of North East, Ministry of Home Affairs wrote to the Chief Secretary of Assam to immediately stop construction work and called for maintaining status quo[3]".

The village where incident took place is known as Chauldhua in Assam which has not existed till year ago. This village has come recently in the month of November and December 2013 to occupy the Arunachalee land. They were camping under the banner of Arunachal Agrisan Pratirod committee (English equivalent is an Anti Arunachal encroachment committee). The committee derived a membership of more than 1500 people from various corner of the Assam for illegal land encroachment at Taraso circle under Arunachal Territory and deployed in a Sango village under Taraso circle and started to cut and cleared of the jungle at the aforementioned village. In that regard, District Administration of Papum Pare of Arunachal Pradesh and Sonitpur of Assam was conducted as series of meeting for vacating the land encroacher of Assam counterpart, but no any action was taken from Assam part. In fact, since the late 1980s, a significant migration of poor, landless Bodo tribal people has occurred in the area under the patronage of the Bodo nationalist groups agitating for a separate state for the Bodos by dividing Assam. In a bid to create contiguity among the Bodo inhabited areas of Assam, which they lacked in their proposed area for the separate state, the Bodo groups – especially the insurgent group National Democratic Front of Bodoland (NDFB) – actively facilitated the settlement of the landless Bodo people in areas with no Bodo population. The forest reserves in the northern region of Assam were their prime target. As a result of this, a large forest under various forest reserves in northern Assam completely disappeared in a matter of a decade or so (Sharma, 2017, p. 16). Thandapani village inside Behali reserved forest was established by the forest department during 1984–86 and the inhabitants of the village are the Santhals, who are ex- tea garden labourers. They were brought from some other parts of the state by the forest department evidently to protect that area from encroachments by the Arunachal tribes (Ibid).

Just after the dispute, economic blockade was imposed by the Communist Party of India (Marxist–Leninist) CPI (ML), Krishak Mukti Sangram Somiti (KMSS) and Assam Jatiyatabadi Yuba Chatra Parishad (AJYCP), All Assam Gurkha Student Union (AAGSU), Adibashi Student Association of Assam etc for nearly 8 days on National Highway-39 (NH-39), NH-52 and NH- 53, the vital lifelines to Arunachal from the rest of the country. But after a series of joint press conferences and negotiations between Assam Jatiyatabadi Yuba Chatra Parishad (AJYCP), All Assam Gurkha Student Union (AAGSU), Assam-Arunachal Labour Union Joint Committee, Assam Arunachal Border Committee, Adibashi Student Association of Assam, Minority Student Association and Student Union Movement of Arunachal (SUMA), All Papum Pare District Youth Association and All Arunachal Pradesh Student Union (AAPSU) at different places, the economic blockade was lifted. The organizations criticized the governments of both the states for such violence in the border regions. The role of the Student Organizations is important in maintaining peace and tranquility along the Arunachal-Assam border. These student organizations play a vital role in making the people aware of their constitutional rights and pressurizing the government. They also contribute towards the unity of the people.

One cannot deny that vigilantism is a general phenomenon throughout Assam-Arunachal borderlands. It is an open secret that the Assam government allows the Nepalese, the Adivasi, Bodos and the Rajbongsis to settle in the forest areas of Assam-Arunachal borderland. Bhalukpong is known for Bodo militant activity such as the National Democratic Front of Bodoland (NDFB). The Communist Party of India (Marxist–Leninist) activity in borderland is also well known. The used of forest areas along the Assam-Arunachal border as a training ground for United Liberation Front of Assam (ULFA) is widely reported in the past. Recently, the Arunachali Agrason Pratirodh Samiti (AAPS–Committee for Resistance against Arunachalese Aggression) formed by the villagers of the foothill areas from the Assam side to resist the encroachment on Assam's land. More recently, the National Liberation Council of Taniland (NLCT) is also said to be active along the Assam-Arunachal borders. There was no report of any activity of this outfit in the recent past but after the killing in Behali the name of the outfit cropped up once again. In the Tirap and Changlang border areas, the presence of Naga outfits is widely known. The All Arunachal Pradesh Border Students' Union since formation in 2003 has actively served the affairs of border students of Arunachal Pradesh. But it is difficult to state with any certainty that they are main cause of the border dispute. However, it is clear that these vigilant groups and militant outfits seem to have intensified the border conflict.

Likabali, the oldest towns in the foothills of Arunachal Pradesh, which is located at the Assam-Arunachal border, is the nodal centers of market related activities of the entire foothills area of the entire Siang districts. But it is also one the most dispute prone areas along the Assam Arunachal border. The dispute has always been reported on Likabali area since the British days. Even after Independence, disputes had been reported on 1959, 1979, and 1987. However, in 1997 dispute turn very aggressive when the Assam Forest department tried to evacuate some agricultural field from the old Telam village (20 km from Likabali) that the villagers retaliated. Again in 2010, Forest officials of the Assam raid and ousted many areas whom they considered as their territory and established an Assam police training centre (Riba,

2014). According to Tao (2014) "The Govt. of India Act 1914 recognized the boundary of the then Frontier tract from Akajan which is 12 km away from the Likabali town. There was a NEFA gate at Akajan, which is now totally under the control of Dhemaji district in Assam. At the gate it was written, 'NEFA begins from here' which was destroyed in 2011 and a dedication to the BRO staff has been erected thereafter. The first time national flag hoisting in Arunachal Pradesh (the then Frontier Tract) was hosted by Lt. Moji Riba at Dipa Lire in 1947 which is now occupied by the Assam and renamed as a Somkong village under Jonai Sub-Division, Dhemaji District of Assam".

On April 6, 2012, the Assam officials led by Additional Deputy Commissioner Dhemaji, UK Baruah illegally raided Malini Mela complex and destroyed structures including erected pandal for Malini Mela celebrations. According to the people, the Malinithan Mela ground is within the Arunachal territory and since late 60's, the Mela has been celebrated every year at the same location. Ajum (2012) writes "the area was declared as protected area vide notice RES (H) 124/75 dated 12th October 1981 by the Govt. of Arunachal". Rina (2012) writes: "Whatever claims they make, the fact remains that all plain land in Likabali have been encroached by Assam and the people of the area are forced to pay land tax to Assam govt. If it was not for the local people, by now the entire township would have been captured by Assam".

Again on January 18, 2014, Assam police officials destroyed the boundary wall constructed by one Mime Riba around her commercial plot inside the Arunachal territory in Likabali area. On 2nd February 2014, Kamcham village under the Kangku circle of West Siang district was asked to vacate their agriculture field. Dharna was called by Akhil Gogoi, a well- known RTI activist of Assam and few CPI (ML) activists. A deadline was also given on 2 February to vacant the Arunachalee paddy field. Although proposed eviction was not carried out, but the mega public meeting was convened at Vijoypur Assam near Kamcham village. The Assam side has set up police chowki units along the Assam-Arunachal border at every 10 metres, but there are no such security provisions on the Arunachal side.

These incidents are extremely serious and clearly demonstrate the sense of impunity with which the Assam police and forest officials operates. The researcher, however, did not find any reports to demonstrate that any effective steps have been taken by the Governments on either side of the border to hold the security personnel accountable for their criminal actions. Since these are often in the guise of 'forest eviction', these security forces cannot be held to account under any law for such violations. These and other incidents, some of them major and others minor show what a conflict can lead to conflict. The security forces are sent to protect them but they can become a threat to the people. Whatever the case, it is clear that there is lack of trust between the people and the neutral force.

Claims and Counter Claims

Bhattacharyya (1995, p. 218 & 221) "The people of Arunachal and the Arunachal Administration had not penetrated into Assam territory at one or two places but the intrusion by encroachment has been widespread along almost the entire border and encroachment in some places had extended to more than 5 kilometers inside Assam. Such encroachments are pronounced at Kimin, Dirpai, Likabali, Dullungmukh and Jonai areas. Arunachal Administration established a Circle office, PWD and Forest Office in Kimin well inside Assam; constructed a Health Center at Telam in Jonai area and built an Anchal Samiti House at Likabali. They settled their people and set up illegal villages inside Assam and are making totally illegal and un- constitutional bid to administer the areas". He further writes: "Apart from the occupation of land deep inside Assam territory, the people of Arunachal, mainly the Adis and Nyishis have been constantly harassing the Assamese inhabitants by intimidation, mischief, kidnapping, assault and arson etc. The theory of 'status quo' as understood by Arunachal appears to be that it should apply to Assam only and not to them. It is breach of status-quo by Assam, according to them, when some local officers of Assam Government obstruct their advancing encroachment" (1995: p. 236 & 237). However, Rina (2011) writes the root cause of Assam-Arunachal border disputes is that" it was created by main land Indians accompanied by the governor of Assam who was a stranger to the region, appointed by the Indian government to divide a state which they had never seen, who arrived here in July 1951 and carried out the imaginary boundary within a month – and that also without the right map and right respective local peoples to do it with".

While according to Bezbaruah (2010, p.180) "Although the British stepped into the shoes of the Ahoms after the annexation of Upper Assam, their regular administration did not cover all the territories earlier administered by the Ahoms. Only the areas suitable for wet cultivation, tea plantation or homestead were brought under settlement and regular administration. Hills, interior forests, and even earlier flourishing parts of the plains once rule by Ahoms, were left out of the regular administrative jurisdiction". Similarly, Hazarika[4] (1995) noted "when we come to the problems of inter-state borders, one pertinent fact all must appreciate that the constitutional boundaries of Assam with all the sister states, which were parts of greater Assam till recent past, are well defined leaving hardly any ambiguity for interpretation. But the neighboring states have seen claiming territories basing their claims on a hypothetical theory of old usage and practices which are difficult to define and impossible to accept".

Interestingly, on June 5, 2013, in a press statement, "Bamang Tago, Political Advisor to Chief Minister of Arunachal Pradesh denying the accusation that the state Government was not doing enough to resolve the boundary disputes with Assam, claimed that the Arunachal Government has been constantly pursuing with both Assam and Central Governments to end the tension along the boundary with a permanent solution. He claimed that all these efforts failed entirely due to Assam's uncompromising stand"[5]. Whereas the Government of Assam claimed that all these effort failed due to misconception of some people and the officials of Arunachal Pradesh about constitutionally defined boundary. According to Minister of State (Assam) Siddique Ahmed: "over 80,000 hectares of Assam's territory are illegally encroached and occupied by Arunachal Pradesh, Nagaland, Mizoram, Meghalaya and Tripura…out of these encroached hectares 15,000 hectares of Assam's land have been encroached by Arunachal Pradesh[6]".

The fact of the matter is the state of Assam has failed to assess any ground realities. This is evident from the fact that the Survey of India could identify as many as 30 villages falling within the territory of Arunachal Pradesh and 7 others along the constitutional boundary which

Assam continue to deny. Hence, the state of Arunachal Pradesh has submitted before the local boundary Commission indicating the names of 123 claimed villages situated all along the inter- state boundary which Assam has failed to indicate. There are many villages that fall under the territory of Assam but the Govt. of Arunachal Pradesh administers the villages. There are also such villages which agricultural fields are located on the Assam side of the boundary. There are also villages, which have similar names creating a problem for identification for both the state such as Telam, Boka/Buka, Gorubandha, Tarajuli, Likabali, Ruti or Ratigaon. As a matter of fact, still today in many portions of West Siang, East Siang, and Lower Dibang Valley border areas-the area which I personally visited, people pays land revenue for their agriculture land to Assam government which is of course, constitutionally right and proper. But the problem arises from the Assam police and forest officials continued evictions unabated in the name of 1951 notification and in the name of the Forest Eviction Drive. Citizens living in areas which share a boundary of Assam like Rayang, Telam, Depi, Debing, Likabali and much more, are often been harassed by police officials of Assam without any reason.

The arguments advanced by Arunachal Pradesh Government fall into three categories. First, it is argued that the 1951 treaty was not legally binding since no Arunachal representatives were present in the commission. Secondly, that in any case the tribal traditional boundary accepted by Britishers should be respected and enacted. Thirdly, further encroachment should be stopped by Assam side, which encouraged boundary problems. With these arguments, in 2007, the state of Arunachal Pradesh by its Letter No-HMB (B) 69/2006 Vol. I, dated 26-12-2007 has submitted its proposal for making certain adjustments in the Assam Arunachal Pradesh Territorial Boundary.

Areas claimed by Arunachal Pradesh through the proposal of boundary adjustment

Sl. No.	*Name of District*	*Area transferred to Assam as per 1951 Notification*	*Area claimed by Arunachal Pradesh for adjustment*
1.	West Kameng (Bomdila)	587.70	75.80 Sq Km
2.	East Kameng (Seppa)	662.00	25.35 Sq Km
3.	Papumpare (Yupia)	-	252.665 Sq Km
4.	Lower Subansiri (Ziro)	257.00	56.25 Sq Km

(*Contd...*)

5.	West Siang (Aalo)	-	187.57 Sq Km
6.	East Siang (Pasighat)	833.85	135.16 Sq Km
7.	Lower Dibang Valley (Roing)	978.30	101.96 Sq Km
8.	Lohit (Tezu)	-	8.65 Sq Km
9.	Changlang (Changlang)	330.00	96.296 Sq Km
10.	Tirap (Khonsa)	-	179.579 Sq Km
	Total	3648.85 Sq Km	1085.82 Sq Km

Source: Government of Arunachal Pradesh, Home Department, Itanagar, 2007.

The Arunachal government argued that the boundary drawn with 1951 notification was a completely biased and one sided decision to the detriment of rights of the hill people over part of foothill plains. It argues that the Ahom rulers paid Posa to many tribes of the North East Frontier Tract for keeping peace in the border and not raiding the plains or in recognition of customary claims on the local inhabitants or territories in the adjoining plains of the hills is an indisputable historical fact. This system was continued by the British rulers and also by Independent India in 1950s and therefore apart from an acknowledgment of the claims of the hill people over the foot hill plains and acknowledgment of their customary rights over the adjoining territories. But this vital aspect was completely overlooked while transferring large areas of the Frontier Tract Territory to the state of Assam by the Notification of 1951. It also argues that the existing constitutionally notified Inter-State Boundary following more or less the Inner Line is a notional boundary.

The argument that the Assam Government advanced so far fall into two categories, firstly, historically North East Frontier Tract (NEFT) was part of Assam and were controlled once very recently. Secondly, the 1951 boundary is a constitutional boundary. In reply to the state of Arunachal Pradesh the state of Assam by its letter No-BD.3/08/320, Dated 29th October, 2009 argues that the claim of the state of Arunachal Pradesh for adjustment of the Inter State Boundary is meaningless. The state of Assam argues that the proposal of the State of Arunachal Pradesh for readjustment of the Inter-State Boundary in the light of traditional and customary rights exercised by different tribes of the state in the foothills adjoining the state of Assam is unacceptable. The state of Assam reiterates that the state of Arunachal Pradesh does not have a right any customary right over the territory of the state of Assam. There is no historical evidence of any hill tribes of Arunachal Pradesh acknowledging any sort of authority of Ahom Kings over them. The State of Assam has also refuted the claim of the State of Arunachal Pradesh for adjustment of Inter State Boundary on the ground that such boundary stands defined by the Constitution of India and therefore, the determination of the Inter State Boundary should be on the basis of what is stated in the Constitution of India.

The problems of Assam Arunachal boundary lie in various factors. Among them first is the inexact definition and of course, in a single word, it is a product of faulty demarcation. Sharma (2017, p.9) noted that "a mutually acceptable division of the states would be difficult to achieve was already known. Despite this, the cavalier and arbitrary manner in which the inter- state border was demarcated was incredible. A stream here, a tree there became the markers of the inter-state border. When the stream changed its course or the tree fell due to some reason over the years, without any proper markers, the boundaries became disputed sites". Besides, Assam claims all the plain territories of Arunachal as their own, Arunachal on the other hand, claims many areas were transferred to Assam in 1951. Arunachal argues that Assam ruled six years Arunachal (1950-56) during those years they have taken an undue advantage. Arunachal argues that the boundary delimited in this award was based on imperfect geographical information. The award was not, in fact, based purely on the geographical and history of people who lived on the boundary. The boundary was surveyed by Survey of India and started demarcation in the years 1971 but unfortunately, in 1973 the demarcation process was abandoned because of the opposition of people from both sides.

The Local Boundary Commission

In India, boundary disputes are resolved through negotiated agreement or by trial in court. Article 3 & 4 of the Indian Constitution provides that boundary disputes should be settled by negotiation, enquiry, mediation, conciliation, arbitration, judicial settlement, and resort to peaceful means. "It confers, on the Supreme Court of India, exclusive jurisdiction to deal with disputes involving legal rights between two or more States among other disputes" (National Commission to Review the Working of the Constitution, July 6, 2001)[7]. Consequently, a local boundary commission was set up on 25th September 2006. This three member commission is headed by retired High Court judge Tarun Chatterjee and M. Kamal Naidu, a retired Indian Forest Service Officer, and S.K. Goel, additional surveyor general of India. Ironically, nothing much has happened over these years because the states refuse to agree to a point. What has so far happened is hearing and objection. The façade will continue while the people residing at border continue to bear the brunt of encroachment after encroachment.

In north east India, a number of commissions were appointed to settle various inter-state boundary problems. However, these commissions have failed to settle any disputes so far because the states refuse to agree with the commission[8]". Some even say that these commission instead of solving rather crated problems in the region. Moreover, there a strong criticism on three counts, firstly, they are involving inordinate delay in securing settlement of such disputes, secondly, there is no provision for an adequate machinery to enforce the award of the Tribunal and lastly people were not involved in the dialogue process.

Hence it is very unlikely that this Local Boundary Commission also would come up with anything substantial. Moreover, the Local Boundary commission while they may give consent, it is just an opinion and they have no jurisdiction over demarcation and delimination of boundary and it is unlikely that we would see any solution from such commission. And more importantly, when both Assam and Arunachal government is so adamant and flexing their muscles across the border, making claims and counter-claims of territory, the situation don't seems will improve in the years to come. Even if local boundary comes up with "give and take" mechanism the people of the border region will not going to comply because in none of the meetings people were involved in the dialogue process. In fact, this Local Boundary Commission in one of their meeting at Hotel Donyi Polo Ashoka on 10th November, 2013 turn down All Papum Pare District Student's Union request to submit a memorandum on behalf of people of Dissing Passo and Seijosa stating meeting of official representatives only. As a matter of fact, Assam-Arunachal border dispute cannot be settled by governmental negotiations rather it will only be settle in consultation with the public living in the border areas.

Conclusion

It is apparent that the Britisher initially was hesitant to administer this borderland. During the colonial period, present Arunachal Pradesh was administered as an "excluded area". But with the anxious to provide security to the tea plantations and the coal mines and oil fields which developed along the foothills, it was found necessary to keep away the hill tribes inhabiting the frontiers, for the Company's Government was reluctant to assume responsibility for them. Hence, they have drawn the Inner Line and the Outer Line, which over the years becomes the present day border between Arunachal Pradesh and Assam. Zou & Kumar (2011, p. 159) noted colonial cartography endeavored to establish and calibrate exact boundary lines between disparate tribes and their territories. This line of thinking understandably ended up enacting inner and external lines in a border zone of overlapping sovereignties and nationalities. They made boundary just to rule the land, they annexed tribal land wherever they want to. Whenever the hill people out of frustration attack their people living on the British side or territory, the punitive expedition was carried out, burning and killing the hill men. Choudhuri (1982, p. 78) noted that the British rulers did not succeed easily in taking control of their areas. Several conflicts followed and gradually, the region and the boundary line of the present day Arunachal Pradesh was brought under British administration at different times and in different ways. Scott (2009) even goes on to argue that historically the people in this area have made consistent attempts to evade the states that tried to lay claim to them and to the territories in which they live.

The colonial policies had a disjunctive effect on the traditional hills–plains relationship. It relegated these processes and the role of foothill tribes to the periphery in the imagination of the plains people (Sharma, 2017, p. 6). With the passing of time the political influence of "dividing line" has grown stronger. It ultimately helps in developing a sense of distinctiveness among the people and a sense of imaginative communion –"Arunachali". After independence, India followed colonial policy and created webs of internal boundaries between Indian states half heartedly (Gohain, 2007). Today, many of these borders operate like international borders, restricting mobility of people and goods as well (Kikon, 2008). The boundaries as objects of cultural differences in Arunachal peoples in opposition to midland Indian started with the announcement of tribal policy by Pandit Jawaharlal Nehru (Elwin, 1959). However, after independence, some of these dividing walls were pulled down. But soon thereafter another force inimical to natural assimilation made its appearance, and that is forced assimilation. This forced assimilation effort of the Government of India upset the tribes. Now, the hegemony of the discourse is maintained through perceptions of influx, the fear of being dominated by the plains culture through the influx of 'outsiders'. But it is not hard to gauge why exclusionary laws are popular with tribal people of the state, since it is the largest state in North East India area wise and with negligible population.

The Assam Arunachal boundary dispute is an age old disputes. No doubt, to solve the problem a series of meetings at different level have taken place and a number of agreements have been signed between the two states but there has been no effective result till date. However, in order to understand this boundary problem understanding the history of border areas is a must. The entire problematic areas of Assam-Arunachal border was a no men land till the Britisher came into the region. The Britishers saw these areas promising for tea cultivation. As a result, Britisher started annexing huge land under their occupation and notified many foothills forest areas as Reserved Forest and Sanctuary for the purpose of grabbing the forests areas wherever they want. Consequently, there were many instances of disputes over the outposts, barricades and blockades and later over the jurisdiction of "Inner Line boundary of 1873" from hillmen. This policy of notifying foothills areas as Forest and Wildlife Sanctuary was even continued by the Governor of Assam, who acted at the behest of President of India. It is ironical that in none of the colonial or post-colonial historical record one will find what made these hillmen attack villages' lies across the borders.

In any case, the quest for the understanding and resolution of Assam-Arunachal's boundary problems need thorough historical analysis and people to people dialogues. Part of the problem of Assam Arunachal borderland lies in the intermingling of the population across the border, which Assam often used to claim to the areas. For instance, there are many Arunachalee who are settled deep inside Assam territory even before the demarcation was made. For instance, there is a village called Abor Leku in Jonai Circle of Dhemaji District of Assam. The Gam Burah (Headman of the village) is Tanya Rina. He came to the village in the 1940s before the great earthquake of 1950. The Government of Assam appointed him as Gam Burah in 1970. He informed, only Galos tribe earlier inhabited the village, now most of them went back to neighboring Arunachal villages. Only six Galos families stayed today in the village. They are living there for at least 8 decades, even before boundary demarcation, paying land revenue to the government of Assam.

There are many such villages all along Assam Arunachal borders. As per the official report as many as 123 villages along Assam-Arunachal borders are disputed. The State of Arunachal Pradesh has submitted before the Local Boundary Commission headed by Justice Tarun Chatterjee on dated 5th April 2010[9] indicating the names of 123 claimed villages/areas situated all along the inter-state boundary between State of Arunachal Pradesh and Assam. Survey of India findings corroborate the stand of Arunachal Pradesh to a great extend which Assam has failed to indicate and continue to deny.

There are also many villages that fall under the territory of Assam but the Govt. of Arunachal Pradesh administers the villages. There are also such villages which agricultural fields are located on the Assam side of the boundary. There are also villages, which have similar names creating a problem for identification for both the state such as Telam, Boka/Buka, Gorubandha, Tarajuli, Likabali, Ruti or Ratigaon. As a matter of fact, many portions of East Kameng, Papumpare, West Siang, East Siang, and Lower Dibang Valley border people pays land revenue for their agriculture land to Assam government which is of course, constitutionally right and proper. But the problem arises when the Assam police and forest officials starts evictions unabated in the name of 1951 notification and in the name of the Forest Eviction Drive. Citizens living in areas which share a boundary of Assam like Torajan, Tarraso, Gumto, Rayang, Telam, Depi, Debing, Likabali and much more, are often been harassed by police officials of Assam without any reason.

It is high time that the Central government must take a bold initiative to settle the problem once and for all. It can do so by either persuading the concerned states to come to the negotiating table and seek a solution through ground level study on nature of land holding system and implication of forest laws in boundary area. A onetime reinforcement is not a solution. It must come up with a tangible solution even if it means give and take. Or else everyone at the helms of affairs might as well give up and let the people at the border decide how they want to take forward the issue.

References

1. Acharya, S. K. (1988). Ethnic Processes in North-Eastern India. *Economic and Political Weekly*, 23 (21), pp. 1068-1077.
2. Administrative Reforms Commission Report on Study Team on Administration of Union Territories and NEFA. (1968). New Delhi.
3. Ajum, T. (2012, April 6). Likabali tense as Assam officials destroy Malini Mela structure. *The Arunachal Times*, p. 1.
4. Barth, F. (Ed.) (1969). *Ethnic groups and boundaries: the social organization of Culture difference.* Middleton: Waveland Press.
5. Baud, M. and W. V. Schendel. (1997). Toward a Comparative History of Borderlands, *Journal of World History,* 8 (2), pp.211-242.
6. Baruah, S. (1989). Minority Policy in the North-East: Achievements and Dangers. *Economic and Political Weekly*, 24 (37), pp. 2087-2091.
7. Barpujari, H.K. (1981). *Problem of the Hill Tribes; North-East Frontier, Inner Line to the Mc Mohan Line*. Guwahati: United Publishers.
8. Bezbaruah, P. (1958). History Yells: The Hills and the Plains of Assam are but one. In P. Chaliha (Ed), *The Outlook on NEFA*. Jorhat: Asam Sahitya Sabha.
9. Bezbaruah, R. (2010). *The Pursuit of Colonial Interests in India's North East*. Guwahati: Eastern Book House.
10. Bhattacharyya, B. (1995). *The Troubled Border*. Guwahati: Lawyer's Book Stall.
11. Blackburn, S. (2003). Colonial contact in the 'hidden land': Oral history among the Apatanis of Arunachal Pradesh. *The Indian Economic and Social History Review*, 40 (3), pp. 335-365.
12. Borah, D., Parixit, K., Tangjang, S., Das, A.P. (2018). Population structure and conservation of endangered Citrus indica Yu.Tanaka (Rutaceae) in Behali Reserve Forest of Assam, India. *Pleione* 12(2), p. 181-186.
13. Border Affairs. 2010. Government of Arunachal Pradesh, Home Department letter to Justice Tarun Chatterjee, Chairman, Local Commission, Dated 5th April 2010.

14. Bose, M. (1979). *British Policy in the North East Frontier Agency*. New Delhi: Concept Publishing Company.
15. Burman, B. K. Roy (1989). Problems and Prospects of Tribal Development in North-East India. *Economic and Political Weekly,* 24 (13), pp. 693-697.
16. Chakravorty, B.C. (1964). *British Relations with the Hill Tribes of Assam since 1958*. Calcutta: Firma KLM Private Ltd.
17. Chakravarti, B.C. (1971). *The Evolution of India's Northern Borders*. London: Asia Publishing House.
18. Chandrika, S. (1989). *Emergence of Arunachal Pradesh as a State*. Delhi: Mittal Publication.
19. Choudhury, J.N., (1982). *Arunachal through the Ages: From Frontier Tracts to Union Territory*. Calcutta: Navana Printing.
20. Danda, A. K. (1991). *Ethnicity in India*. New Delhi: Inter-India Publications.
21. Daphne, B. (1999). *Where the World Ended: Re-Unification and Identity in the German Borderland*. London: University of California Press.
22. Donnan, H. & Wilson T. M. (1999). *Borders: Frontiers of Identity, Nation and State.* Oxford: Berg Publishers.
23. Dunbar, G. 1984 (1932). *Frontiers*. New Delhi: Omson Publication.
24. Elwin, V. (1959). *India's North East Frontier in the Nineteenth Century*. London: Oxford University Press.
25. Gellner, D. N. (2013). *Borderland lives in northern South Asia*. London: Duke University Press.
26. Gohain, H. (2007). Violent Borders: Killings in Nagaland-Assam. *Economic and Political Weekly*, August 11, 2007, Pp. 3280-3283.
27. Government of Arunachal Pradesh. 2007. Home Department, Itanagar, Proposal for adjustment of areas along the Inter-State Boundary between Arunachal Pradesh and Assam, File No.- No. HMB(B)69/2006 Vol. I, Dated Itanagar, the 26th December, 2007.
28. Government of Arunachal Pradesh. 2013. Documents. Retrieved from http://arunachalpradesh.nic.in/csp_ap_portal/arunachal-assam-to-solve-boundary- issue.html on 9th February, 2014.
29. Government of Assam. 2009. Border Areas Department-Dispur, Guwahati, Reply to the rejoinder submitted by Govt. of Arunachal Pradesh before the state of Assam, File No.- NO.BD.3/08/320, Dated Dispur, the 29th October, 2009.
30. Hazarika, K, (1958). The Nebula of the Northeast Frontier. In P. Chaliha (Ed.), *The Outlook on NEFA*, Jorhat: Asam Sahitya Sabha.
31. Heyman, J. (2004). Ports of Entry as Nodes in the World System, *Identities,* 11(3), Pp. 303-327.
32. Johri, S. (1962). *Where India, China and Burma Meet*. Calcutta: Thacker Spink & Co. Private Ltd.

33. Kar, B. (2009). 'When was the Postcolonial? A History of Policing Impossible Lines.' In Baruah, S. (Ed.) *Beyond Counter-Insurgency: Breaking the Impasse in Northeast India.* Oxford: Oxford University Press.
34. Karlsson, B.G (2011). *Unruly Hills: a Political Ecology of India's Northeast.* Oxford: Berghahn Books.
35. Kikon, D. (2008). Ethnography of the Nagaland–Assam Foothills in Northeast India. In W. Fernandes & S. Barbora (Eds.), *Land, People and Politics: contest over tribal Land in northeast India*. Guwahati: North Eastern Social Research Centre International Workgroup for Indigenous Affairs.
36. Khamrang, L. (2015). Geography of Insurgency: Contextualization of Ethno-Nationalism in Northeast India, *Open Journal of Social Sciences,* 3, pp. 103-113.
37. Konrad V., Laine J.P., Liikanen I., Scott J.W., Widdis R. (2019). The Language of Borders. In Brunn S., Kehrein R. (eds) *Handbook of the Changing World Language Map*. Basel: Springer.
38. Kumar, P. (2013). One-man Bordoloi Commission: Boundary row haunts people, Cong wields BC, *Arunachal Front*, 12/06/2013, p.1.
39. Mishra, S. (2011). *Becoming a Borderland: The Politics of Space and Identity and in Colonial Northeastern India*. New Delhi: Routledge.
40. MHA directs Assam Govt. to stop encroachment at Tarasso (2014, April 23). *The Arunachal Times*, p. 1.
41. Nagaland seeks reviewing of border pact with Assam (2014, June 1). *The Echo of India*, Siliguri, p. 4.
42. Nagaraju, N. (2007). Border Negotiations, in Tamo Mibang & M. C. Behera (Ed.) *Tribal Studies: Emerging Frontiers of Knowledge*. New Delhi: Mittal Publications.
43. National Commission to Review the Working of the Constitution. (2001). A Consultation Paper on Constitutional Mechanisms for settlement of Inter-State Disputes, Vigyan Bhawan, New Delhi, the 6th July, 2001, p. 10.
44. Pachuau, J.L.K & Schendel, W.V. (2016). Borderland Histories, Northeastern India: An Introduction. *Jawaharlal Nehru University: Sage Publication Studies in History,* 32(1), pp. 1-4.
45. Prescott, J.R.V. (1987). *Political Frontiers and Boundaries*. London: Allen & Unwin.
46. Rahul, R. (1970). *The Himalaya Borderland.* Delhi: Vikas Publications.
47. Reid, R. 1983 (1942). *History of the Frontier Areas Bordering on Assam: From 1883-1941*, Delhi: Eastern Publishing House.
48. Riba, R. (2014, February 15). Time to get united. *The Arunachal Times*, p. 4.
49. Rina, T. (2012, April 7). Likabali fends for itself. *The Arunachal Times*, p. 1.

50. Rina, T. (2011, November 30) Arunachal and its Boundaries. *The Arunachal Times*, 30/11/2011, p. 1.

51. Report of the States Reorganization Commission, New Delhi, (1955), p. 193. Retrieved from https://www.mha.gov.in/sites/default/files/State%20 Reorganisation%20Commisison%20Report%20of%201955_270614.pdf

52. Sharma, C. K. (2017). Political Economy of the Conflicts along Assam-Arunachal Pradesh Foothill Border: A Study with Special Reference to the Behali Foothill of Assam, *North East Resources Study Series*, 1 (1) 2015-16. Guwahati: Action Aid India.

53. State Govt denies accusation, says pursuing with Centre, Assam to solve boundary issue (2013, June 6). *The Arunachal Times*, p. 1.

54. Tao, I. (2014, April 25). Assam- Arunachal boundary row. *The Arunachal Times*, Editorial Column, p. 4.

55. Tayeng, O. (2012, March 29). 15,000 hectares of Assam's land encroached by Arunachal: Assam Minister, *The Arunachal Times*, p. 1.

56. Tayeng, R. (2018). *Living on the Edge: An Anthropological Study of the Mishing Community of Arunachal-Assam Borders*. An unpublished PhD thesis submitted to Department of Anthropology, Rajiv Gandhi University, Itanagar.

57. Tayeng, R. & Sonam, T. (2014). *Interstate Boundary Dispute between Arunachal Pradesh and Assam*. In a International Conference Proceedings, *Media's Role in Facilitating Peace in Conflict Situation in Northeast India and Neighboring Countries, Media Watch*, pp. 124-135.

58. Wouters, J.J.P., (2012). Keeping the Hill Tribes at Bay: A critique from India's Northeast of James C. Scott's paradigm of state evasion. *European Bulletin of Himalayan Research* 39, pp. 41-65.

59. Zhoto, T. & J J. P. Wouter. (2016). India's Northeast as an Internal Borderland: Domestic Borders, Regimes of Taxation, and Legal Landscapes. *The NEHU Journal,* 14 (1), pp. 1-17.

60. Zou, D.V. & M.S.K. (2011). Mapping a Colonial Borderland: Objectifying the Geo Body of India's Northeast. *The Journal of Asian Studies*, 70, pp. 141-170.

Notes

2. 10 killed, eight hurt at Behali Reserves Forest (2014, January 30). *The Assam Tribune*, p. 1.

3. MHA directs Assam Govt. to stop encroachment at Tarasso (2014, April 23). *The Arunachal Times*, p. 1.

4. Jatin Hazarika, in his forward to the book "The Trouble Border" by Bhubaneshwar Bhattacharya, 1995, Lawyer's Book Stall, Guwahati.

5. State Govt. denies accusation, says pursuing with Centre, Assam to solve boundary issue (2013, June 6). *The Arunachal Times*, p. 1.

6. Tayeng, O. (2012, March 29). 15,000 hectares of Assam's land encroached by Arunachal: Assam Minister, *The Arunachal Times*, p. 1.
7. National Commission to Review the Working of the Constitution. (2001). A Consultation Paper on Constitutional Mechanisms for settlement of Inter-State Disputes, Vigyan Bhawan, New Delhi, the 6th July, 2001, p. 10.
8. Nagaland seeks reviewing of border pact with Assam (2014, June 1). *The Echo of India*, Siliguri, p. 4.
9. Border Affairs, Government of Arunachal Pradesh, Home Department letter to Justice Tarun Chatterjee, Chairman, Local Commission, Dated 5th April 2010.

11

Urbanization and Its Implication in Tribal Society of Apatani

— *Dr. Padi Hana*

Introduction

Before the independence Ziro valley was a sanctuary for the Apatani tribe of Arunachal Pradesh. Politically it was not administered by any state machinery or company. The tribal society remained self-administered with their indigenous system of village councils - Builyang system. Builyang system was not a democratic in nature it is ascribed status transferring from generation to generation. Every clan of the village has their Builyang representative in any matter of disputes and ceremonial occasions.

In Haimendorf's book 'The Apa Tanis and their Neighbours' written from his ethnographic work among the Apatani tribe in 1944-45, Haimendorf had elaborately tried to explaine the agriculture pattern, the value of the agriculture land according to distance from the main village. The economy of the people was simple and traditional in nature. Agriculture was the main occupation along with forest activities practice by the men folk. People could exchange and barter their necessary items. The valley was enriched by terrace cultivation of paddy crop. The population was fed sufficiently by the farming system and from the forest product. Some of the goods did go for exchange with their neighbouring Nyishi tribe. The valley was not known by the outsider and it came into limelight only when a semi – military expedition known as the Miri mission was made in the year 1911-12 and surveyed the Subansiri region.

The Subansiri district was bifurcated several times for creation of new districts till now four new districts have come out – Upper Subansiri, Papumpare, Kurung Kumey and Kamle. Due to timely demarcation for new district out from the district the headquarters of Subansiri could not able to attain the urban status. As several of the machinery, infrastructure and population was distributed after the declaration of new districts. So to say Ziro as headquarter was not stable those days and to retain the status of urban. It's been a decade after the declaration of Ziro as urban area by the state in 1991. Since then the valley is experiencing a phenomenal change in physical structural and socio cultural structure.

Understanding Urbanization in tribal society

In the process of learning and understanding one ought to ask oneself, what is urbanization? How to understand the process of urbanization? Can we generalize the concept as it took place in western countries for the tribal society? Why urban studies are necessary in tribal society?

Understanding urbanization as a phenomenon is explained differently in different level by social science disciplines. Ultimately it always ends in explaning about population and economy dimensions. Without population there cannot be a city or town. Population becomes a mechanism of declaring the status of city to town or town to city by its varying population growth. Secondly there cannot be dynamism with the city population if there are no economic advantages for the vast population who are different from each other in terms of their economic specialization. Concentration of population is one of the major criteria of urbanization. Urbanization is a worldwide process and it has been considered not only as an index of economic development but also as an important factor of social. The city relies on division of labor and specialization. The economy of the urban depends on the services provided by the division of labor. Thomas (1984) Urbanization which led to large human settlement and new living environment largely divorced from natural things.

However, any single criterion fails to define urban in a satisfactory manner. Some authors – notably Sorokin and Zimmerman have, therefore, adopted various criteria and have given a 'multiple' or 'compound' definition of the word, Urban. In their opinion, Urban may be distinguished from rural in respect of occupation, size, density, heterogeneity, mobility, social differentiation and stratification and system of interaction of population.

Gibbs observes that "there is some hazard, on the theoretical level, in using compound definition which mixes. Thompson uses the term just in the same census when he writes, "Urbanization is characterized by movements of people from small communities concerned chiefly or solely with agricultural to other communities generally larger, and whose activities are centered in Government, trade, manufacture, or allied interests.

Definition of urbanization in terms of population concentration may at first seem too limited, but an investigation of the possibilities of broader or different definition will show that this is the only one which does not lead to any kind of ambiguity (Hope Tisdale Elridge, 1956).

The impact of urbanization on economic activity and its structure is largely developed. The degree of changes in the economic structure of tribal society depends on the movement of population from other state and the existence of opportunity to engage in different sectors. One cannot ignore the impact of the process in contemporary time. To large extent the society is leaping from traditional life towards rational, acceptability, tolerance of the new elements in their life and society. Thus, Lerner (1958: 43-48) and his associates among others contend that urbanization is a key variable in the "System of Modernity." They argue that it is with urbanization that the modernizing process begins. (Ibrahim, 1972). Studying the impact of urbanization on the economic structure and function of the Apatani community at Ziro is very significant to understand the new face of the society in the wake of modernization and urbanization. In the process of urbanization, a number of noteworthy changes have been observed in Ziro valleys particularly in terms of infrastructure growth, migration, occupational diversification, market activity, consumption pattern, production process and so on and so forth.

With the dawn of modern life the Apatani tribes are struggling to comprehend with new technology and accommodation of others culture into the fabrics of traditional culture. Gradually the society has responded positively by accommodating several aspects of other culture like element that is evidently found in all walks of tribal life. In due course of time there arose a several community based organization protecting the encroachment and washing off the practices and values of traditional practices. Some of the organization are playing vital role in preserving the rich tradition of the people by taking out seminar, organizing and producing learning material for education institution. The rationality of the organization is that the discussion and decision are not arbitrarily nor made by the single person. The finalization of the event takes places when the entire process is taken into consideration from the experts and likeminded groups that are workable and logical in nature that is acceptable by the mass. It is pertinent to observed that all the programmers are coming from educated, holding government officials who are also member of the community based organization and they all are found to be not villagers but hailing from urban community. So basically the traditional knowledge and its practices are now access and process by those groups of educated and elite class as the guardian of the custodian. In the olden times the village councils and priesthood could act on this line.

The infrastructure building in the early part of post independence has transformed the future of the Apatani tribe. The tribe remained isolated until the road infrastructure came into being by 1952. No, doubt the Apatani had the chance of visiting the foothills of Assam, had worked as paid labor during the agriculture season. Even they had traded with the southern part of Tibetan tribe. Eventually the rate of mobility from valley to other parts of the world could be brought to a very meager individual that could do this as a professional line.

The coming of road link became the medium of distancing between the traditional ways of life to modern life. The road communication was responsible for the frequency of people moving out from the valley that was intensified as well additional outsiders came into the valley as a government posting and to run the business. Before the road was constructed advance landing ground was operating for official purposes at old Ziro but it could not attempt to bring any drastic change as did by transport road building. Till today the impact of road transport is phenomenal at the state level especially for Ziro valley.

Road way is a vein for economic development without the road infrastructure the economy of the place could be difficult to grow and advance. The locals have changed their farming occupation to other non farming occupation especially by the men folk in the early part of the valley history. Women were still engaged with their household choir and agriculture. The possibility of social mobility among the men were more high in compare to women at large maybe it was notion of men are bread earner for family which is generally found in all type of society.

The persons who did not engage in agriculture were occupied with their new endeavor like opening petty shops like tea stall, grocery, retail shops of basic items, radio with photo studio and watch shop. There were also contractors and suppliers having good relations with the officials and public leaders. Other than the above, the third group of people belongs to labor working class. They work as physical laborer during the construction of roads, and building government quarters and offices. Many of the Apatani went out from the valley to work as laborer in different parts of the districts. Today, in addition to the above groups of people engaged in different fields of non agriculture we have another section of people engaged in white collar, and blue collar type of jobs.

The changing occupation has given a better and stable income for a person. With this the attitude and beliefs have change in their value outlooks. As per the study of the people it had shown that majority of the respondents declared that doing agriculture is economically unproductive and cost effective. They could prefer doing non agriculture work and encourage their youngster to look for government service, business, and any professional line. Therefore parents have started sending their children to private, missionary and few other good government schools.

Lately, inter generation gap is already build in terms of transferring the art of doing agriculture and forestry. The percentage of the Apatani farmers in the agriculture field is dropping down drastically. More or less the elderly women are found active and many women from other communities from Nepali, Miri, muslim Bengali are joining them. In future, the agriculture as practice will be a history for apatani society if the importance is not given be it culturally or economically. Considerably education and literary based occupation is replacing traditional skill based occupation among the youths. It is found in every organizations be it public or private prioritized education qualification criteria for employability.

Table 11.1: Total population and Schedule Tribe Population of District, Ziro town and Old Ziro

Sl. No.	*Name of Circle*	*Person*	*Male*	*Female*
1.	Lower Subansiri District	72911	35803	37108
2.	Ziro (Sadar)	17742	8433	9309
3.	Old Ziro	18177	9057	9120

Source: District Statistical Handbook, 2013-14.

Administrative center and urban infrastructure

Ziro was declared as an administrative headquarters in the year 1952 for the undivided Subansiri district at Old Ziro. Due to lack of transportation system and infrastructure the administration was organised and function from North Lakhimpur and then Kimin. Ziro was declared urban in the year 1991. The administration centre was later shifted from Old Ziro to Haoplyang which is known by the name Ziro. The land for administrative infrastructure was donated by the Bamin Michi village. The greater part of the Haoplyang land belong to Bamin Michi village.

The landscape of the valley began to change with the growth of administrative infrastructures. The coming of development brought face to face of traditional and modernization. The phase of development followed the ideals of Nehru Elwin policy by gradually integrating the tribal into civilization without uprooting their tradition and culture directly in the name of development.

The Apatanis have largely benefitted from the allocation of headquarter in their valley. Gradually the isolated swampy land was being converted into one of the modern administration centre. The land began to establish and form with several other economic area consisting of market area, residential area, health centres, education institution, and transport station.

Provision for getting employment and earning began to flourish. People have started coming from their village to do business in Haoplyang, to buy essential items like rice, tobacco, safety pin, iodised salt, sugar, tea leaves etc., repairing of machines- transistor, watch, bicycle. People could go to movie hall enjoying Bollywood films and listen to news and song from transistor.

Now, the headquarter town is densely settled area because of the growth and development of urban infrastructures. The settlement pattern in town area is not in a planned way, there is haphazard building structure located in paddy fields, hills, swampy area and bamboo groves. People from different villages migrate towards town and buy the land to establish their own residence, and commercial buildings at the centre of the town– shopping complex, show room, hotels and restaurants, rent houses.

Commercial transport and private vehicles is plying in and out from the valley to different parts of district and state. The valley is well connected with the Capital city and Assam part. There is easy movement of people from other state and district of the state. This has further led to dynamism in demography of the valley.

With the benefits of roadways and transportation system the closeness among the kin group and neighbors is gradually diminishing due to physical distancing. Now instead of face to face interactions virtual and digital modes are taking over. The sense of obligation and bondage are still intact with the people when it comes to family problem, ceremonial observation, and marriage rituals. Apatani people reached out their family members staying outside with the wireless and telecommunication technology. Wireless telecommunication has solved the problem of travelling, everything is now being consulted and decisions made.

Ziro valley attracts both domestic and foreign tourist because of its scenic beauty, culture mosaic and people. Government and local groups are giving due importance to expand tourist infrastructures. In recent years there is growth in numbers of hotels and tourist lodges located in different parts of the villages and town area. So far the significant of tourism industry and its capacity to solve the problem of unemployment and income generation is not percolated to grass root level. Culturally the tribe is very vibrant and unique, is one of the reason foreigners comes for their research purpose and site seeing the valley. Ziro valley is getting recognized globally because of the Ziro Music Festival event held every year. The event attract tourist from all over the world and shared their culture. Newly created artificial lake *Siikhe* is one of the beautiful places visited by different walks of life. The vibrancy of the valley is drawing more people to visit the place creating demographic change.

Consumption

At the large extent the consumption pattern has drastically changed since the beginning of modern administration and urbanization too place. Urbanization has brought the culture of different caste and creed into common place. Urbanization is the medium in which the isolated Apatani tribe has come into contact and inherited others culture practice and knowledge.

The growing consumption has greatly altered in recent times it is found that the Apatani society which was based on simple stratification is now classified and stratified into complex class groups. The social interaction of different class is blending towards more complex form. It is happening due to life styles of a person according to their occupation and income accordingly to regular government job, business in terms of opening medium scale and small scale firm business with the help of government schemes and financial support and personnel investment, running dealership, showroom of branded company, contractors – supplying government orders, civil constructions, running educational institution, health clinic, advocating profession etc are the modern occupation offering the people to engage in consuming to large extend.

The distinction among the high income and low income class groups of Apatani can be identify from their living style and possession of the property. Several of the good earning people are found of constructing their storey houses in concrete style or modern housing system. The limitation of the concrete house at village and few other at town is that during the ritual observation especially during the Myoko festival and performing of *Takho Bela* became difficult because the sliced bamboo stick cannot insert into concrete floors which should be in arc shape surrounding the dwelling house, so the bamboo stick are laid flat around the house. During the *Myoko* and *Murung* ritual observation many of the family perform *Meping Pala* as a sign of offering by those who had done Ali Lao during *Myoko* and *Subu Murung*. While performing *meping Pala,* the interior decoration (painting) of the house gets spoil because smeared rice mix with wine has to be put in the walls of the house including doors and windows. Visitor from outside may not understand the paste on the walls it looks messy in modern style house.

The study revealed that 96.54% of the respondents agreed that the pattern and mode of consumption are drastically changing in the Apatani society with the coming of non-tribal population, and accessible road transportation to other parts of the world. The marketing system has opened the varieties of commodities for the locals other than their local products. Gradually the market and industrial produce goods have over taken or replace the traditional tools and technique. Leaving ritual material which is still depended on forest resources now rest of the preparation and construction are done with the help of industrial product like plastic ropes for binding purpose during repairing of bamboo fences, houses, any other domestic works.

The consumption patterns at the level of nutrition intake and popular food like fast food, pastries and cake among, and wine alcohol is raising high with the growing new generation and it is quite contrasting with their elder generation dietary system. Now, besides local cuisine every household have recipe of making any type of food which can be made by spice and vegetable which is available from the shops. Before Ziro becoming a town the Apatani people could have their meal twice a day as a regular pattern, the content of nutrition value in the meal was simple and poor. These days, Apatani people are taking their food according to their office work following a day time meal – breakfast, lunch and dinner. The nutrients value in the meal is richer than earlier system of food habit. This habit has given the local people a proper amount of nutrition based diet for a healthy life. The diseases related to vitamin and mineral deficiency in the valley has greatly reduced and the longevity of life span is improved. With this the monthly expenditure budget on household items of the family is increased. It was found out that none of the family head was making any budget preparation for household expenditure per month. Making a budgetary plan and calculation seems not a part of their simple life.

Becoming wealthy and rich is an ideal life for every Apatani. Since the time there were wealthy people who could display their possession of their land, arable land, slave, cattle and forest. The dressing and housing style was similar for the rich and poor. The dual of the wealthy individuals could show their wealth by destroying their property as a kind of challenge and competition. The winners could take away the claims of the disputes.

Both the urban and rural life is influenced by materialist culture. The lives become easier and complicated with the advance in technology. The houses are filled with electronic based machines and gadgets. The interior of the house is decorated with sofas, center tables, television, kitchen, toilet with shower room, parking garage, Iron Gate, heater, gas, and computer. The maintenance of the machines becomes lot easier for those residing in urban area because of their easy access to facility and specialist. The rural people faces problem as they have to hire the expert from the urban site and it cost higher than urban rate.

The Apatanis never thought that their popular rice beer could be replaced by tea in the future. Drinking of tea became an ideal beverage for the community; it is available in every household and offer to any visitors any time. It is often drunk in or without occasion which had replaced local rice beer (*Apong*). Tea has come to be enjoyed in different verities – milk, black tea, green tea, lemon tea etc. Most commonly milk and black tea are served in any gathering and occasion. Chewing of betel nut is another level of popular edible items that is taken commonly by the old and young adults. Factory made cigarette and *bidi* replaced pipe tobacco. Whiskey and rum have replaced local *apong*. Apong was one of the economic sources of income for poor family. A number of Apatani families inside and outside the district survived by doing *apong* business. Gradually it was closed down due to growth of hotel and bars and superior quality of factory liquor. There are still few houses running the business.

There are several traditional based culture materials which are today replaced by modern materials or techniques. Use of beacon during the

Myoko festival for giving it to ceremonial friends and kin group is replaced with currency note. The value of traditional practices is improvised by some other value which is more convenient and efficient for any person involved. In other sense mental and physical concern about maintaining the beacon is greatly reduced. The families who are staying outside the valley can now easily send the amount to their relatives to formalize the Myoko celebration.

Lapang a wooden slates having sacredness is brought to the village by each clans during the Myoko celebration from the forest. Earlier clan male members including of both young and old in numbers visit their clan forest stayed overnights and prepare *lapang* slate the women carry the food for them from the village. After finishing the work male participant of the particular clan bring the *lapang* slate to the village by dragging with wild ropes and cane rope. In the process of *lapang* preparation the elders teaches younger generation the knowledge about their forest boundaries where and about, types of trees, plant and animals found and that is useful for ritual purpose, fire woods and taboo plants. During the gathering social integration is held high among the clan members.

Nowadays, the process is very rarely seen performing by the clan members in bringing the *lapang* slates from the clan forest. The clan members give an order to saw mill to cut the *lapang* slates and in place of physical work of bringing it the village truck is used instead.

Modern financial institution

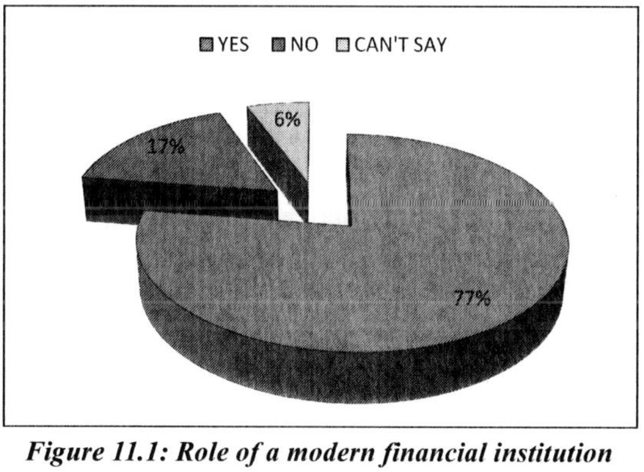

Figure 11.1: Role of a modern financial institution

Before the introduction of modern financial institution there was no idea of currency notes, economic value of currency, and the idea of saving and investment account. The society was under the system of exchange, and barter. Along with economic exchange of ideas social ideas and interaction were also involved which had strengthened the communication capacity and brought into a new relationship. The community people did not have any proper storage system to keep their valuable belonging and cash to keep safe at their house. Due to introduction of bank by the government the people are having the opportunity to interact with new financial system and its facilities.

Now every kind of financial transaction and business are done by the financial institution. The cooperative banks are providing loans and credits from the government schemes which have been benefitted by most of the unemployed youths, married couple and entrepreneurs. The study also revealed that 17.0% of the respondents are not getting any kind assistance from the bank in spite of several application submissions. The financial institutions have well documented terms and requirement but lack proper action to support the poor families. It provides grant to those who are having security, regular income and property. The villagers and uneducated are not aware of about the available government schemes and facilities as found in the other states.

There is ever growing of micro finance groups or fund group based on family, clan, friend circle, neighbors etc. the members belong to similar category of life history or pattern of their life style. They raised the fund among themselves with few amount and lend out the money to any individuals at certain percentage. The interest rate varies with members and non-members during the loan. It is less formal than the financial institution with paper works. It is not only an economic institution it also function as social institution and social interaction. Members conduct the meeting annually to update the amount that is loan out and income generated. In certain occasions members distribute the profit amount among themselves as a kind of bonus. The interaction among the members in annual meeting is socially significant it becomes a platform to met each other some travel from other districts and states for the meeting.

Labour

The human resources are coming from the other states especially those workers dealing with barber, washer man, cobbler, mansion, carpenter, sweeper, trolley puller, electrician, plumber, cable boy, etc. gradually the local youths are taking over the skills and using it to earn with dignity. But still large number of non-tribal population holds those manual occupations. In the study it also found, respondents agreeing that local youths is gradually growing in numbers and taking up skills and unskilled works. Basically, local youths received their training from Industrial Training Institute (ITI), short term course provided by District Industrial Units (DIU), and by self-learning from others during the work. In this way the economic relationships and structure is changing. The changing economic structure and relation has led to variance in distribution and circulation of income in the valley.

Land value

The land value and land tenure system is unique part of apatani society. If we look at the land tenure system the value of the land decreases from centre of the village to periphery of the village. Haopolyang the district center was once isolated and deserted place is becoming one of the expensive places to live in since urbanization has taken place. The land value of Ziro valley is having the equivalent value of capital complex. Accordingly the plot of land cannot be sold out to any other community than Apatani. In recent time few of the wealthy individuals from other tribe have bought the land. The center of the town act as important place for any commercial and administrative works the cost of land is very high and it is not easy to get the land. The commercialization has already began in the urban area there are few isolated places like bamboo groves, forest, public or clan based land are exceptional areas which are still not being commercialized.

Commercialization of indigenous products

Below given diagram is the response given by the respondents during the survey about the local products and its capacity for commercialization.

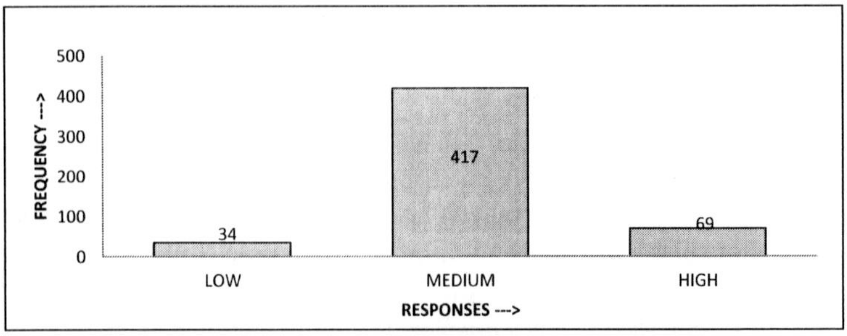

Figure 11.2: Growth and sell of indigenous products.

The local product are those goods that is made in the valley or having some properties in relation to Apatani tribal culture. The local products especially embroidery and handloom section are displayed during the time of traditional celebration, fashion and modeling shows, cultural events etc. There are ample of emporium retail stores in the Ziro valley and capital complex deals with traditional dresses and ornaments. The products are necktie, shawl, coat, waist coat, shirts, skirts, maplar, bangles, kurta, etc. over the period of time there has been moderately demand and increase of selling and youths having the skill and knowledge are getting engaged and few others are having set up of their own units of production.

With the growth of urbanization and population increase in the valley and tourist inflow, the demands for local items/goods have increased. Some well-known local goods besides embroidery are agriculture products, horticulture product and handicrafts. There are few industries run globally, Kiwi wine industry has come up to trap the local kiwi products. There are several households preparing their own home made kiwi wine. Spice Ziro industry is producing the local cuisine and spicy items of traditional Apatani at global market. Restaurants and hotels are also offering the local dish of Apatani. Gradually things are shaping into market oriented if proper diagnosis of market situation and advertisement are made. To encourage the local farmers and people market sheds are arranged by the district administrator in Ziro town to sell their products. The development activities are also found in disbursing loan to farmers, and involving in MGNREGA.

In the recent development process, people are indulging in horticulture activities. The vast tracts of private forest land are converted into horticulture field for cultivating cardamom, kiwi fruits, pears, Ginger, and apple are some of the major items grown. The government is assisting the local with the help of incentives and subsidies to engage in horticulture farming for self-employment and income generation. The climatic condition of Ziro valley is considered to be a good place for doing horticulture.

The demand for horticulture products is coming from the other states. The product quality is good and the buyers are buying at low cost price for the goods. On the other hand the reason for increasing demand is due to the growth of shops, broker and demand. The customers are generally belongs to both indigenous people and outsiders.

Handicraft and woodcraft are available in the form of baskets, mat, machete handle, machete cover, cap, toys. The items could be obtained from the shops and outlets store in the market and websites are created for easy purchasing. The numbers of emporium shops have increased which has significantly affected the growth of employment and skill workers among the Apatani youths. The administrative center is becoming the hub of center providing structural change in socio-economic dimensions.

Table 11.2: The classification of Main workers of Lower Subansiri District and Urban (Ziro)

Sl. No.	*Category*	*Total*
1.	**Total Main workers of Lower Subansiri District**	
	Urban(Ziro)	4518
	(a) Male	3034
	(b) Female	1484
2.	**Total Main Cultivators of Lower Subansiri District**	9552
	Urban(Ziro)	164
	(a) Male	62
	(b) Female	102
3.	**Total Main Agriculture Laborers of Lower Subansiri District**	826
	Urban (Ziro)	26
	(a) Male	19
	(b) Female	7

(Contd...)

4.	**Total Main household Industry of Lower Subansiri District**	244
	Urban (Ziro)	39
	(a) Male	27
	(b) Female	12
5.	**Total Main other workers of Lower Subansiri District**	8226
	Urban (Ziro)	3821
	(a) Male	2748
	(b) Female	1073
6.	**Total Marginal Workers of Lower Subansiri District**	7533
	Urban (Ziro)	468
	(a) Male	178
	(b) Female	290
7.	**Total Non-workers of Lower Subansiri District**	52828
	Urban(Ziro)	8288
	(a) Male	3349
	(b) Female	4939

Source: Statistical Handbook of Lower Subansiri District 2013-14.

Conclusion

The paper focuses on the process of urbanization and modernization interaction in a tribal society. It tries to interpret the role of the state and its relations with different type of infrastructural development. The case of Ziro valley under the process of urbanization is unique. The circumstances of urbanism growth in the valley is gradually replacing the traditional practices.

Basically the Apatani tribe is undergoing transformation at the structural level of the social system with the coming of other community groups and exposure to outside world. Only the older generation is left with the knowledge of traditional especially farming activities which is rapidly dying away. The non-farming sectors are playing an important role in engaging the younger generation in new kind of occupation. While there is slowing down of total entry into the agriculture sector and non-tribal families are being hire to till and cultivate the land. Even if opportunity for employment emerge a large number of the population in agriculture will be 'professionally stranded' (McGee, 1973) unable to utilize the opportunities for alternative employment.

The urbanization and contact with the outside people and exposure has given the Apatani tribe a privilege of globalizing their traditional art, products and practices. Several individuals are taking up to become an entrepreneur and enterprises generating employment avenues for the local people. With the help of financial institution and emergence of local micro finance groups has led to ease of doing and taking up business. In this way the money is circulated within the valley, and indirectly restraining the out flow of cash to other states.

References

Anderson, Nels. (1959). Urbanism and Urbanization. *American Journal of Sociology*, 65(1), 68-73. Retrieved from www.Jstor.org/stable/2773622

Arunachal Pradesh: Development Report. (2009). Planning Commission, Government of India. New Delhi: Academic Foundation.

Barooah, Jeuti. (2007). *Customary Laws of the Apatanis of Arunachal Pradesh.* Shillong: North Eastern Council,

Behera, M.C. (1995). State sponsored urbanization in Arunachal Pradesh: participation of autochthons in this process. In J.B Ganguly (ed.): *Urbanization and development in North East India.* New Delhi: Deep Publication.

Bhagat, R. B. & Mohanty, Soumya. (2009). Emerging Pattern of Urbanization and the Contribution of Migration in Urban Growth in India. *Asian Population Studies,* 5(1), 5-20.

Bhagat, R. B. (2011). Emerging Pattern of Urbanization in India. *Economic and Political Weekly*, XLVI (34).

Bhatachargjee, R.P. (2002). Urbanization in Arunachal Pradesh. *Arunachal Review*, V(4), Itanagar: IPRP Govt. of Arunachal Pradesh.

Bora, D.K. et al. (1997). *Impact of urbanization in Arunachal Pradesh.* Directorate of Research, Government of Arunachal Pradesh. Itanagar.

Chakravarty, L.N. (1995). *Glimpse of the early history of Arunachal Pradesh* (2nd Ed.). Directorate of Research Government of Arunachal Pradesh, Itanagar.

Choudhary, S. Dutta, (1981). District Gazetteers, Subansiri District-Arunachal Pradesh Government of Arunachal Pradesh.

Chaudhuri, S. (1999). Urbanization and Identity: Emerging Situation in Indian Metropolises. *Indian Anthropologist*, pp. 37-66.

Das, Gupta. (1998). Capital, the State and Petty Trading in Calcutta' in Patel, S and Deb K (ed) book *'Urban Studies'.* OUP, New Delhi.

District Census Handbook of Lower Subansiri, (1991). Director of Census Operations, Arunachal Pradesh, Part XII – A&B, Series-3.

Elwin, Verrier, (2012). *A Philosophy for NEFA* (4th Reprint), Itanagar: Department of Cultural Affairs, Directorate of Research Government of Arunachal Pradesh.

Gist, Noel P. (1961). Cities without Industry. *Economic Development and Cultural Change*, 9(4), Part 1, 660-662. Retrieved from www.Jstor.org/stable/1151878.

Hoselitz, Bert. F. (1962).The Role of Urbanization in Economic Development; Some International Comparison. In Turner, Roy (ed.), *India's Urban Future,* Bombay: Oxford University Press.

Hana, Padi, (2019). Understanding the Impact of Urbanization on Apatani tribe of Ziro valley, Arunachal Pradesh: a sociological study unpublished PhD thesis.

Ibrahim, S. E. (1972). The relationship between urbanization and modernization in yugoslavia. *International Review of Modern Sociology*, pp. 143-160.

Imitiyaz, M. H. (2018). URBANIZATION CONCEPTS, DIMENSIONS AND FACTORS. *International Journal of Recent Scientific Research*, pp. 23513-23523.

Kani, Takhe. (1993). *The Advancing Apatanis of Arunachal Pradesh*. Ziro: Mrs. Takhe Omang.

Mibang, Tamo. (1994). *Social Change in Arunachal Pradesh.* (The Minyong) 1947-1981. New Delhi: Omson Publication.

Sutton, Anthony Giddens. (2017). *Sociology 8th edition.* New Delhi: Wiley.

Phillip Modi. (2011). A Case Study on Informal Micro Finance Houses among the Apatani Tribe in Twin Capital Cities of Arunachal Pradesh. *Journal of Asian Research Consortium*, 1(3). 1-15. retrieved from www.Jstor.org/stable/2768859.

Zhang Baiping, M. S. (Aug., 2004). Urbanization and De-Urbanization in Mountain Regions of China. *Mountain Research and Development*, pp. 206-209.

12

Homestay as an emerging mode of accommodation for tourists and exploring the experiences of tourist: "A case study of Ziro valley, Lower Subansari District, Arunachal Pradesh"

— *Dr. K. Sotechand, Mr. B.P. Sarma Barua,*

Introduction

Accommodation is a fundamental factor of the tourism product to the tourists. The type, extent and nature of accommodation determine the volume and value of tourism that is possible at any destination (Henning and Willemse, 1999). Homestay is defined by the World Tourism Organization as 'people who travel to and stay in places outside their usual environment for more than twenty four hours and not more than one consecutive year for leisure, business, and other purposes not related to the exercise of an activity remunerated from within the place visited' (Kadir et al., 2010. Lynch, McIntosh and Tucker (2009), give a definition of Homestay by referring to it as commercial homes whereby visitors or guests pay to stay in private homes where interaction take place with a host or family. It is a very unique characteristic as this concept promotes interaction between host families and tourists and acting as a development tool to raise awareness on the cultural exchange and respect for the host's culture (Jamilah and Hamzah, 2007). Wang

(2007) stated that homestays appeal to travellers searching for novelty, personalized service and genuine social interaction with the hosts. Dolezal (2011) analyzed that rural Homestays permit guests to catch a glimpse of the daily lives of village residents and therefore serve as a means of experiencing a local community in ways that differ from conventional tourism interactions and settings. Kumar, Gill & Kunasekaran (2012) opined that homestays are places where the tourists stay with the host's family and experience their way of life in a direct and indirect manner. Homestay is very different compared to other modes of accommodation such as a hotel, motel or bed and breakfast which is normally located in the city or suburban areas whereas the location of the homestay is normally situated in rural areas where the whole community is still practicing the traditional way of life and embracing strong culture and traditional practices (Salamiah, Othman and Maheran, 2011). Dahles (2000) indicates that in most cases, the homestay operation is a source of supplementary income for the operators since they often take on other forms of employment and also maintain their social and religious responsibilities. Ideally, the homestays program allows the local people to experience other people's cultures from all over the world without leaving their own homes. Indeed this can be considered as an important strength of this particular product, no other tourism product offers a similar experience (Kayat, 2009). Colton and Whitney-Squire (2010) conclude that the homestay program has the potential to address many of the economic, environmental and socio-cultural challenges that communities face. Precise benefits include preservation of cultural and natural heritage, increased training and capabilities in business development and tourism, education, increased economic diversification, enhanced environmental integrity, sharing of local culture, improved infrastructure, allowing of traditional ways of living in a sustainable way, and diminishment of existing social problems. Levitt (1996) concludes that the important components of the homestay program are education, entertainment, enrichment, food, accommodation and hospitality.

Experience is a key aspect of a tourist destination's offering because tourists accumulate experiences throughout a journey. Carlson (1996) defined experience as a constant flow of thoughts and feelings that occur during moments of consciousness. Experiences are ultimately created within the person; the outcome dependent upon how the individual, in a specific mood and state of mind, reacts to his or her interaction with an event (Csikszentmihalyi, 1990; Pine & Gilmore, 1999; Wang, 2002; Mossberg, 2003). Furthermore, according to McCabe and Foster (2006), travel activities become embedded within the totality of one's lived experiences because tourists visit different places in order to interact with people from different cultures and to accrue valuable memories. Therefore, the tourist experience is socially constructed; the product of multiple interpretations based on the social, environmental, and physical components of the overall experience.

The success of a tourism service provider is dependent upon their knowledge of how a destination can provide the right mix of circumstances that can enhance the experiences of tourists. In this study, we sought to identify activities and factors that might attract tourists to a specific destination and to stay at homestays. In light of it, we chose Ziro Valley, a well-known homestay destination in the state as our case study. Ziro Valley was shortlisted for inclusion in the in the tentative list for further nomination to UNESCO for inscription in the World Heritage Site and as such, Ziro valley represents a developing and a very promising tourism destination that can benefit from added value by learning from tourist experiences.

Objective of the study

(i) To understand the scenario of homestay tourism in Ziro valley and identify the major challenges.

(ii) To study the key reasons why tourists visiting Ziro valley prefer homestay.

(iii) To examine the experience of tourist staying in homestay, Ziro valley.

(iv) To offer practical suggestions/recommendations so as to make the homestay tourism more viable.

Research design

The study has been conducted in Ziro valley, Lower Subansari District, Arunachal Pradesh's homestay tourism industry. The intrinsic features of Ziro fitted very well considering the development of homestay as a strong tourism option. The study is based on primary data as well as secondary data sources such as previous studies, journals, books, reports, magazines, government publications and several online data sources. The data collection instrument had two sections. Section-1 was designed to gather personal details of the tourists and Section-2 had 20 variables on which the respondents had to respond. The variables were identified from the literature review and expert opinion from tourism academics and professionals.

Data was collected from 21 respondents through the help of a self-administered questionnaire followed by an indepth interview. The selection criteria for respondents were that they must have stayed at least an overnight in homestays. An attempt to collect data from all the 17 registered homestay had been made but data could only be collected from 12 homestays as 2 homestays were lying unoccupied and the occupants from 3 homestays could not be contacted during the time frame. Furthermore, data could only be collected from domestic tourist only (4 tourists from the state and 17 tourists from other states). No international tourists were found to be staying at homestays during the study period.

The data was collected from 26-29th September, 2019 coinciding with the four days "Ziro Festival of Music (ZPM)" which is regarded to be amongst one of the biggest outdoor music festival of India

Overview of homestay tourism in Arunachal Pradesh

Tourism in Arunachal Pradesh has grown rapidly in the recent years with eco and adventure tourism, cultural tourism and religious tourism being the major areas of interest. Major sports of interest to travellers include angling, boating, rafting, trekking and hiking. The concept of Homestay was launched in the state only during the last few years. As in the year 2016, there are 106 registered homestays in the state covering few districts (given in below table-12.1). The Government of Arunachal Pradesh in its new tourism policy has launched "restructured Chief Minister's Paryatan Vikas Yojna" on 7th of August, 2016. Under this flagship program, beneficiaries can avail loans to start homestays. The department of Tourism, Govt. of Arunachal Pradesh is doing its best to encourage other districts to start homestays.

Table 12.1: List of Registered Homestays of Arunachal Pradesh as on 2016

Sl. No.	*Districts*	*No. Of Registered Homestays*
1	Tawang	18
2	Lower Subansiri	24
3	East Siang	10
4	West Siang	21
5	East Kameng	02
6	West Kameng	24
7	Dibang Valley	01
8	Lower Dibang Valley	01
9	Changlang	05
10	**Total-**	**106**

Source: Department of Tourism, Govt. Of Arunachal Pradesh, Itanagar.

Homestays in Ziro

Ziro, nestled in the mountainous folds of Central Arunachal Pradesh, is one of the most picturesque places in all of North East. The bowl shaped valley with colorful mosaic rice fields, interlaced by canals, makes for a very pretty sight. The beauty of the land is further accentuated by the friendly Apatani tribe, who reside over here. The culture and traditions of the Apatani tribe is still pretty intact as most of them are still animists following Donyi-Polo (Sun and Moon). And it is not uncommon to spot elder men with long hair tied up in a peculiar way, and old women with wooden nose plugs. To get a glimpse of their culture one must visit some of their villages spread across Ziro valley. The villages of Hong, Hari, Hija, Duta and Baman Michi are the most interesting ones.

Since the past few years, Ziro has also become quite famous for the Ziro Music Festival which happens here in the third week of September. During this festival, people from all over, come to listen to nationally and internationally renowned artists.

1. Key highlights of Ziro as a Tourist Destination

- Breathtaking landscape & vibrant culture.
- Mesmerizing paddy fields and colourful community forests.

- In the month of September every year, Ziro festival of music (ZFM) is held here which is an international festival and attracts a lot of people.
- Fish, butterfly and caterpillar farming are done in Ziro which can be witnessed.
- There are bastis (small villages) near Ziro which can give a real exposure to rural life.

Homestays in Ziro is still a new concept but in the past few years, many homestays have sprung up. Marketing and promotion of the home stays at Ziro is handled by Department of Tourism, Government of Arunachal Pradesh. Also, the homestay owners use various social media platform as promotional tools. The bookings of home stays are done through telephone, travel agencies and online platform such as goibibo, makemytrip etc. The benefits flowing to homestay owners are immense. It gives an additional income to the family other than the regular income. The homes that are unable to directly serve as homestays are also given the opportunity to supplement their income by acting as guides for tourists. The room rate of the homestay is not fixed. It varies in the range of 500-2500 INR per night.

2. Key highlights of the homestays in Ziro

- Authentic Apatani meal can be enjoyed on order.
- Organic vegetables are grown and served in some homestays.
- Consumption of non-veg meals and alcohol beverages is also allowed.
- Can participate in daily and seasonal chores of the host family.
- Can spend time relaxing in the village and interacting with villagers and host family.
- Can participate in local rituals, festivals, functions, traditional games and sports.
- Traditional kitchen with fireplace in centre so that guest can relax besides warmth of bonfire while enjoying ethnic tribal delicacy.

3. List of registered homestays in Ziro valley

Table 12.2: List of registered homestays in Ziro valley

Sl. No.	*Name of the Homestay*	*Address*	*Room Details*
1.	View Point Homestay	Duku Abulyang, Old Ziro	Single-5, Double-3
2.	Dogindo Homestay	Hari Village, Old Ziro	Single-2, Double-2, Suit-1
3.	Tam Yamyang	Hong Village, Old Ziro	Single-2, Dormitory-1
4.	Dolo Mondo	Bamin Village, Ziro	Single-1, Double-1, Dormitory-1
5.	Suchusi Homestay	Siiro Village, Ziro	Double-2
6.	Rose Homestay	Mudang Tage, Ziro	Single-1
7.	N.K Homestay	Hari Village, Ziro	Single-2, Double-2
8.	Buhang Homestay	Hong Village, Old Ziro	Double-1
9.	Abasa Homestay	Siiro Village, Ziro	Single-2, Double-4
10.	Jajang Nello	Siiring Village, Ziro	Double-3, Dormitory-1
11.	Ngunu Ziro Homestay	Siiro Village, Ziro	Double-2
12.	Yanya Homestay	Hija Village, Ziro	Double-2
13.	Ark Homestay	Hari Village, Ziro	Single-2
14.	Tamo Homestay	Bamin Village, Ziro	Double-1
15.	Danyi Piilo Homestay	Hija Village, Ziro	Double-2
16.	Nehabo Homestay	Nehabo Village, Ziro	Single-1, Double-1
17.	Hage Hinda Homestay	Hari Village, Ziro	Double-1

Source: arunachaltourism.com

Key challenges of homestay in Ziro

1. Poor infrastructural facilities such as good roads, electricity, healthcare, communication and other residential.
2. Lack of skilled human resources such as guides, entrepreneurs, hospitality professionals and this is due to lack of availability of education and training institutes.
3. There is lack of proper legal regulations for example registration of homestay, booking of homestay and other relevant policies.
4. Marketing and promotion of homestay tourism is also not satisfactory in the region.
5. There is poor coordination among different tourism participants such as government, tourism players, tourism intermediaries and other non-government bodies associated with homestay tourism.

6. Less awareness regarding conservation of natural as well as cultural resources among locals.
7. Improper management of resources at the destination is also a big challenge in extension of homestay viability.
8. Poor maintenance of security, chaos situations at times, frequent bandhs, unpredictable weather conditions etc., which demotivate foreign tourists to visit India and more particularly north-east India.
9. The host families find that the tourists are coming from different cultural backgrounds. At times they fail to respect the local traditions and customs. They fear that in times to come, people may get materialistic in their approach. The young population tries to copy the foreigners which may in times to come change the lifestyle of local community and hence might become a threat to the sustainability of culture.

Findings

1. Source of information about Homestays

Out of 21 respondents, 41% of the respondents came to know about homestays in Ziro from electronic media like websites followed by

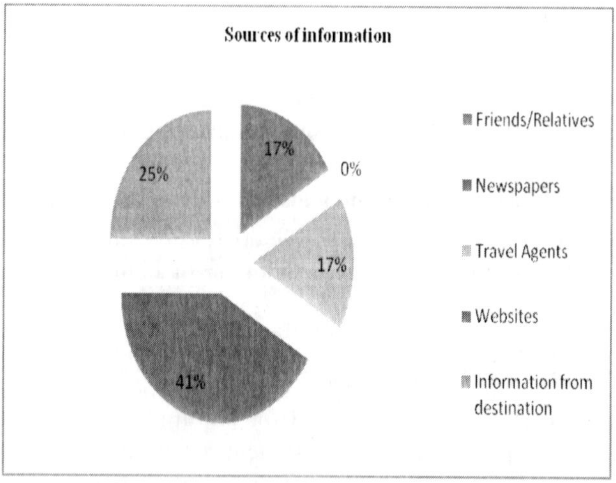

Chart 12.1: Source of information about Homestays

information from travel agents at 21 %. Information from destination and friends/ relatives stood equally at 17%. None of the respondents got information from newspapers.

2. Reasons for tourists staying at homestays

Figure 12.1: Reasons for tourists staying at homestays (in terms of no. of respondents)

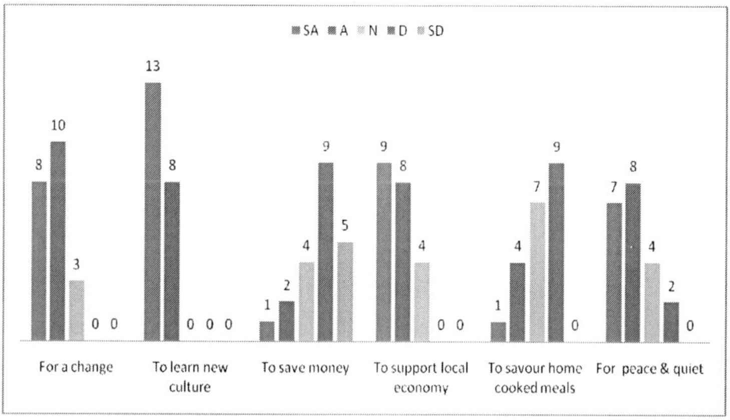

3. Reasons for tourists staying at homestays (in terms of % of respondents)

Chart 12.2: Reasons for staying at Homestays

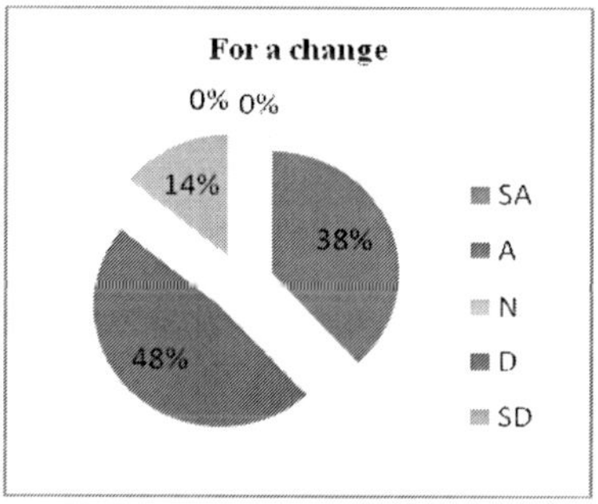

Chart 12.1: For a Change

From Chart 12.1, we can understand that a majority (86%) stayed at homestays because they wanted a change. It may be because hotels may have become too commonplace and boring to them.

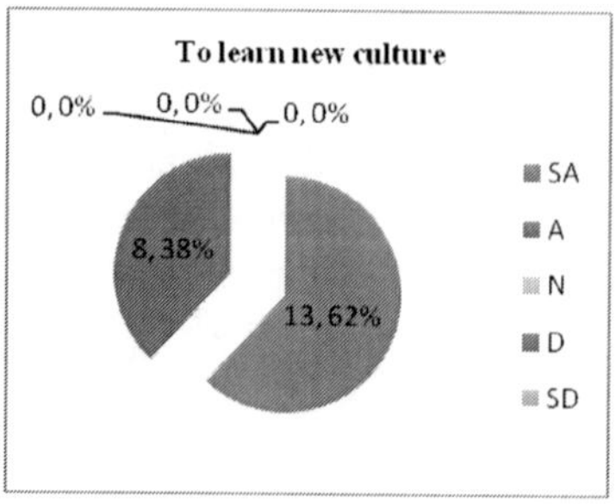

Chart 12.2: To learn new culture

It can be observed from Chart 12.2 that 100 % of the respondents agree that they stayed at homestays because they want to learn new culture of the destination. One can live through the authentic culture of a place, witness how people live on a daily basis, how they communicate, celebrate and dress up by staying at homestays.

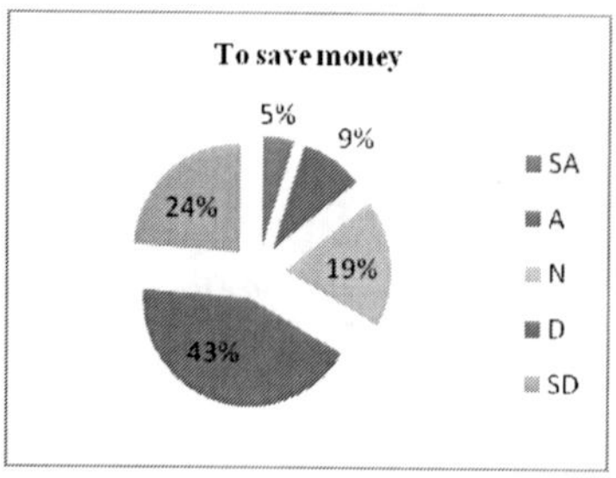

Chart 12.3: To save money

Chart 12.3 portrays whether the respondents stayed at homestays to save money or not. As is evident in the chart, a minority of the respondents stated that they are staying at homestays to save money whereas a large majority i.e., 67 % of the respondents do not agree with it.

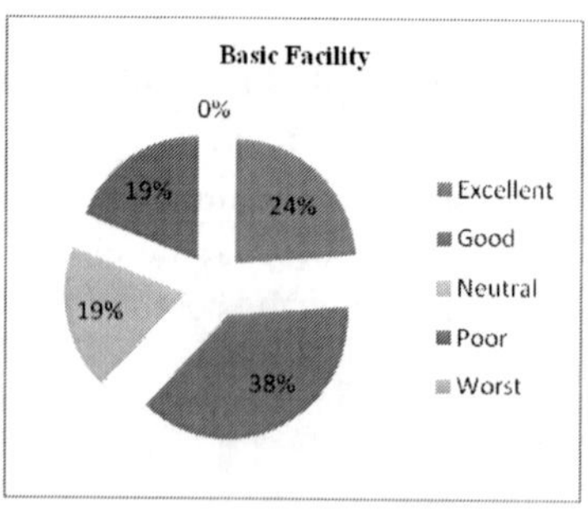

Chart 12.4: To support local economy

As can be seen from Chart 12.4, a majority of the respondents feel they stayed at homestay because they wanted to support local economy. By staying at a homestay, tourists are contributing to the livelihood of the local community. Often, tourist also end up buying handicraft from local artisans that the hosts may point to and, best of all, return and spread the good word around.

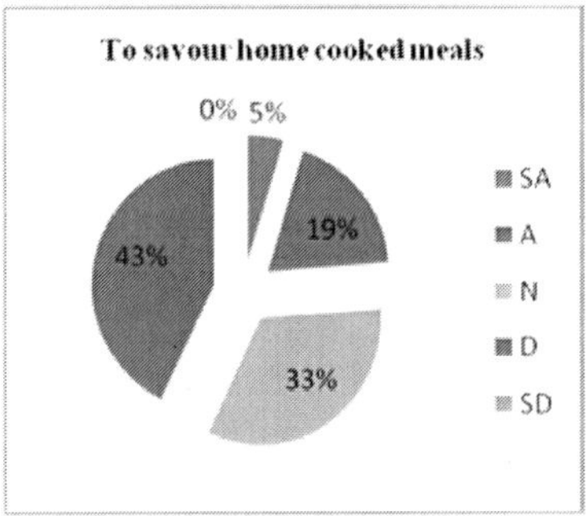

Chart 12.5: For home cooked meals

As can be observed from Chart 12.5, it is clear that a majority of the respondents are staying in homestays not because they want to savour home cooked food but rather for some other reasons. One of the best part about staying in a homestay is undoubtedly the delicious home-cooked food but in this study, the majority of the respondents were from outside the state and they may have thought that they may not be used to eat what the local populace eats.

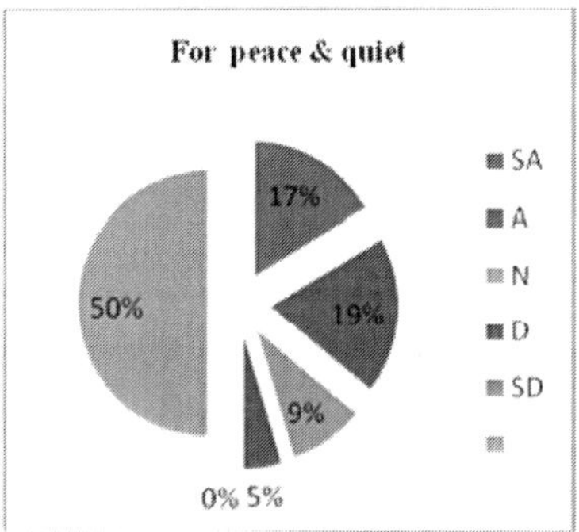

Chart 12.6: For peace & quiet

A large majority of the respondents agree that they stayed at homestays for peace and quiet. They may be staying at homestays to get away from the noise and clutter of hotels. Homestay operations are small, at any point they normally won't have less people around. Thus, tourist will get more peace and quiet and more quality time spent with himself/herself, or with their family and friends.

4. Rating of the experience by tourists staying at homestays (in terms of no. of respondents)

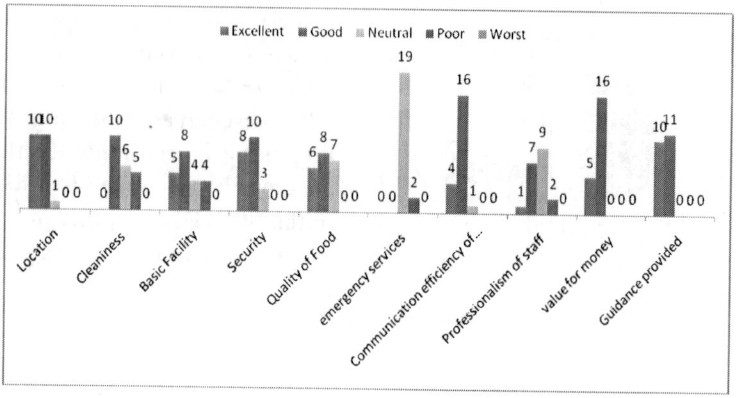

Figure 12.2: Rating of tourist experience.

5 Rating of the experience by tourists staying at homestays (in terms of % of respondents)

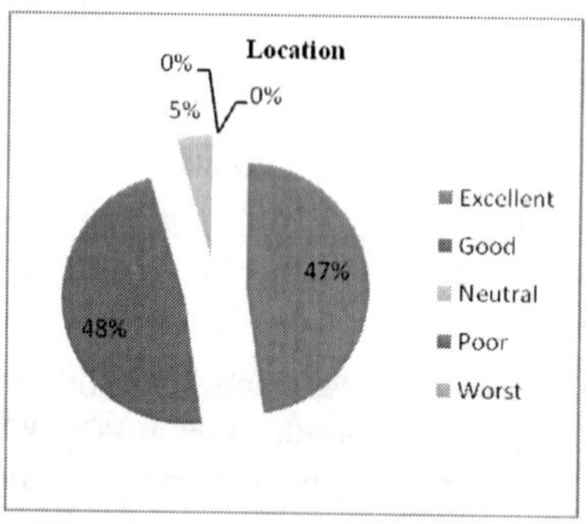

Chart 12.7: Tourist experience with regard to location of the homestay.

As the chart reveals, 48 % & 47 % of the respondents strongly agree and agree that the homestay they are staying is located at a very good location respectively. Only 5% of the respondents neither agree nor disagree with the convenience of the location of the homestay they are staying. Thus, we can conclude that the experience of the tourist with regard to the location of the homestay is satisfactory.

It is observed that a 48% of the respondents felt that the cleanliness of the homestay was

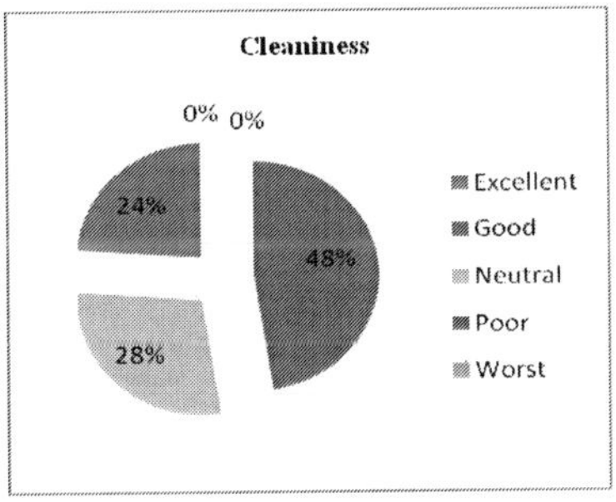

Chart 12.8: Tourist experience with regard to cleanliness of the homestay.

good whereas 28% responded that it was average and 24% said that the homestay was poor in respect of cleanliness.

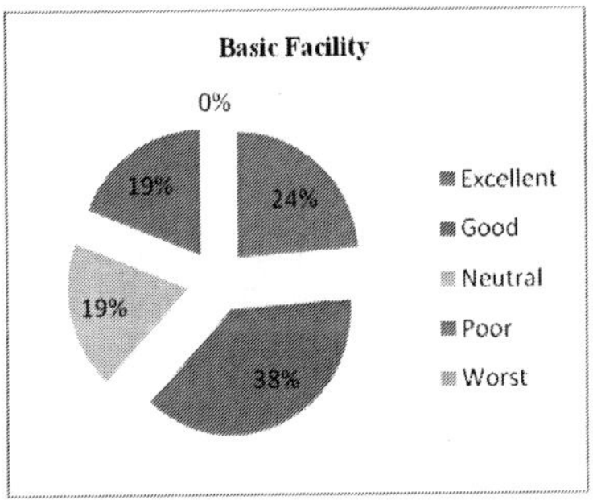

Chart 12.9: Tourist experience with regard to basic facilities at the homestay.

It can be observed a majority of the tourist are happy with the basic facilties provided by the homestay like separate toilet, warm water, shower etc. as 24 % of the respondents rate their experience as excellent and 38% of the respondents rate their experience as good.

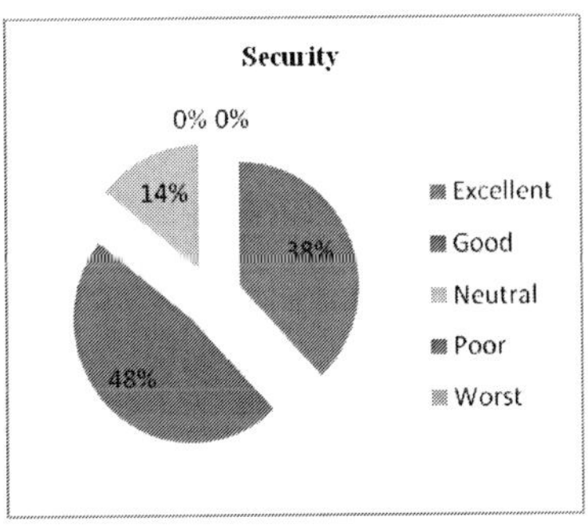

Chart 12.10: Tourist experience with regard to security of the homestay.

Chart 12.10 shows that a large majority of the respondents were satisfied with the level of security/safety provided at the homestay.

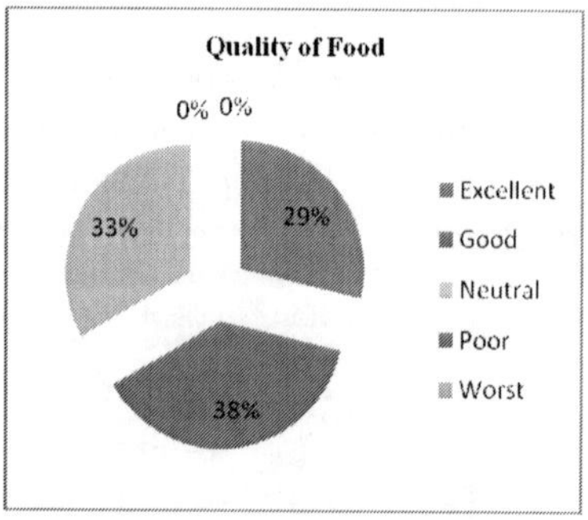

Chart 12.11: Tourist experience with regard to quality of the food at the homestay.

As can be observed from the chart on the left, the majority of the respondents are satisfied with the quality of food given to them. On the other hand, 33% of the respondents did stated that the quality of served to them was neither good nor bad.

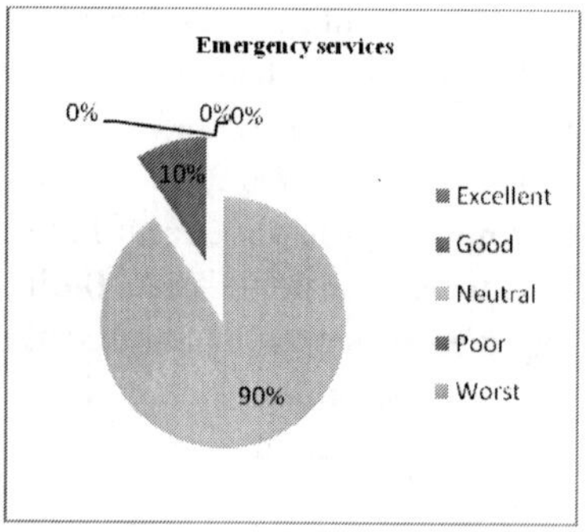

Chart 12.12: Tourist experience with regard to emergency services at the homestay.

90 % of the respondents are neither satisfied nor dissatisfied with the level of emergency services provided such as doctor on call, transporting ill documents to nearby hospitals. The neutrality in their opinion may be because they may have never been in such a situation before and thus may not be having any experience in this regard.

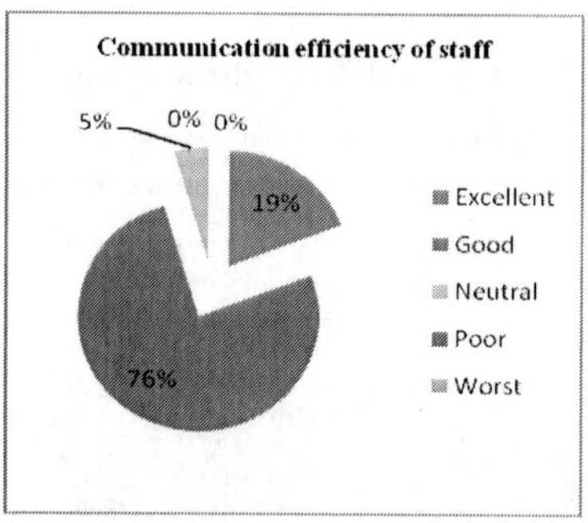

Chart 12.13: Tourist experience with regard to communication efficiency of staffs at the homestay.

19 % and 76 % of the respondents said that the communications efficiency of staff is excellent and good respectively.

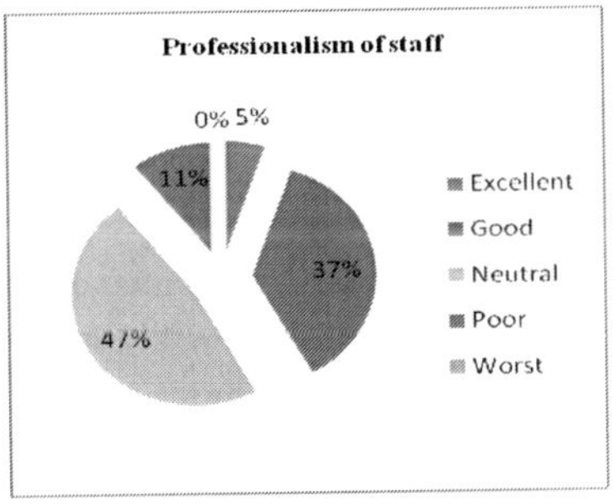

Chart 12.14: Tourist experience with regard to professionalism of the staff at the homestay.

37 % the tourist opined that they are good when it comes to professionalism. On the other hand, 47 % said that the staffs were neither professional nor unprofessional. 11 % and 5 % responded that the staffs were unprofessional.

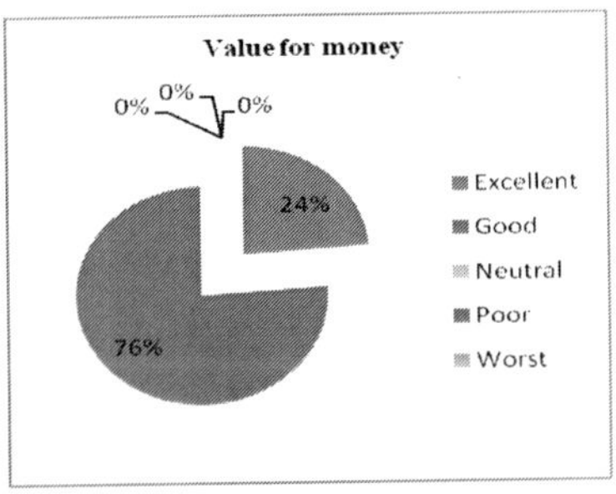

Chart 12.15: Tourist experience with regard to value for money at the homestay.

As can be seen from the chart, a large majority of the respondents opined that they got the value of the money paid by them from the homestays they are staying.

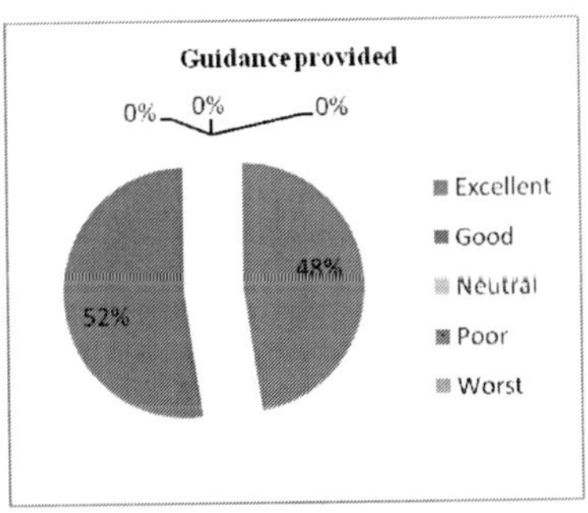

Chart 12.16: Tourist experience with regard guidance provided at the homestay.

The chart reveals that 48% and 52% of the respondents responded excellent and good respectively with the level of guidance provided at the homestay they are staying.

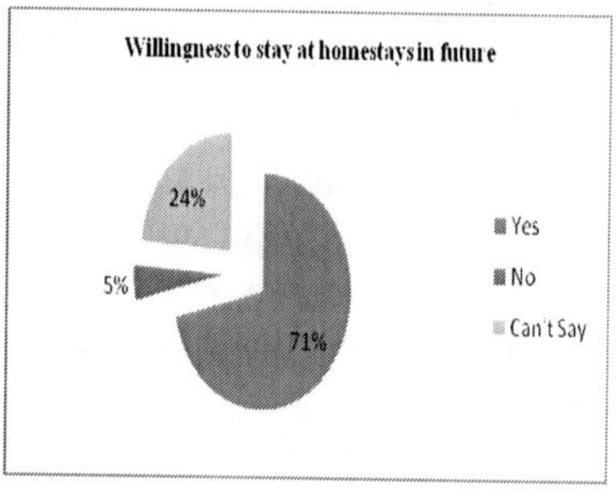

Chart 12.17: Willingness to stay at homestays in future.

A whopping 71 % of the respondents showed willingness to stay at homestay in the future whereas only 24% are undecided. Only 5% showed no willingness to stay at homestay in the future.

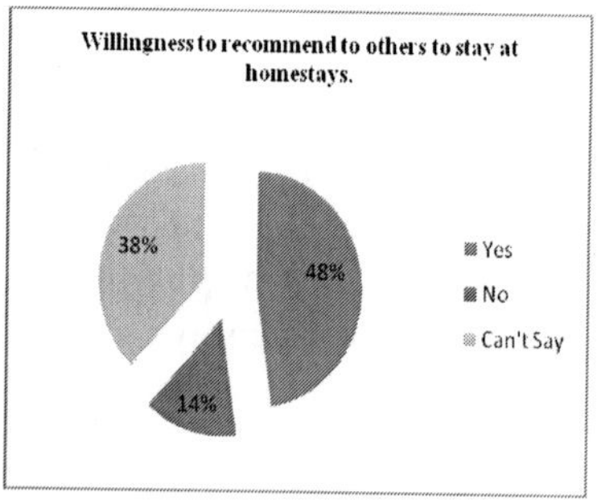

Chart 12.18: Willingness to recommend to others to stay at homestays.

48% of the respondents are willing to recommend others to stay at homestay.

38% of the respondents are not sure whether they will recommend others to stay at homestay.

Only 14 % of the respondents opined that they will not recommend others to stay at homestay.

Recommendation and suggestions

(i) The quality of infrastructure and surface connectivity to Ziro valley should be developed to enable tourists to have better accessibility to the destination. The roads leading to Ziro valley are all in bad shape which only worsens during the monsoons. As such infrastructural facilities needs to be revamped and improved because without these facilities it is difficult to establish and promote better service to existing as well as potential homestay visitors.

(ii) Some of the home stays are located at a distance from well-populated places. Enhancement of safety and security measures for visitors such as a well-fenced perimeter, support services for visitors, offering travel advice and aiming for visitor satisfaction will go a long way in reassuring visitors. The homestay operators and service personnel should be made familiar with the standard operation procedures (SOP) to be followed in the wake of natural calamities and disasters to ensure safety of guests and visitors. This is what will help the Homestays to sustain and flourish.

(iii) The locals of the homestay tourism should be given training on leadership and hospitality along with food and beverage so that the tourists can get satisfactory service. It is recommended that the Homestay operators invest in some kind of professional training for their employees so that they are better equipped to handle guest requests and requirements i.e., creating a unique experience for the guests with a professional touch. There is a need of preparation of homestay planning and development for the local people. Hence, the local people of the proposed homestay tourism destination should be technically assisted to prepare homestay planning and development.

(iv) The homestay units operating in Ziro valley should be able to offer more recreational and interesting activities to visitors and guests to make their stay interesting and memorable. Participation of guests in cultural activities, agricultural activities, local sports and other outdoor recreational pursuits like trekking, bush walking, jungle safari, river rafting, fishing, etc can create memorable experiences for visitors and guests staying in Ziro valley. Homestays can also showcase local handicrafts, souvenirs, cane and bamboo made products to attract the interests of visitors which can be a source of income generation for the locals. The promotion of local cuisine and delicacies also has a tremendous scope in homestay tourism.

(v) The operators should ensure that proper standards of hygiene and cleanliness are followed in their property, as guests do not want to compromise on this important aspect at any given point of time.

(vi) Loan subsidy and other incentives should be enhanced and provided to the local homestay operators for upgrading their existing facilities i.e. bedrooms, bathrooms, interior fittings and appliances, cleanliness etc.

(vii) The homestay operators in Ziro valley should have effective linkages with tourism organizations and service providers based in national as well as international source markets. The use of ICT tools and destination management systems (DMS) can provide a suitable platform for the homestay units to have an electronic presence and facilitate e-marketing of their products and services. This would enable tourists from anywhere in the world to easily explore, choose, and book their accommodation in homestays located in Ziro valley.

Conclusion

Homestay accommodation is an excellent way of experiencing the authentic style of living of a destination. Guests staying here can truly get to live the life as the locals do, in a way that they would not be able to in a hotel. They get to know about the culture and history of the destination. Homestay operators however need to work on the hygiene levels as well as provision of basic amenities to the travellers. They should also take care to have enhanced security measures that will greatly enhance the comfort levels of their guests. The present study revealed that the state government is encouraging unemployed youths of the state to start Homestay by providing loan through various schemes. There are also many challenges in homestay and the homestay owners and the department of tourism as well as state government need to focus on such challenges and bring out some solutions at the earliest. Evaluation of visitors' experiences can assist the management and operators of the Ziro homestay programme in improving their range of services, business viability, and infrastructure. Infrastructure limitations also severely constrain the capacity of the local community in providing high-quality homestay experience and competing with more established commercial operators.

References

Carlson, M. (1996). *Performance: A critical introduction*. London: Routledge.

Csýkszentmihalyi, M. (1990). *Flow: The psychology of optimal experience*. New York: Harper & Row.

Colton, J. W., & Whitney-Squire, K. (2010). Exploring the relationship between aboriginal tourism and community development. Journal of Leisure Studies, 34(3), 261-278.

Dahles, H. (2000). Tourism, small enterprises and community development. In G. Richards and D. Hall (Eds.), Tourism and sustainable community development (pp. 154-169). London: Routledge.

Dolezal, C. (2011). "Community-Based Tourism in Thailand: (Dis-) Illusions of Authenticity and The Necessity For Dynamic Concepts Of Culture And Power". ASEAS: Austrian Journal of South-East Asian Studies, 4(1).

Henning, R., & Willemse, C. (1999). Effective guest house management. Kenwyn: Juta & Co.

Jamil, J. & Hamzah, A. (2007). KPW and Women roles in Banghuris Homestay; Rural Tourism Research in Malaysia. Retrieved Nov 19, 2019, from http://www.ritsumei.ac.jp/acd/re/k-rsc/hss/book/pdf/vol02-03.

Kadir, R. A., Rashid, M. S. A., Yusoff, S. R. (2010). Homestay as a Factor in Sustaining the Traditional Malay Culture in Heritage Tourism Industry. *Arte-polis 3 International Conference – Creative Collaboration and the Making of Place*. Bandung: Institut Teknologi Bandung.

Kayat, K. (2009). Customer orientation among rural home stay operators in Malaysia. ASEAN Journal on Hospitality Tourism, 6(2), 65-78.

Kumar, S., Gill, S., & Kunasekaran, P. (2012) "Tourism as a Poverty Eradication Tool for Rural Areas in Selangor, Malaysia", Global Journal of Human Social Science Research, 12(7), 20–26.

Levitt, T. (1996). The marketing imagination (1st ed.). New York, NY: Free Press.

McCabe, S. and Foster, C. (2006). The role and function of narrative in tourist interaction. *Journal of Tourism and Cultural Change,* 4(3), 194–215.

Mossberg, L. (2003). A marketing approach to the tourist experience. *Scandinavian Journal of Hospitality and Tourism*, *7*(1), 59–74.

Pine, B. J. & Gilmore, J. H. (1999). *The experience economy*. Massachusetts: Harvard Business School Press.

Richardson, K. (2003). International Education: Home Stay Theory versus Practice. In Educational Research, Risks, & Dilemmas. *NZARE/AARE Conference*. Auckland, New Zealand. Retrieved from. http://www.aare.edu.au/03pap/ric03173. pdf.

Salamiah AJ, Nor' Ain Othman, Nik Maheran Nik Muhammad (2011) Tourist perceived value in a community-based homestay visit: An investigation into the functional and experiential aspect of value. Journal of Vacation Marketing 17 (1), 5-15.

Suraj Bhan & Lakhvinder Singh (2014) Homestay Tourism in India: Opportunities and Challenges African Journal of Hospitality, Tourism and

Leisure Vol. 3 (2) - (2014) ISSN: 2223-814X Copyright: © 2014 AJHTL - Open Access- Online @ http//:www.ajhtl.com

Wang, N. (2002). The tourist as peak consumer. In G. M. S. Dann (Ed.), *The tourist as a metaphor of the social world* (pp. 281–295). Wallingford: CABI Publishing.

Wang, Y. (2007). "Customized Authenticity begins at Home", Annals of Tourism Research, 34(3).

Zaki, M., Johan, A., Affendi, I., & Norria, Z. (2011). Inap desa sebagai agen pembangunan sosio ekonomikomuniti: Menelusuri perspektif pelajar pengurusan pelancongan UUM, Prosiding PERKEM V1, Jilid 2, 81-93.

Websites

http://greenerpasturesind.wordpress.com/2019/08/19/eco-tourism-in-north-east-india-5-responsible-cottages-and-homestays/retrieved on 04.08.2019 at 11:25

http://www.ecotourismsocietyofindia.org/index.asp retrieved on 15.07.2019 at 10:18.

http://www.arunachalpradesh.gov.in/

http://www.arunachaltourism.com/2019/10/19/toursim/retrieved on 15.08.19 at 11:15

http://tourism.gov.in//2019/10/19/toursim/retrieved on 15.08.19 at 11:05

http://tourism.gov.in/sites/default/files/arunchal%20pradesh.pdf/2019/10/19/toursim/retrieved on 15.08.19 at 11:30

http://tourism.gov.in/sites/default/files/policy/National%20Tourism%20Policy%202002.pdf/2019/10/19/toursim/retrieved on 15.08.19 at 14:15

13

Growth and Development of Adult Women among the Ahom of Dhemaji district, Assam

— *Chayanika Hazarika*

Growth is the sign of life. Growth is the most important and fundamental attributed of all living organism. It is the harmonic increase in size and weight of the body through multiplication of cells, in relation to age and in proportion to other parts of the body. Studies on growth and development of adulthood are important as they provide determinants of a nation's health.

Individuals experience great changes from childhood to old age in respect of several physical and physiological traits. There is actually no clear static point in actual age or particular time of human being, when the morphological body features do not change (Astrand *et al.,* 1973). The definition of a period of complete maturation as well as the starting point of ageing process is difficult to assign. Adulthood is not a stable physiological and bio-chemical period; changes are numerous and constantly observed at anthropometric and physiological levels.

Ageing is a process involving many changes in the body; they are molecular, cellular and organism. These changes are measurable and can be explained. After the active phase in the span of life, there is a declining process resulting in old age or senescence.

The cessation of height is regarded as a sign of maturity. Height ceases to grow when the long bones e.g., tibia, fibula etc., lose their capacity to increase in length. Usually males attain the height at about 21 years of age and females at 18 years of age. Body weight attains its peak after thirty; girths and some functional characteristics reaches its peak more or less the same time; width measurements increases slowly but steadily arriving the peak at the later ages of life (Prokopec,1987).

The variation of anthropometric measurements in adulthood are primarily related to the osteological changes, changes in the fat and muscle tissues, although nutritional status has a great role in making all the changes. Most of the anthropometric studies on adults are often cross-sectional and it is difficult to separate the changes due to secular changes or resulting from continuing growth or due to aging (Susanne, 1977).

The works on the adult growth with the ageing process were confined to some basic parameters like height, weight and some physiological variables (Mukherjee and Gupta, 1930; Risley, 1931; Mason, 1931). There exists a good number of works on adult growth coupled with the aging process. Laskar (1953) worked on the age factor in bodily measurements of adult male and female Mexicans. Borzek *et al.,* (1963) studied the skin fold distribution in middle aged Americans. Noris *et al.,* (1963) and Wassel *et al.,* (1963) studied the body composition in aged men and women in New York. Wolanaski and Pyzuk (1972) studied morpho-physiological characters and physical working capacity in inhabitants of low mountains in Poland. Floris *et al.,* (1977) conducted a study on morphometric changes in Sardinians of different age. Relethford and Lee, (1981) studied the effects of aging and secular trend on adult stature in rural western Ireland. Fosenbaum *et al.,* (1985) conducted a survey on stature and weights of adults in Great Britain.

In India, Sidhu *et al.,* (1983) studied the processes of maturation and senescence in two communities of Punjab (India) taking into consideration some morphological measures. Joyee and Kapoor (1995) studied the changes in physiological parameters and their relation with physical traits among Rajput females. Begum and Barman (1998) studied adult sexual dimorphism among the tea garden labourers of

Dibrugarh, Assam. Begum (1998) studied in nutritional and economic status in relation to changes in adult growth among the Assamese Muslims of Kamrup district, Assam. Roy (1999) and Roy and Pal (2003) studied age changes in anthropometric characters among the tea garden labourers of northern West Bengal. Tungdim and Kapoor (2003) studied morpho physiological changes among the high altitudes aged. Sikdar and Ahmed Das (2006) studied growth progression with ages in physical and physiological variables among the Bengali population of Dibrugarh, Assam. Sengupta and Hussain (2014) studied the changes in somatometric characters among the adult Boro Kacharis of Assam.

Investigation carried out under different conditions by various research groups have shown positive correlation between blood pressure and age (Reddy *et al.*, 1991), body composition (Sambasiva Rao, 1983) and Sex (Celine and Mathur, 1979).

The present study was conducted to evaluate the structural and functional changes with the process of ageing with respect to ten somatometric characters and one physiometric trait - blood pressure among the adult Ahom women of Dhemaji District, Assam.

The Ahom

The Ahoms are the major ethnic groups of Assam. The Ahom people in India are mostly confined to the state of Assam and Arunachal Pradesh. The Ahoms is the biggest community in the state Assam, which has been selected for the study. These wonderful people stepped their footprint in the great Brahmaputra Valley from the east (initially from Muang Mao, Chaina through the Shan state of Burma) in the 13th century. In Assam, this very significant wave of Mongoloid migration has been brought by the Ahoms. The Ahom belongs to a major population of Assam and ruled Assam for nearly six hundred years. The Ahom community ethnically belongs to the Mongoloid racial group, which belong to Other Backward Class under Indian Constitution. The Ahom people are found mostly in upper Assam district of Gulaghat, Jorhat, Sibsagar, Dibrugarh, Dhemaji, Tinsukia and Lakhimpur.

Material and Methods

The sample for the present study is collected from the Ahom inhabiting

Gugamukh Chetia Gaon, Dhemaji district, Assam. The village is bounded by Subansiri river in the west. On the estern side lies the Nepali village. Towards the northern side of the village lays the Mohori camp village. On the south of the village is the Gugamukh Chariali.

The materials for the present study were collected from 21-70 years adult Ahom women. The total sample was 250 adult females. Requisite information on socio-demographic profile for each subject were collected by interview method, which include age, sex, family size, marital status, education etc.

A total of ten somatometric measurements were taken from each subject following standard anthropometric techniques as proposed by Martin (1968). A standard non elastic tape was used to measure the mid upper arm, waist and hip circumference. Mid upper arm circumference was measured at the midpoint in between radiale and acromeon. Waist circumference was taken at the minimum circumference between umbilicus and xiphisternum, while hip circumference was measured at the maximum width of the greater trochanter.

In the present study the blood pressure of the subjects were measured and classified following the standard of American Medical Association (JNC-VII) like Normotensive (mmHg) SBP < 120 and DBP < 80; Pre-hypertensive (mmHg) SBP 120 - 139 and DBP 80 – 89; and Hypertensive (mmHg) SBP e" 140 and DBP e" 90 – 99 (Chobanian *et al.*, 2003).

Body Mass Index (BMI) and Waist Hip Ratio (WHR) were computed using standard equations (WHO, 1995). Body Mass Index was calculated as body weight in kilograms divided by height in meters squared. Waist Hip Ratio was calculated as waist circumference divided by hip circumference. BMI is an indicator of overall obesity, and WHR, is a good indicator of abdominal fat accumulation. The cut off points recommended for the Asia Pacific region (WHO, 2002) was followed.

Nutritional status was also assessed on the basis of mid upper arm circumference (MUAC) following the standard recommended by James *et al.*, (1988). Truncal obesity is diagnosed when waist hip ratio > 0.92 in males and > 0.82 in females is categorised as higher.

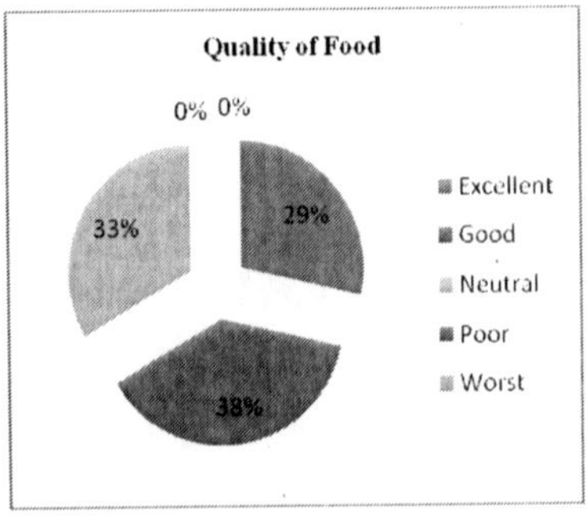

Result and Discussion

Table 13.1. Statistical constants of anthropometric and physiometric traits according to age

Age category (in years)	*Sample size*	*Stature (cm)*	*Weight (cm)*	*Circumference (cm)*			*Blood Pressure*	
				Mid Upper Arm	*Waist*	*Hip*	*Systolic*	*Diastolic*
21-30	67	152.12±0.53	48.37±0.57	24.07±0.13	74.95±0.79	83.61±0.81	119.14±2.01	76,75±1.40
31-40	44	153.33±0.83	47.93±1.03	23.87±0.29	75.57±1.10	84.35±1.02	119.14±2.00	76.74±1.40
41-50	48	152.75±1.01	48.72±1.54	24.56±0.47	76.21±1.31	87.20±1.21	121.91±3.62	75.91±2.06
51-60	36	151.39±0.83	45.22±1.28	23.32±0.31	73.43±1.09	82.29±1.56	121.45±3.34	75.73±1.74
61-70	55	152.80±1.21	44.86±1.24	23.25±0.46	71.36±1.21	81.57±1.26	120.09±3.10	73.71±2.51

Table 13.2. Statistical constants of some skin fold measurements according to age

Age group (in years)	*Sample size*	*Skinfold Measurement*				
		Biceps	*Triceps*	*Scapular*	*Supra-iliac*	*Calf*
21-30	67	6.78±1.07	8.42±0.17	9.89±0.21	11.11±0.25	9.70±0.22
31-40	44	6.89±0.22	8.40±0.19	10.10±0.36	11.52±0.47	9.72±0.29
41-50	48	7.13±0.32	8.60±0.33	10.11±0.42	11.31±0.88	10.18±0.68
51-60	36	6.64±0.19	8.08±0.18	9.50±0.30	10.38±0.25	8.84±0.20
61-70	55	6.68±0.26	8.15±0.37	9.72±0.20	10.03±0.13	8.67±0.27

From the Table 13.1 shows the height of adult Ahom females reveals the gradual increase in height from 21-30 years age group to 31-40 years. However, gradual decrease in height is noted in them from 41-50 years onwards.

The mean values of weight along with their statistical measures among the adult Ahom females. The weight of adult female gradually increases up to 50 years of age then it sharply falls and remains constant. The mean value of the mid upper circumference gradually increases from 21-30 years up to 41-50 years and then gradually decreases from 51-60 years onwards.

The mean value of waist circumference increases from the age group 21-30 to 41-50 years and then decreases from 51-60 years to 61-70 years. The mean value of hip circumference increases from the age group of 21-30 to 41-50 years, however, from 51-60 years to 61-70 years the mean value of hip circumference remains almost constant.

The mean value of the systolic and diastolic blood pressure increases from the age group of 21-30 which continue till 41-50 years and then both of them decreases from 51-60 years to 61-70 years.

Table 13.2 shows the mean value of skin fold measurements of Ahom women. The mean value of biceps skin fold increases from the age group of 21-30 to 41-50 years and then decreases from 51-60 years onwards.

The mean value of skin fold at triceps clearly shows that with the increase of age the mean value of skin fold at triceps also decreases.

The mean value of scapular skin fold increases from 21-30 years to 31-40 years and then it decreases from the age group of 41-50 to 61-70 years. With the increase of age, the mean value of skin folds at supra-iliac and calf region gradually decreases.

Table 13.3 show the blood pressure types in Ahom adult female reveals that the incidence of Normotensive type is highest in the age group of 21-30 years and which then decreases constantly.

The frequency of Ahom females belonging to pre-hypertensive category gradually increase from 21-30 to 41-50 age group and then gradually decreases. The hypertensive category increases with the increase of age.

Table 13.3. Variation in blood pressure types according to age

Age category (in years)	Sample size	Normotensive (SBP<120 and DBP <80)		Pre-hypertensive (SBP 120-139; DBP 80-89)		Hypertensive (SBP≥ 140 DBP ≥ 90-99)	
		No	%	No	%	No	%
21-30	67	31	46.3	25	37.3	11	16.4
31-40	44	20	45.5	18	40.9	5	11.4
41-50	48	12	25.0	22	45.8	14	29.2
51-60	36	9	25.0	10	27.8	17	47.2
61-70	55	13	23.6	17	30.9	25	45.5

Table 13.4. Variation in Body Mass Index according to age

Age category (in years)	Sample size	Body Mass Index							
		Under weight (<18.5)		Normal (18.5-22.99)		Overweight (23-24.9)		Obese (>25)	
		No	%	No	%	No	%	No	%
21-30	67	10	14.9	25	37.3	17	25.4	15	22.4
31-40	44	3	6.8	11	25.0	14	31.8	16	36.4
41-50	48	5	10.4	7	14.6	19	39.6	17	35.4
51-60	36	5	13.9	4	11.1	11	30.6	16	44.4
61-70	55	6	10.9	11	20	20	36.4	18	32.7

Table 13.4 shows the nutritional status of the Ahom adult females as per Body Mass Index. From the table it is clearly seen that the Ahom females belonging to 21-30 years age group, the percentage of underweight is quite high i.e. 14.9 percent. In underweight category, the number of females decreases from 21-30 years to 41-50 years and then increases with the increase of age group 61-70. In the normal category of Ahom female gradually decreases with the increase of age. The incidence of overweight Ahom females increases with the increase of age. In the obese category of adult Ahom female increases from 21-30 to 51-60 age group and then it is decrease in the age group 61-70.

Table 13.5 shows results on two nutritional indices among the Ahom female. In the mid upper circumference, the females are all showing higher values. With regard to waist hip ratio, all also showing high waist hip ratio (truncal obesity).

In the present study the analysis of the data with regard to blood pressure and other variables considered recorded considerable number of fluctuations with regard to age, which is a regular feature of all growing individuals.

Table 13.5. Variation in Nutritional Characters and Indices according to age

Age category (in years)	*Sample size*	*Mid Upper Arm Circumference* <22.00 No	%	*Mid Upper Arm Circumference* >22.00 No	%	*Waist Hip Ratio* Male <0.92 Female<0.82 No	%	*Waist Hip Ratio* Male >0.92 Female>0.82 No	%
21-30	67	12	17.9	55	82.1	2	2.9	65	97
31-40	44	2	4.5	42	94.5	0	0	44	100
41-50	48	0	0	48	100	6	12.5	42	87.5
51-60	36	0	0	36	100	2	5.6	34	94.4
61-70	55	0	0	55	100	0	0	55	100

The height of adult Ahom females reveals the gradual increase in height from 21-30 years age group to 31-40 years. However, gradual decrease in height is noted in them from 41-50 years onwards. In this regard, Roy (1999), Joyee and Kapur (2003), Begum (1998), Tungdim and Kapoor (2003) and Sikdar and Ahmed Das (2006) has reported a decreasing trend in stature with advancement of age. Studies conducted by Kazoka and Vetra (2013) found that the body height for the urban women show a considerably higher mean value than the rural women at the age group of 21-25 years, whereas for the rural women a reverse trend is noticed from the age group of 26-35 years. Roche *et al.,* (1981), Roy and Pal (2003) noted almost similar trend which corroborate with the present study. According to Roche *et al.,* (1981), the stature decreases after about 36 years of age in both the sexes. Roy and Pal (2003) reported that after 25 years of age the stature begins to decline.

The weight of adult female gradually increases up to 50 years of age then it slightly falls and remains constant. Similar trend in male has also been reported by Tungdim *et al.*,(2003); Miall *et al.*, (1967); Choudhary (1981); Roy and Pal (2003), all of them noted that the weight increases up to 35 years of age, then it declines. Sikdar and Ahmed Das (2006) on the other hand found that the weight in male increases up to 40 years then it decline. Roy and Pal (2003) also reported that in female weight decreases from 35 years of age. On the other hand, Sikdar and Ahmed Das reported that the mean weight increases up to 50 years, then it decline.

The mean value of female, the mid upper circumference increases from 21-30 years to 41-50 years which ultimately shows decreasing trend from 51-60 years onwards.

The present finding has been supported by Begum (1998), Sikdar and Ahmed Das (2006) who also noted a similar trend in the males but in females they found the declining trend which started after 50 years of age. It was found that the waist circumferences of Ahom females, it increases from 21-30 years till 41-50 years which then decreases from 51-60 years onwards. While focussing on the growth of the hip girth among the Ahom females, in the age group from 21-30 to 41-50 years, the values in females increases while a reverse trend is noted,

C.M. Law and his associates (1992) in the *Journal of Epidemiological and Community Health* mentioned that the growth of hip girth closely depends on BMI of an individual. According to them, the hip girth increase up to 30 years of age which has close similarity with the Ahom females of the present study.

The mean value of both systolic and diastolic blood pressure increases from the age group of 21-30 which continue till 41-50 years and then sharply decreases from 51-60 years to 61-70 years.

Ulijaszek and Kozeiel (2003) reported that the mean blood pressures of Rarotonga, the Cook Islands exhibit no statistical significant differences in blood pressure between males and females. Studies conducted by Kazoka and Vetra (2013) reported that in the age group of 21-25 years, the mean values of both systolic and diastolic blood pressure shows consistently higher values in the urban women than the rural women.

The mean values of skin fold at biceps in Ahom female, it increases from age group of 21-30 to 41-50 years and then decreases from 51-60 years onwards. Roy and Pal (2003) reported that after 25 years of age, the fat at biceps shows gradual decline in both males and females. Roy (1999) reported that after 20 years, fat at biceps declines. On the other hand, Sikdar and Ahmed Das (2006) reported that the fat at biceps declines after 50 years of age in both males and females.

In case of skin fold at triceps, the female shows irregular trend in different age groups. The mean value of triceps decreases with the increase of age. Roy and Pal (2003) reported that the fat at triceps declines after 25 years of age in males where as in the females, it fails to show any uniform declining trend. Sikdar and Ahmed Das (2006) recorded a gradual decrease with the advancement of age in the males and in the females it decreases after 50 years of age.

The mean value of skin fold at scapular region in female decreases from the age group of 21-30 years to 31-40 years but it records an increasing trend from 41-50 years onwards. The mean value of skin fold at supra iliac and calf region in female records gradually decrease with the increase of age. It is worthwhile to be mentioned here that Roy and Pal (2003) reported from among the Oraon male that the skin fold at calf declines after 44 years whereas it is after 25 years in case of females. Roy (1999) found that the fat at calf in the tea garden labourers of North Bengal gradually decreases with the advancement of age, more particularly from the age group of 20 years in both the sexes. Sikdar and Ahmed Das (2006) reported that after 30 years in Bengali Kayastha males, the calf girth declines and in female they show a similar trend with the present study.

The blood pressure types in Ahom adult female reveals that the incidence of Normotensive type is highest in the age group of 21-30 years in both of the male and female which then decreases constantly. The frequency of Ahom females belonging to pre-hypertensive category gradually increase from 21-30 to 41-50 age group and then gradually deceases. The hypertensive category of Ahom adult women increases with the increase of age.

The blood pressure in human being is influenced by a large number of intrinsic and extrinsic factors. The deviation from the expected trend observed in the present study, therefore, must have been due to the differences in body composition, habitual physical activity, diet, income, ageing, smoking etc.

The nutritional status of the Ahom adult women as per Body Mass, belonging to 21-30 years age group, the percentage of underweight is quite high i.e. 14.9 percent. In underweight category, the number of females decreases from 21-30 years to 41-50 years and then increases with the increase of age group 61-70. In the normal category of Ahom female gradually decreases with the increase of age. The incidence of overweight Ahom females increases with the increase of age. In the obese category of adult Ahom women increases from 21-30 to 51-60 age group and then it is decrease in the age group 61-70.

Studies among the elderly adults of Southeast Brazil (Barreto *et al.,* 2003) reveal that underweight was significantly more common among men than women and the incidence increased dircctly with age irrespective of sex. It also revealed that obesity was more common among women, and its prevalence decreased with age.

In this regard, in North East India, Kulkarni and Sharma (2001) studied the Karbi population of Assam; Khongsdier (2001) studied twelve population groups of North East India; Basu (2006) studied the Dimasa population of Assam; Boruah (2007) studied the Mishing population of Brahmaputra valley, Assam; but all these studies failed to show prevalence of obesity among these population groups. Dutta and Sengupta (2008) reported prevalence of overweight and obesity among the Kalita, Mishing and Sonowal Kacharis of upper Assam.

In the present study, the values of Body Mass Index (BMI) indicate that the Ahom women have high nutritional status. The mean values of BMI were compared with the standard chart of WHO (1995). The nutritional indicator like mid upper arm circumference and waist hip ratio among the Ahom women also reveals satisfactory nutritional status.

Acknowledgement

Authors are deeply indebted to all the participants for their unhesitating help and sincere co-operation during data collecting.

References

Barreto, S.M.; Passos, V.M.A. and Lima-Costa M.F.F. 2003, Obesity and underweight among Brazilian elderly. The Bambui Health and Ageing study. *Cad. Saude. Publica*. 19: 605-612.

Basu, D. 2006, 'Nutritional anthropometric assessment of nutrient's intakes in the Dimasa Kachari adult population of Assam'. In: D. Basu; B. Francis Kulirani; and B. Dutta Roy (Eds): *Agriculture, Food Security: Nutrition and Health in North East India,* Akansha Publications: New Delhi.

Begum, G and Barman, R., 1998. 'Adult sexual dimorphism among the tea garden labourers of Dibrugarh, Assam'. *Jr. Hum. Ecol.* 9, 5: 521-523.

Begum, G, 1998, 'Nutrition and economic status in relation to change in adult growth among the Assamese Muslim of Kamrup District. Assam'. *Jr. Hum. Ecol.* 585-591.

Brozek, J.K; Khilbeg, H.L; Taylor and Keys, A., 1963, 'Skin fold distribution in middle aged American men: A contribution to norms of leanness and fatness'. *Annals of New York Academy of Sciences,* 110: 492-502.

Celine, V.J and Mathur, S.B.L., 1979, 'Blood pressure variation in ageing: A study in a central Indian population', *Journal of Indian Medical Association,* 55: 129-130.

Chobanian, A. V.; Bakris, G.L; Black, H.R; Cushman, W.C; Green, L.A.; and Izzo, J.L. Jr. 2003. 'The seventh report of the joint national committee on prevention, detection, evaluation and treatment of high blood pressure: The JNC-VII report' *Journal of American Medical Association*, 282, 19: 2560-2572.

Choudhury, B., 1981, 'Changes of some somatometric characters in adult Rabhas of Kamrup district, Assam due to ageing'. *Bull. Dept. Anthrop. Dibrugarh Univ.*, 10: 87-93.

Dutta, D and Sengupta, S. 2008, 'Prevalence of overweight and obesity among three ethnic groups of Assam: A preliminary appraisal'. *Bulletin of the Department of Anthropology, Dibrugarh University,* 36: 1-16.

Floris, G,; Maxia, C; Cosseddue, G.G and Vona G., 1977, 'Morphometric changes in Sardinians of different ages'. In O.G. Eiben (Ed): *Growth and Development Physique.* Symposium of Human Biology – Akademiai Kiadio Budapest, pp. 315-323.

Fosenbaum, S; Skinner, R.K., Knight, I.B., and Garrow, J.S., 1985, 'A survey of heights and weights of adults in Great Britain 1980', *Ann. Hum. Biol.* 12: 115-128.

James, W.P.T.; Ferro-Luzzi, A and Waterlow, J.C. 1988. 'Definition of chronic energy deficiency in adults'. *European Journal of Clinical Nutrition,* 42, 12: 969-981.

Joyee, K.P. and Kapoor, S., 1995, 'Age change in physical parameters and their relation with physical traits among Rajput females'. *Man in India*, 75.4:

Khongsdier, R. 2001. 'Body mass index of adult males in twelve populations of North East India', *Annals of Human Biology*, 28: 374-383.

Kulkarni, S and Sharma, E.R. 2001, 'Nutrition among the Karbi tribe of Assam: An anthropometric assessment'. *Journal of Indian Anthropological Society,* 36: 223-229.

Lasker, G.W., 1953, 'The age factor in bodily measurement of adult male and female Mexicans' *Hum. Biol.,* 25-50.

Law, C.M.; Barker, D.J.P; Osmond, C; Fall, C.H.D. and Simmonds, S.J. 1992. 'Early growth and abdominal fatness in adult life'. *Journal of Epidemiology and Community Health*, 46, 3: 184-186.

Martin, R. 1928. *Lehrbuch der Anthropologie,* Jena, Verlag: von Gustav Fischer.

Mason, E.D.1931. 'The basal metabolism of South Indian women'. *Indian Journal of Medical Research.* 19-75.

Miall, W.E.; Ashcroft, M.T.; Lovell, H.G. and Moore, F. 1967. A longitudinal study of the decline of adult height with age in two Welsh communities. *Human Biology,* 39; 445.

Mukherjee H.N and Gupta D.C. 1930 'The basal metabolism of Indians (Bengalis)'. *Indian Journal Medical Research, 18:307.*

Norris, A.H.; Lundy, T; and Shock, N.W., 1963, 'Trends in selected indices of body composition in men between the ages of 30 and 80 years'. *Ann New Tork Acad. Sci.*, 110:623.

Prokopec, M., 1987, 'Changing patterns of growth, development and ageing in the population of Czechoslovakia'. *Collegium Anthropologicum,* 11: 91-115.

Reddy P.C., Bulliyya, G, Ramachandrayya, T., Kumar K.S. and Reddarma, 1991. Serum lipids and lipids peroxidation pattern in industrial and rural worker in India', *Age*, 14: 33-38.

Relethford, J.H.; and Lees, F.C., 1981, 'The effect of ageing and secular trend on adult status in rural western Ireland', *Amer. Jr. Phy. Anth.* 55: 81-88.

Roche, A.F.; Garn, S.M.; Reynolds, E.L.; Rainbow, M and Sontag, L.W; 1981, 'The first seriatim study of Human growth and middle aging'. *Amer. Jr. Phy. Anthrop.* 54: 23-24.

Roy, S.K and Pal, B., 2003 'Anthropometric and physiological traits: Age changes among the Oraon agricultural labourers of the Jalpaiguri District, North West Bengal, India'. *Anthrop.Anz*, 61, 4: 445-460.

Roy, S.K., 1999, 'A note on age changes in anthropometric characters among the tea garden labourers of Northern West Bengal', *Jr.Ind. Anthrop.Soc.,* 34, 2:191-195.

Sambasiva Rao, R. 1983. 'Blood pressure and triceps, skin fold thickness', *Ann. Hum. Biol*; 10: 191-193.

Sengupta, S and Hussain, Sayeeda U. 2014. 'Age changes in somatometric characters among the adult Boro Kacharis of Assam: A preliminary appraisal'. *Bulletin of the Department of Anthropology, Dibrugarh University*, 42: 81-88.

Sidhu, L.S.; Singhal, P; and Bansal, D.K., 1983, 'Processes of maturation and senescence in two Communities of Punjab (India) as studied from some morphological measures'. *Anthrop.Anz.*41; 149-159.

Sikdar, M and Ahmed Das, F., 2006 'Growth progression with ages in physical and physiological variables among the Bengali population of Dibrugarh, Assam'. *Bull. Dept. Anthrop. Dibrugarh Univ.* 34: 45-49

Susanne, C., 1977, 'Individual age changes of the morphological characteristics', *Jr.Hum.Evol*. 6: 181-189.

Tungdim and Kapoor, S., 2003, 'Morpho-physiological changes among height altitude aged'. *Ind. Jr.Phy.Anth.Hum. Genet.* 22, 1: 73-86.

Ulijaszek, S.J. and Koziel, S. 2003. Association between blood pressure and economic modernization among adults on Rarotonga, the Cook Islands. *Przeglad Antropologiczny – Anthropological Review,* 66: 65-75.

Wessel, J.A.; Ufer, A; Van Huss, W. D.; and Cederquist, D., 1963, 'Age trends of various components of body composition and fluctuational characteristics in women aged 20-69 years'. *Ann. New York Acad. Sci.*, 110: 608.

Wolanski, N, and Pyzuk, M., 1972, 'Morpho-physiological characters and physical working capacity in 15-72 years old inhabitants of low mountains, Lieniny Range, Poland'. *Hum. Biol.,* 44: 595-612.

World Health Organization, 1995, *The Use and Interpretation of Anthropometry.* Report of the WHO Experts Committee, Technical Report Series, No. 854. World Health Organization, Geneva.

World Health Organization, 2002, *Health Situation in South East Asia Region,* 1998-2000.WHO Regional Office for South East Asia, New Delhi.

14

A Study on Cephalic Index and Head shape among the Deoris of Dhemaji District of Assam, India

— *Milonjyoti Borgohain, Prof. H. Vokendro S.*

Introduction

Anthropometry deals with the measurement of physical size and shapes of human body. Cephalic index is one of the very useful measurable anthropometric variables used in physical or biological anthropology to determine gender, age and ethnic variations. The cephalic index and shape of head is vary with race in sex. Cephalic index is also called as cranial index or index of breadth. It is one of the parameter that helps to differentiate between different human races.

The cephalic index was defined by Swedish professor of Anatomy Anders Retzius and first used in physical anthropology to classify ancient human remains found in Europe. The measures, when applied to living individuals are known as cephalic index and when referring to dry skulls are known as cranial index.

Comparison of changes in cephalic index between parents, offspring and siblings can give a clue to genetic transmission of inherited traits. On the basis of cephalic index, head shapes are grouped into four international types, namely dolicocephalic (long and narrow), brachicephalic (short and broad), mesocephalic (intermediate length and width) and hyperbrachicephalic (very short and broad). Australian aborigines and Southern Africans are Dolicocephalic, Europeans and the Chinese are mesocephalic and Mongolians and the Andaman Islanders have brachicephalic head.

Review of Literaure

Several studies have been carried out to classify hade shapes based on cephalic index into four internationally acceptable categories that include dolicocephalic (< 74.9), mesocephalic (75-79.0), brachycephalic (80.0-84.9), and hyperbrachycephalic (85.0-89.9). A research study has shown that the people of Gurung community of Nepal of India are brachycephalic with cephalic index of 80.42. Bhils and Barelas are mesocephalic (76.98 and 79.80). The Iranian are predominantly brachycephalic and hyper brachycephalic.

Aims and Objectives

The aim of the present study is to provide a baseline data of cephalic index and head shape of Deoris of Assam. The data were analysed statistically and results presented in tabular form. The present data is also compared with some available national and international populations.

Materials and Methods

A total of 100 Deori adult individuals (50 males and 50 females) were randomly selected for the present study. The age of the individuals was between 18-50 years. To obtain the cephalic index, the maximum head length was measured from glabella to opisthocranion, while the maximum head breadth was measured from the transverse diameter between the two eurya using a spreading calliper. The anatomical landmarks were defined as, glabella (g): a point above the nasal root between the two eyebrows and intersected by mid-sagittal plane, euryon (eu): most lateral point placed on the side of the head. The measurements were taken with the subject sitting on a chair, in a relaxed mood, and the head in the anatomical position. All the measurements were recorded in the nearest centimetre. The data were analysed statistically and results presented in tabular form.

About the Study Population

The present study deals with the cephalic index and head shape of the Deori tribe inhabiting in Kapahtali Deori village under Sisiborgaon Development Block, District Dhemaji, Assam .The Deories are one of the major tribal group in Assam. The Deories are found in the Districts of Dibrugarh, Sibasagar, Jorhat, N. Lakhimpur, Tinsukia, Sonitpur, Dhemaji and in some parts of Arunachal Pradesh. The Deores are one of the four divisions of Chutiyas and they represents the priestly section of the whole chutiya community. They have a unique cultural and traditional heritage. They are mongoloids, with very strong religious character and are known to be a brave, tradition loving and cultured people with deep agricultural roots.

They are hard-working people, and agriculture is the main source of their livelihood. Like other tribal communities of this region, rice is the staple food. The Deories also consume the meat of pigs, ducks, fowls, etc. Fish is eaten regularly and dry fish is also well liked. All the families in the Deori village produce rice beer, which is considered very healthy.

The Deori tribe comprises of four main subsections or *khel* (territorial group), namely the Dibongiya, the Tengapaniya, the Borgonya and the Patorgonya. The people who lived on the bank of the river Dibong, were called Dibongiya. The people who lived on the bank of the river Tengapani, were called Tengapaniya. They are animist and their chief deities are Kundimama or Burdha-Burdhi, Bolia-Baba, Tamreshwari or Keshaikhati. The Deoris are patrilineal tribe and their descent, inheritance, succession, authority and residence after marriage are traced in male line.

Table 14.1: Distribution of head breadth in males and females.

Head breadth (cm)	*Males*		*Females*		*Total*	
	Frequency	*%*	*Frequency*	*%*	*Frequency*	*%*
12.01-13.00	01	2.00	02	4.00	03	3.00
13.01-14.00	12	24.00	17	34.00	29	29.00
14.01-15.00	24	48.00	24	48.00	48	48.00
15.01-16.00	13	26.00	07	14.00	20	20.00
16.01-17.00	-	-	-	-	-	-
Total	50	100.00	50	100.00	100	100.00

The area of the present study is Kapahtali Deori village, Dhemaji District, Assam, India. The village is located about 10 km away from Dhemaji town. It falls under Dhemaji Development Block.

Table 14.2: Distribution of head length in males and females.

Head length (cm)	*Males*		*Females*		*Total*	
	Frequency	*%*	*Frequency*	*%*	*Frequency*	*%*
15.01-16.00	-	-	03	06.00	03	03.00
16.01-17.00	04	08.00	14	28.00	18	18.00
17.01-18.00	23	46.00	27	54.00	50	50.00
18.01-19.00	20	40.00	06	12.00	26	26.00
19.01-20.00	03	06.00	-	-	03	03.00
Total	50	100.00	50	100.00	100	100.00

Table 14.3: Distribution of cephalic index in males and females.

Head length (cm)	*Males*		*Females*		*Total*	
	Frequency	*%*	*Frequency*	*%*	*Frequency*	*%*
70.01-75.00	07	14.00	02	04.00	09	09.00
75.01-80.00	17	34.00	12	24.00	29	29.00
80.01-85.00	15	30.00	21	42.00	36	36.00
85.01-90.00	11	22.00	15	30.00	26	25.00
90.01-95.00	-	-	-	-	-	-
Total	50	100.00	50	100.00	100	100.00

Table 14.4: Distribution of the mean values of the head length, head breadth and cephalic index of the study.

Parameter	*Males*	*Females*	*Total*
Head breadth (cm)	14.48 ± 0.54	14.22 ± 0.75	14.35 ± 0.56
Head length(cm)	17.94 ± 0.36	17.22 ± 0.61	17.58 ± 0.61
Cephalic index(cm)	80.06 ± 0.66	82.04 ± 0.57	81.05 ± 0.62
Sample size	50	50	100

Table 14.5: Classification of head types according to Martin and Saller (1957).

Head type	*Male*	*%*	*Female*	*%*	*Total*	*%*
Dolichocephalic	07	14.00	03	06.00	10	10.00
Mesocephalic	22	44.00	18	36.00	40	40.00
Brachycephalic	12	24.00	18	36.00	30	30.00
Hyperbrachycephalic	09	18.00	11	22.00	20	20.00
Total	50	100.00	50	100.00	100	100.00

Table 14.6: Cephalic index or length- breadth index of head (according toMartin and Saller, 1957).

Classes	*Ranges*	
	Male	*Female*
Dolichocephalic	71.01-75.9	72.0-76.9
Mesocephalic	76.0-80.9	77.0-81.9
Brachycephalic	81.0-85.9	82.0-86.4
Hyperbrachycephalic	86.0-90.9	86.5-91.9

Table 14.7: Comparative data on cephalic indices of various populations.

Racial/ethnic groups	*Cephalic index (mean ± SD)*	*Sample size*	*References*
Ijaw males	80.98 ± 6.11	63	Oladipo and Olotu, 2006
Ijaw females	78.24 ± 6.33	37	Oladipo and Olotu, 2006
Igbo males	79.04 ± 5.75	53	Oladipo and Olotu, 2006
Igbo females	76.83 ± 4.94	47	Oladipo and Olotu, 2006
Urhobo males	86.50 ± 9.06	250	Oladipo and Paul, 2009
Urhobofemales	86.09 ± 11.30	250	Oladipo and Paul, 2009
Itsekiri males	94.51 ± 34.44	250	Oladipo and Paul, 2009
Itsekiri females	82.16 ± 44.74	250	Oladipo and Paul, 2009
Ogoni males	111.18 ± 10.28	400	Oladipo et al., 2009
Ogoni females	75.09 ± 7.09	400	Oladipo et al., 2009
Yoruba males	75.02 ± 4.78	493	Oladipo et al., 2014
Yoruba females	73.75 ± 5.13	427	Oladipo et al., 2014
Tiwa males	79.80 ± 0.57	100	Sarma, R. et al., 2014
Tiwa females	82.04 ± 0.44	100	Sarma, R. et al., 2014
Deori males	80.06 ± 0.66	50	Present study
Deori females	82.04 ± 0.57	50	Present study

SD: Standard Deviation

Results and Discussion

The results of the present study are presented in Table 14.1- 14.5. A total of 100 human subjects (Deoris) were studied, of which 50 were males and 50 were females. The ages of the subjects were between 18-50 years. Table 14.1 and 14.2 shows the percentage frequencies of the distributions of head breadth and head length, respectively. Table 14.3 represents the distribution of the cephalic indices of the Deoris while Table 14.4 contains the mean values of the head length, head breadth and cephalic index of the study. Table 14.7 indicates the cephalic indices of various ethnic groups earlier investigated.

The mean head breadth was 14.35- 0.56cm and the mean head length was 17.58- 0.61cm. For males, the mean head breadth and head length were 14.48- 0.54 and 17.94- 0.36 cm respectively, while for females, the mean head breadth and head length were 14.22-0.75 and 17.22-0.61cm respectively (Table 14.4).

The total mean cephalic index was 81.05- 0.62. The mean cephalic indices of males and females were 80.06- 0.66 and 82.04-0.57 respectively.

The head breadth, head length and cephalic index between males and females were tested for significance. The mean in the head length, head breadth and cephalic index between males and females were statistically significance ($p < 0.05$).

In the present study, the mean cephalic indices of Deori males and females resident in Dhemaji District, Assam are 80.06-0.66 and 82.04-0.57 respectively. Thus, the Deori males fall under the mesocephalic head type while females are under the brachycephalic head type. The Deori population irrespective of gender with cephalic index of 81.05-0.62 could be classified as brachycephalic head type. The size of cephalic index varies significantly in different geographical zones. In tropical zones head form is longer (dolicocephalic) but in temperate zones, head form is more round (mesocephalic and brachycephalic).

Table 14.5 shows that 14% of males are dolichocephalic, 44% are mesocephalic, 24% are brachycephalic and 18% are hyperbrachycephalic heads while in case of females, only 6% are of dolochocephalic, 36% are of both mesocephalic and brachycephalic and 22% are hyper brachycephalic heads.

Conclusion

The result of the present study shows that, in general the Deori tribe can be classified under as brachycephalic head. There is, however, found sexual dimorphism ($p < 0.05$) where with females showing slightly higher cephalic index than males (females 82.4-0.57, males 80.06-0.66, respectively). The overlapping distribution of head shape between males and females makes sex determination from the present study impossible.

References

Anupama M, Baljeet SK, Seema, Arvinder PSB. 3010. The study of cephalic Index in Punjabi students. *Journal of Punjab Academy of Forensic Medicine and Toxicology.* 10: 24-26.

Oladipo GS, Olotu EJ. 2006. Anthropometric Comparision of Cephalic Indices between the Ijaw and Igbo Tribes. *Global Journal of Pure and Applied Sciences*. 12 (1): 137-138.

Olotu EJ, Eroje A, Oladipo GS, Edibamode E. 2009. Anthropometric study of the facial and nasal length of adult Igbo ethnic group in Nigeria. *The Internet Journal of Biological Anthropology*. 2: 80-87.

Sekla B, Soukup F. 2005. Inheritance of the cephalic Index. *The American Journal of Physical Anthropology*. 30 (1): 137-140.

Shah GV, Jadhav HR. 2004.The study of cephalic Index in students of Gujarat. *Journal of the Anatomical Society of India.* 53 (1): 25-26.

15

Virtual Accelerator: A Review of Current Issues

— *Gautam Huidrom, Sunil Koijam*

Introduction

Entrepreneurship has emerged as one of the important drivers of economic development. The development of regional entrepreneurship ecosystem has become imperative to create the environment for new start-ups to come up in the region. In a developing country like India, where there is the challenge of unemployment among the youths, entrepreneurship if nurtured well, it could be a game-changer. India in particular in recent years have seen a healthy growth of entrepreneurship firms. However, this agglomeration of entrepreneurship firms with high growth potential is mainly an urban area phenomenon. This is because the tier I cities in India have created a vibrant entrepreneurship ecosystem in the cities (Dey, 2013). The entrepreneurship support programs such as incubator, accelerator, angel funding, co-working space, etc., are widely available in the cities (Lall, Bowles, & Baird, 2013).

Therefore, the next leap in entrepreneurship growth in India must come from rural regions. This is the challenge for a big developing country like India with diverse geographical regions. The challenges are to spread the idea and grow the phenomenon of entrepreneurship ecosystem in the rural areas. The duplication of the entrepreneurship support system will be a costly proposition, considering the diversity of the country. This is where the emergence of virtual accelerator globally could play a crucial role in providing entrepreneurship education to a vastly diverse country like India.

Virtual accelerators are a new generation of entrepreneurship support programs that have incorporated the principles of MOOC (Massive Open Online Course) to deliver entrepreneurship support programs using digital technologies (Rippa & Secundo, 2018). By using digital technologies and blending the concepts of MOOC, virtual accelerators can provide entrepreneurship support programs that are accessible, affordable and available to a new population of entrepreneurs (Mcauley, Stewart, Siemens, & Cormier, 2010). This paper examines the detail of the potential of the virtual accelerator in supporting entrepreneurship, especially in geographically challenging areas. The paper will delineate the difference between incubator and accelerator, thus, highlighting the role of each type of entrepreneurship support program that could play in entrepreneurship development. Further, this paper will examine the characteristics of virtual accelerators with special attention to the usage of MOOC principles in democratizing the dissemination of entrepreneurship education to a new set of entrepreneurs in rural areas.

Entrepreneurship Support Program

Some of the typical entrepreneurship support programs are incubator, accelerators, and co-working spaces. These programs provide a structured approach to entrepreneurship development (Cohen & Cohen, 2013). These support programs play a crucial role in stimulating the growth and development of early ventures. Since, early ventures face many challenges such as liability of newness, funding, human resource challenges, and product development; these support systems can play an important role in making them as viable business enterprises (Cohen & Hochberg, 2014). This paper will go in detail on the similarities and differences between incubators and accelerators programs. One of the reasons for looking at the similarities and differences of these two types of entrepreneurship support programs is because in practice we tend to express the concept of entrepreneurship support program as an incubator or accelerator and thus inferring that they are similar. Both types of entrepreneurship support programs are a structured approach to entrepreneurship development. Both of them offers mentoring and networking opportunities for start-ups. Each of them could provide desk space for start-ups (Dempwolf, Auer, & D'Ippolito, 2015).

Incubator type of entrepreneurship support programs is widely adopted all over the world. An entrepreneurship incubator is typically a pre-venture entrepreneurship support program. Usually, the support system occurs from the business idea itself. Thus, an incubator is an early-stage start-up entrepreneurship support system (Bone, Allen, & Haley, 2017). In general, funding for the incubator is grant-based funding or it has a revenue-generating model such as rent model, royalty model or debt-based model. Generally, an incubator does not take an equity position in the early start-ups. Incubators are sector agnostic, they support incubators from various sectors (Cohen & Cohen, 2013). There different types of incubators depending on the location, sponsor, and purpose so on, there are various types of incubators. Some them are Business Innovation Centres (BICs), University Business Incubators (UBIs), Independent Private Incubators (IPIs), and Corporate Private Incubators (CPIs) (Grimaldi & Grandi, 2005).

Accelerators, on the other hand, are entrepreneurship support system typically for a little more matured stage of the early venture development (Cohen & Hochberg, 2014). Typically start-ups that join accelerators have a viable business model, minimum viable product or services and sometimes a revenue-generating firm. The main purpose of joining an accelerator is to scale up the business (A. Isabelle, 2013; Dempwolf et al., 2015). A characteristic of an accelerator is a cohort-based entrepreneurship development program with a fixed time frame. A typical accelerator has a selective application process, e.g., one of the pioneer accelerator Y Combinator selects only 2% of the applicants' early venture start-ups (Pauwels, Clarysse, Wright, & Van Hove, 2016). Usually, the program is three months to six months in length. In this time frame, there will be a mix of common entrepreneurship workshops and individualized attention will also be given to the early start-ups. One of the main objectives of an accelerator is social learning, that is, much of the learning will be absorbed from one another (Levinsohn, n.d.). Thus, the learning and problem-solving process will be accelerated because of the diverse nature of talent in the program (Hallen, Bingham,

& Cohen, 2014). Accelerators typically target a particular industry, e.g. Level 39 based in London is known to target fintech companies. Thus, these industry-specific entrepreneurship support programs can provide specialized knowledge, resources and mentoring service to the early start-ups. The early start-ups are provided with pre-seed or seed funding (A. Isabelle, 2013; Cohen & Cohen, 2013; Cohen & Hochberg, 2014; Lall et al., 2013). This is usually done at the end of the program when the start-ups are provided a platform to showcase their companies to investors. Usually, angel investors, venture capital fund and even, private equity funds are part of the process.

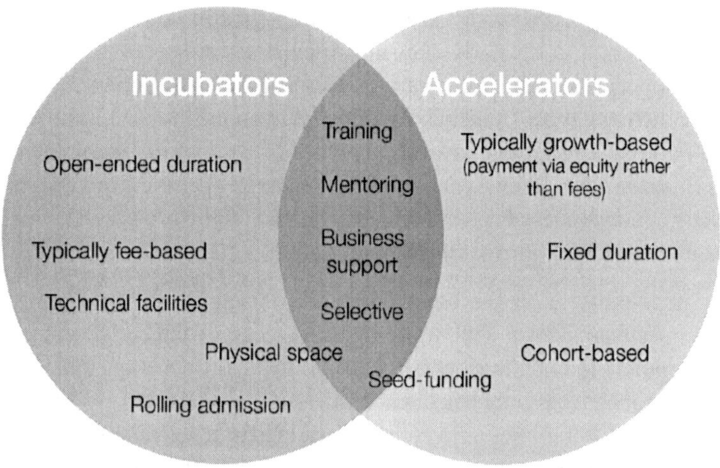

Source: Dempwolf, et al. (2014)

The growth of accelerators throughout the world has been a diverse phenomenon, in many countries, accelerators have grown over the years (Lall et al., 2013; Roberts, Thomas, Manager, & Chao, 2017). This growth has led to the realization that there is not a single template form for organizing an accelerator. Each country and even sub-national level context demands different ingredients to make accelerators successful in terms of funds raised or survival of the nascent ventures. Taking into consideration the aspects of two contextual factors, i.e., participant's location and frequency of interaction of the participants and the mentors, a topology of accelerators is being described by Levinsohn (2015). The figure below highlights the category of accelerators.

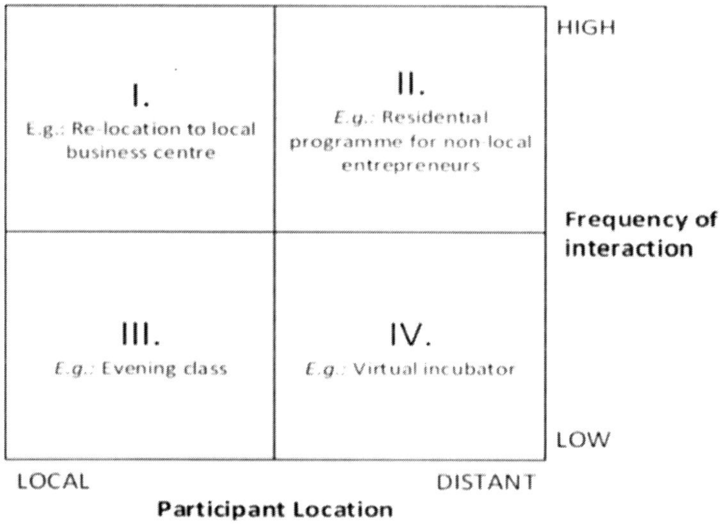

Source: Levinsohn (2015)

According to Levinshon (2015), the topology of an accelerator can be divided based on focus, frequency of interaction and participant's geographical location. In the I & II type, the frequency of interaction is intense, usually, it is a residential cohort type of program. In the I type, the focus is on developing local-based nascent start-ups, therefore, and the participants tend to form a particular local geographical area. The type II is typical of pioneer accelerators like the Y Combinator, in which, participants are usually brought together in a vibrant entrepreneurial ecosystem area or cities like Silicon Valley or Bangalore. In type III, usually occur in accelerator dedicated to a particular industry and usually, the participants are also working professionals trying to start new ventures in the same industry they are working. In this type, the time frame of the program tends to be longer like six months and the interactions tend to less intense as compared to type I & II. When the target participants are from a wider geographical area and one can run a low-intensity cohort program, the IV type virtual accelerator is the format type one can choose from. In this paper, we will be particularly focusing on the IV type of accelerators that is the virtual accelerators.

Whatever be the format of the accelerators, the key role of the accelerators is to scale up the business of the nascent start-ups. From prior studies, it has been inferred that accelerators can help nascent ventures navigates the liability newness by supporting them with established business networking and industry knowledge. It is also observed that though accelerators can act as a complement to experienced founders and team, practitioners and researchers are yet to find an accelerator format that fits all bills (Lewis, Haper-Anderson & Molnar, 2011). Thus, researchers have cautiously stated that diverse contexts will require a different type of accelerator. However, one area the accelerators does an effective job is in compressing the learning time frame of nascent start-ups. This process is aided by social learning. When several motivated individuals from diverse backgrounds are bound together in a cohort manner, it creates an environment of the fast pace learning environment (Levinsohn, n.d.). One impact of participating in the accelerator program is the higher probability of exit via acquisition (A. Isabelle, 2013). Nascent ventures that participated in accelerators programs have a higher chance of exiting by acquisition when compared to other entrepreneurship support programs like angle investors programs. Studies have also shown that nascent ventures that participated in accelerators programs more likely chance of getting venture capital funding relative to participating in other entrepreneurship support programs (Drover et al., 2017).

Virtual Accelerators

Virtual accelerators are a new breed of accelerators that have come up in recent years. The crucial differentiating factor is that it uses digital technologies to deliver entrepreneurship support programs to participants (A. Isabelle, 2013; Carayannis & Von Zedtwitz, 2005; Levinsohn, n.d.). As it has become clear that to stimulate growth and development in a region, entrepreneurship becomes a key component of the exercise. The question is how to deliver entrepreneurship education and support services in diverse and geographically spread areas is a challenge. The forms of accelerators that have been discussed above, generally are intensive, residential and expensive entrepreneurship support programs (Cohen & Cohen, 2013; Cohen & Hochberg, 2014). Typically, these programs are seen in urban areas with a known entrepreneurship ecosystem (Hochberg, Cohen, Fehder, & Yee, 2014). Therefore, the challenge of spreading entrepreneurship education in rural and other geographically diverse regions is a challenge. Without watering down the key components of an accelerator, one must deliver an entrepreneurship support program for the above-said target audience.

The challenge of making entrepreneurship education that is accessible, available, affordable and the awareness of the value of entrepreneurship support program remains a challenge. Thus, virtual accelerators tackle some of the challenges of spreading entrepreneurship education to a new audience so that growth and development are spread in diverse communities. The phenomenon of virtual accelerators, combines aspects of entrepreneurship support program, digital technologies and MOOC (Massive Open Online Course) to deliver the value of accelerator program to scale nascent ventures for livelihood and employment generation in geographically diverse region (Mcauley et al., 2010).

Digital Technologies for Virtual Accelerators

The rapid development of digital technologies has made accessibility, affordability and availability component of entrepreneurship education to the masses a reality. This paper will categorize some key elements of digital technologies that are incorporated in building virtual accelerators. The digital technologies can be broadly classified into three broad categories, namely the digital artefact, the digital platform and digital infrastructure (Rippa & Secundo, 2018).

Digital Artefact	Digital Storytelling Tools, Digital Business Portfolio, Conversational System,
Digital Platform	Intelligent Apps, Mobile Apps, Desktop Applications, Cloud Computing & Social Media
Digital Infrastructure	Broadband Internet, Networking System

The digital artefact tools like digital storytelling are utilized to create awareness and recruitment of participants by the virtual accelerators. The digital business portfolio consists of text data, multimedia data, and other relevant data that are used for the production and dissemination of knowledge and practices. A conversational system is a crucial tool in the bag, they form the interactive basis of a virtual accelerator. The tools under digital platforms such as apps, cloud computing, and social media function as tools for productivity, storage and peer to peer interaction and digital marketing. Finally, the digital infrastructure forms the core backbone technology for the whole process to work.

Adopting MOOC Principles in Virtual Accelerator

The phenomenon of MOOC has a tremendous impact on education. The process of knowledge production and dissemination has taken to a different level. By integrating the principles of MOOCs in creating a new form of virtual accelerators, these new accelerators have changed the landscape of entrepreneurship education (Mcauley et al., 2010). As we can see from the diagram below, online learning has different variations. Starting from simple IT aided face-face learning to blended learning and fully online learning. The virtual accelerators programs range from a blended program to fully online-based learning (Guardia & Sangra, 2013).

By incorporating MOOC principles of competency-based learning, learner empowerment, collaborative learning social networking, peer

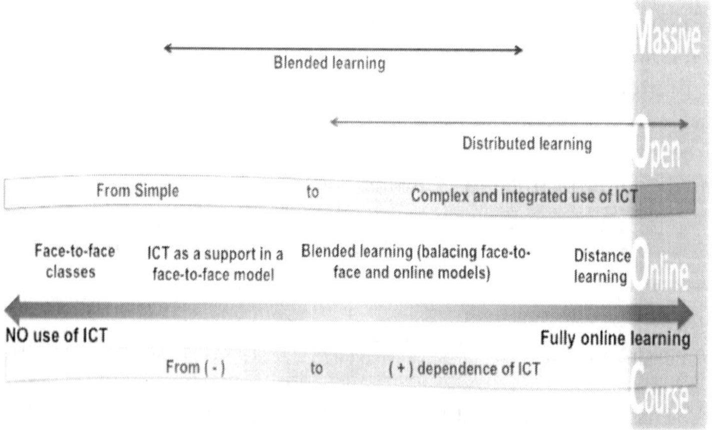

Fig. 1 The interpretation of online learning continuum, Guàrdia (2012). Adapted from Bates & Poole (2003), and Bach, Haynes & Smith (2007, p.34) approaches.

assistance, and media technology-enhanced learning; virtual accelerators have democratized entrepreneurship learning to a new set of participants. Virtual accelerators program content is similar to the location-based accelerator. Thus, the program consists of training, mentoring, business support, seed funding. Typically, the virtual accelerator also is cohort-based with a fixed time frame in conducting its program. It has made entrepreneurship education, especially in the knowledge and practice of scaling business to a larger set of populations. Thus, increasing the chances of creating a new generation of entre-preneurs in challenging geographical location. The virtual accelerator does provide an accessible, affordable and available form of entrepreneurship education to a new set of entrepreneurs to scale their business (Rippa & Secundo, 2018). This democratization of entrepreneurship education is the fundamental objective of virtual accelerators. Geographic location, current employment, and resources challenges are a lesser hindrance to the growth of nascent ventures with help of virtual accelerators. It provides entrepreneurs to pursue entrepreneurship education at his own pace, time and place of his choosing (Carayannis & Von Zedtwitz, 2005; Lall et al., 2013). However, challenges remain, the foremost aspect of an accelerator is to scale business, that means nascent start-ups must secure funding from venture capital or other sources of capital. The lack of face to face interaction with a potential investor could be a challenge. Therefore, for this reason, most virtual accelerators are blended programs as compared to being a completely online learning program. The probability of superficial student engagement is higher as compared to face to face interaction. This can reduce the quality of social learning which is a key aspect of a cohort-based learning program (Levinsohn, n.d.). Despite the challenges, there is a healthy growth of virtual accelerators all over the world. Below is a selected list of virtual accelerators and its description.

Virtual Accelerator	*Country Focus*	*Duration of Programme*	*Sector*	*Seed Funding*
Y Combinator	Global	Six Months	IT	1,20,000 USD
Techstar	Global	Three Months	Multiple	1,20,000 USD
Rerise	India & UK	16 Weeks	Multiple	10% Equity
Oasis	Jordan	One Year	IT	50,000 USD
Faster Capital	**UAE**	**Up to 5 Year**	**IT**	**2,000,000 USD**

Discussion on the Applicability in Arunachal Pradesh & Conclusion

Entrepreneurship support programs have emerged as a critical factor in developing the entrepreneurship ecosystem in any region (Roberts et al., 2017). There are many forms of entrepreneurship support programs depending on the focus and goal. This paper has examined in detail the characteristics of both incubator and accelerator. Both of them support business, gives mentoring and they can be both selective. However, an accelerator is a cohort-based, fixed time frame program with seed funding for start-ups with a viable business model. They are also usually sector agnostic. Incubator, on the other hand, follows an open-ended selection process with a target audience from various industries. Additionally, the incubator takes in early start-ups with the idea stage itself. The goal of an incubator for start-ups is to transition to an accelerator or brings in funding (Cohen & Cohen, 2013; Cohen & Hochberg, 2014; Kohler, 2016).

A virtual accelerator is a particular type of accelerator that uses modern digital technologies to provide entrepreneurship education for a wider audience. A virtual accelerator makes entrepreneurship support system accessible, affordable and available to entrepreneurs from diverse geographic regions of Arunachal Pradesh. A virtual accelerator can disseminate entrepreneurship education democratically by using elements of MOOC traditions (Rippa & Secundo, 2018). Thus, the virtual accelerator has the potential to create entrepreneurs from rural areas and add dynamism to the rural economy. The challenge of remote geographic location will a little bit blunted by the rise of virtual accelerators for the new generation of entrepreneurs.

References

A. Isabelle, D. (2013). Key Factors Affecting a Technology Entrepreneur's Choice of Incubator or Accelerator. *Technology Innovation Management Review*, *3*(2), 16–22. https://doi.org/10.22215/timreview656.

Bone, J., Allen, O., & Haley, C. (2017). Business incubators and accelerators: The national picture. *Department for Business, Energy & Industrial Strategy*, *7*, 1–76.

Carayannis, E. G., & Von Zedtwitz, M. (2005). Architecting gloCal (global-local), real-virtual incubator networks (G-RVINs) as catalysts and accelerators of entrepreneurship in transitioning and developing economies: Lessons learned and best practices from current development and business incubation. *Technovation*, *25*(2), 95–110. https://doi.org/10.1016/S0166-4972(03)00072-5.

Cohen, S., & Cohen, S. (2013). *What do Accelerators do - Cohen*. *8*(3), 19–25. https://doi.org/10.1162/INOV_a_00184.

Cohen, S., & Hochberg, Y. V. (2014). Accelerating Startups: The Seed Accelerator Phenomenon. *Ssrn*, 1–16. https://doi.org/10.2139/ssrn.2418000.

Dempwolf, C. S., Auer, J., & D'Ippolito, M. (2015). Innovation accelerators: Defining characteristics among startup assistance organizations. *Small Business Innovators: Insights From Accelerators, Additive Manufacturing and Supply Chain Analysis*, (October), 93–142.

Dey, S. (2013, July 20). Mentoring, the new seed capital investors bring to startups: Early-stage investors plug the gaps in the start-up ecosystem. *Business Standard*. Retrieved from http://www.business-standard.com/article/companies/mentoring-the-new-seed-capital-investors-bring-to-start-ups-113072000729_1.html

Drover, W., Busenitz, L., Matusik, S., Townsend, D., Anglin, A., Dushnitsky, G.,… Review, A. (2017). A Review and Roadmap of Entrepreneurial Equity Financing Research/: Venture Capital, Corporate Venture Capital, Angel Investment, Crowdfunding and Accelerators Will Drover University of Oklahoma Lowell Busenitz University of Oklahoma Sharon Matusik Uni. *Journal of Management*, 1820–1853.

Grimaldi, R., & Grandi, A. (2005). Business incubators and new venture creation: An assessment of incubating models. *Technovation*, *25*(2), 111–121. https://doi.org/10.1016/S0166-4972(03)00076-2

Guàrdia, L., Maina, M., & Sangrà, A. (2013). MOOC design principles: A pedagogical approach from the learner's perspective. *elearning papers*, (33).

Hallen, B. L., Bingham, C. B., & Cohen, S. L. (2014). *10.5465/ambpp.2014.185*.

Hochberg, Y. V., Cohen, S., Fehder, D. C., & Yee, E. (2014). *2013 Seed Accelerator Rankings*. 1–40. Retrieved from http://seedrankings.com

Kohler, T. (2016). Corporate accelerators: Building bridges between corporations and startups. *Business Horizons*, *59*(3), 347–357. https://doi.org/10.1016/j.bushor.2016.01.008.

Lall, S., Bowles, L., & Baird, R. (2013). Bridging the pioneer gap_the role of accelarators. *Innovations - Quarterly Journal by MIT Press*, *8*(3), 105–137.

Levinsohn, D. S. (n.d.). *No Entrepreneur is an Island*.

Lewis, D. A., Harper-Anderson, E., & Molnar, L. A. (2011). Incubating Success. Incubation Best Practices That Lead to Successful New Ventures, University of Michigan- Institute for Research on Labor, Employment, and the Economy, University of Michigan. *Ann Arbor, Michigan. Available on line at www. nist. gov/sites/default/files/documents/ineap/Incubating-Success-Report. Pdf*

Mcauley, A. A., Stewart, B., Siemens, G., & Cormier, D. (2010). *MOOC_Final*.

Pauwels, C., Clarysse, B., Wright, M., & Van Hove, J. (2016). Understanding a new generation incubation model: The accelerator. *Technovation*, *50–51*, 13–24. https://doi.org/10.1016/j.technovation.2015.09.003

Rippa, P., & Secundo, G. (2018). Digital academic entrepreneurship: The potential of digital technologies on academic entrepreneurship. *Technological Forecasting and Social Change*, (July), 0–1. https://doi.org/10.1016/j.techfore.2018.07.013

Roberts, P. W., Thomas, E., Manager, S., & Chao, C. (2017). *Accelerating Startups in Emerging Markets*. (May). https://doi.org/10.1038/npp.2009.90

16

Religious Experiences within the Meitei context of Manipur towards Sustainability of Plant Resources

Thiyam Rabikanta Singh

Introduction

Culture of a particular people is closely related to their natural surrounding and specific plants are used specially in their religious action. In their worldview, specific plants are considered sacred and are offered to particular God during different religious occasions (Hedge & Bhat 2012). Again, plants and animals are sometimes regarded to be incarnations or symbols of the supernatural beings and commonly worshipped (Niroula and Singh 2015). It brings out the religious plants to be spiritually valued; but, on the other hand it preserves biodiversity that reflexes the society to a sustainable cultural setting. In fact, in non-western cosmovision, real world is understandable in terms of three inter-related and inseparable domains of natural world, social world, and spiritual world (Haverkort 2009). Plants are important natural resources in this cosmovision.

Various plants have been mentioned related to different religions. *Phoenix dactylifera* L., (Date Palm) is an important plant in Islam. Christianity and Judaism also honour it in festivals such as Passover and Palm Sunday (Marwat et.al 2016). In Buddhism, *Saraca sp.*, fig, sal, teak, etc., are important (Buddhism and Plants. 2018). Robinson and Johnson (1970:14) mentioned about an episode of offering food to Buddha mistaking him as the spirit of a sacred tree. In Hinduism, *Aegle marmelos* is used to worship lord Siva, *Oryza sativa* is the plant of goddesses Laxmi and *Anthocephalus cadamba* is associated with lord Krishna (Sarma and Devi 2015). Thus, plants enrich the religio-cultural contents. Contrary, religious plant and forest has positive impacts on ecological and biodiversity balance (Niroula and Singh 2015). So, plant-religion relationship in culture and sustainability is academically an important area of study. The present study has been conducted to discuss the religious belief system concerning a plant-environment of the Meiteis along with the entrenched ethics to preserve plants.

Methodology

The study was conducted by using scheduled and in-depth interview with key informants as *Maiba* (medico-religious man), *Bamon* (Hindu priests), *Arangfam* (attendants of rites and rituals), *Piba* (head of lineage), etc. The study was carried out among the Meiteis living in different parts of Manipur state. It encompassed the belief system of the Hinduism and Meitei traditionalism. In addition, archival scribed works called *Puyas* were referred to as important secondary sources.

People understudy

The Meiteis are the people who inhabit mainly in the north eastern states of India, namely, Manipur, Assam, Meghalaya and Tripura, and in some parts of the neighbouring countries like Bangladesh and Myanmar. The cultural centre of the people lies in the soil of Manipur and the present study was conducted among the Meiteis in the central valley of Manipur.

Ethnic identity and the endemic plants

The formation of the Meitei civil society was enacted at an earlier historical stage when the ancient people of the valley of Manipur lived as subjects of seven chiefdoms, namely, Mangang, Angom, Sarang Leisangthem/Chenglei, Khaba Nganba, Luwang, Khuman and Moirang.

After a long battle for supremacy among these chiefdoms, the earlier chiefdoms were relegated as exogamous kin groups (clans) of the larger Meitei society emerging as the societal base of the new political system. Nevertheless, the fission in the spatial structure of the Meitei fusion is traceable in their offering to respective eponymic ancestors. A uniqueness within the solidarity of the Meitei s is still expressed in worshipping their clan ancestors known as *apokpa.* It is an offering of specific items in particularistic manner which include specific plants (Meetei 1996) to the ancestor or the clan deity. Flowers, leaf, fruit, and fire wood to be offered and shoot to be used for sanctification purpose of the clans are given below.

Table 16.1: The Meitei clans and their specific plants

Clan	***Flower***	***Leaf***	***Fruit***	***Fire wood***	***Sanctification***
Ningthouja	Red lotus	Lotus leaf	Lotus fruit	Sahi (*Pasania dealbata*)	Urung
Angom	White lily	Larong (*Dillenia pentaphylla*)	Heiba (*Ficus sp.*)	Upal (*Quercus sp.*)	Tairen (*Toona ciliata*)
Luwang	Melei (*Dendrobium thyrsiflorum*)	Larong (*Dillenia pentaphylla*	Pineapple (*Annamus comosus*)	Heikru(*Embli ca officinalis*)	Ukhok (*Alhizzia stepulata*)
Khuman	Leisang (*Lycopodium squarossum*)	Kwakla (*Pterospermum accrifolium*)	Fig (*Ficus slomerata*)	Chaokhong (*Polygonum orientale*)	Pungphai (*Dactylocterum aegyptiacum*)
Moirang	Yerumlei (*Dendrobium ochreatum*)	Khangla (*Butea minor*)	Kangrou	Kuhi (*Pasania pachiphyla*)	Naohing
Kha-Nganba	Leisang (*Lycopodium squarossum*), kwaklei (*Vanda coerula*)	Leihoula (*Amomum sp.*)	Heibung (*Garcinia xanthochy mus*)	Chingyensil (*Antidesma diantrum*)	Napu Nasel
Sarang Leisangthem	Leikham (*Sesquipedalus guniothalamus*)	Lotus leaf (Thamna Thayai)		Nongleisang (*Xylosma longfolia*)	Napi, Singbi

A specific Plant-environment in the Religious sphere

The Meiteis are the people who regard plants as beings with soul and worship some plant species like Tulsi (*Ocimum sanctum*), Tairel (*Toona ciliata*), etc., having the power to sanctify from social defilements and wipe out miseries in addition to the uses of *tulsi* as believed by the Hindu-Meiteis and *tairel* by the Traditional followers. Besides, they even worship the spirit of big trees before cutting down. Tylor (1958: 58) finds the idea of plants having souls and partaking phenomena with humans in certain societies. They also use certain species of plants found in their environment as essential items in their life crisis rites and rituals. Some of plants also remain interlacing the oral tradition and consequently, they have become essential items in such rites. Just before the delivery of a child, there needs fumigation of leaves of Khoiju (*Plectranthus sp.*) and Leikham (*Goniothalamus sp.*) to keep the incoming baby free from evil eyes. In the final engagement of marriage, the boy's party would have never failed to bring Heikru (*Embilica officinalis*) and certain indigenous fruits to the house of the bride-to-be. In marriage, the husband-wife bond is publicly marked by adorning a wreath of Kundo (*Jasminum sambae*) by each other. Again, in case of death ritual, if the dead body is missing, cremation is carried out with a piece of Pangong (*Butea frondosa*) representing the corpse. In such ways, the cultural life crises of the Meiteis have unavoidable relationship to the plant world. The numbers of essential plants for the *rites-de-passage* are given in tabular form.

Table 16.2: Essential Number of Plants in the Life Crisis Rites of the Meiteis

Crisis rite	*Total no. of plants*	*For Hindus*	*For Traditionalists*	*Common plants*
Birth rite	37	34	22	18
Solidfeeding rite	11	9	9	6
Ear ring ceremony	29	29	-	
Thread donning rite	26	26	-	-
Rite of initial avowal	11	9	8	6
Marriage	34	29	28	22
Death	24	20	15	9

It is revealed from the above table that despite the differences in religion, the Meiteis use many common plants in their *rites-de-passage* that comprise 48.6 p.c.(per cent) in birth rite, 54.5 p.c. each in solid feeding and initial avowal rites, 64.7 p.c. in marriage, and 37.5 p.c. in death rite. Thus, the religious plants despite question of different faiths are closely related to the local environment.

More than 60 species are used by the Meiteis living in the valley of Manipur for various life crises ritual ceremonies. Some of the dominant families are Poaceae (15 p.c.), Moraceae (8.3 p.c), and Fabaceae (8.3 p.c.). Stem, flower, fruit, leaf, seed, twig, bud, rhizome, vein and fibre are the essential parts of the plants. The sacred fumigation with resin of Makruk (*Canarium bengalensis*) and *tiki* (rounded charcoal cake) or incense thereof comprises an essential part in rites and rituals. Exorcism by burning Khoiju and Leikham is also a common practice. Thus, various plants in religious acts builds up a plant-environment in the comprehensive scale of the Meitei worldview.

A socio-religious complex providing the need of certain plants in their material culture is produced here. A conical basket with lid known as *Phingaruk/phiruk* is an object that depicts social hierarchy as well as social cohesion in certain ritual events. In marriage ceremony, women in luxurious traditional attire carry *phiruk* containing essential items of the solemnization. The *phiruks* for the ritual are carried in procession by socially beautiful ladies exclusively. A socially beautiful woman means a socially good woman who marries following the ideal norm of arranged marriage. However, at present, marriage by elopement is accepted and sanctioned. Besides, a socially beautiful woman is a lady who marries only for one time in her life. A woman who marries more than once is neither socially good nor beauty. If the first child of a mother is a boy, she is preferred to be the leader of transporters' team known locally as *yatra pubi*. Besides, a lady who is the mother of both sexes is also preferred. It is related to the belief domain for the preference of male child or mother issuing both son and daughter in this patrilineal society. In addition, it is a bin used in the procedure of unifying the close consanguinal kins and for seeing predicament of the newly wedded couple. After the marriage ceremony, the fruits containing in the *phiruk* which has been kept at the place of family deity, are distributed to the families of the boy's close descent group signifying the social cohesive and solidarity of the kinsmen. On the fifth day of marriage, the fortune of the newly married couple is also observed from the contents of the *phiruk* brought by the *yatra pubi*. In this way, the conical basket is connected with the inner value of their social structure. In other word, conical basket made of cane and bamboo plus its contents is an item of cultural particularity.

World view on spirit and natural conservation

The Meiteis who own literature of plants and flowers as mentioned in their *puya* known as *Leirol* view for healthy and harmonious nature.

In their traditionalism, sacred groves are created and maintained specially for deities called *umanglai.* For the Meiteis, gods, spirits, ancestors, leaders, sacred groves, lands and shrines, fertility, ritual crops, animals, and food items are all interrelated. In their cosmovision, the natural world provides the habitat for the spirits who sends message to the human world.

The epistemology of the social action may explain the cosmovision of the indigenes of Manipur as the interrelationship of three domains - spiritual, natural and human – to form the real world. Spiritual domain consists of divine supernatural being, invisible world, spiritual forces, ancestors, etc. Natural domain includes thematic fields of natural resources, agriculture, and other practices. Human domain includes culture, social organisation, economy, management of natural resources, language, conflict resolution, etc. The three domains intersected each other and remain interrelated. The intersecting domains form sub sets of human-spiritual, human-natural, spiritual-natural, spiritual-human-natural domains. It means the domains do not remain in isolation and the integration is established firmly through age-long experiences of local tradition.

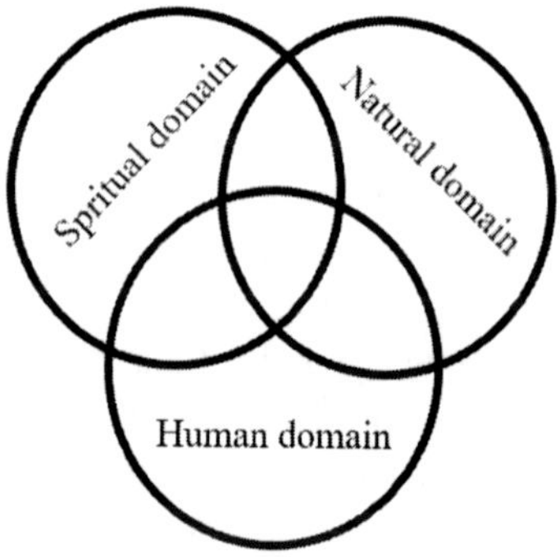

Fig. 16.1: Cosmovision of the Meitei

The cosmovision reflects in making their worldview. It acts upon the daily life of the people. Knowingly or unknowingly people follow the social system in relation to spiritual beliefs in consonance with the underlying conservation of natural resources. *Mayokpha* (*Terminalia arjuna*) is conserved from extinction because of growing sacred grove. Plants like betel, coconut, etc., of natural domain are increasingly in human domain grown not directly from economic value but as consequence of spiritual domain.

The Meiteis do not disturb the ecology of plants on certain days by proscribing social taboos. For instances, trees and bamboos are not cut down on Tuesday, Thursday and Saturday. Again, leaves of *tulsi* cannot be plucked on Sunday and *akadasi* that is, the 11th and 26th day of a lunar month. Above this, no part of any plant is touchable at night. Not only this practical utility, a social fact regarding the felling of bamboo in the region is specification of days. For instance, the Meiteis cut down it on auspicious days – Monday, Wednesday and Friday – for the fear of extinction of personal bamboo grooves. Besides, felling all the bamboo plants at a time is restricted. Commonly these are tabooed by saying *touheide* meaning 'not to be done' without further rational explanation. The cause is wrath of spiritual being and the effect is the protection from extinction. Hence is the conservation of plant resources thereby sustaining to its utility and ecological balance.

Conclusion

It may be concluded from the above discussion that the world view of the Meitei regarding love and affection for plants is immense. And, their normative culture under-carries the conservation of indigenous plants. Rituals are a must in the life of a Meitei identity and coercion in peace. But, in order to complete the rituals, plants are very important. Their cultural ways, in turn, arrange to preserve these plants. So, many flowers and fruits are conserving with great normative value. In cultural ecological enclave, biodiversity is preserving. In the meanwhile, the prominent cosmovision reflects the culture in context to self-aggrandize in sustaining a specific human-nature balance.

References

Anonymous. n.d. *Leirol* [archival manuscript]

Buddhism and Plants. http://www.kepu.net.cn/english/banna/folk/fol405.html retrieved on 15.08.2019.

Haverkort, B. 2009. Towards Co-evolution of Different Ways of Believing: Possible Contributions of Religions and Religious Studies to Sustainable

Development. In *Religion and Sustainable Development: Opportunities and Challenges for Higher Education* Eds. Cathrien de Pater and Irene Dankelman. Berlin: Transaction Publishers.

Hedge, G.T. and Bhat, D.M. 2012. Wild plant species used in Hindu Festivals- A case Study from Uttarakhanda District, Western Ghats, South India. *Centre for Ecological Sciences, Indian Institute of Sciences* Bengaluru, India. *Life sciences Leaflets* 3: 1-6.

Marwat, S. K, Bakhsh, W., Shoaib, M., Khan, E. A., Fazal-ur-Rehman, Javaria, S. and Ullah, G. (2016) Ethnobotanical and Religious Importance of the Quranic Plant-Nakhl (Phoenix dactylifera L.) Review. *American-Eurasian J. Agric. & Environ. Sci.*, 16 (5): 842-851.

Meetei, A.T. 1996. *Meetei Yek Salai (Asuppa).* Imphal.

Niroula, Ghanashyam and Singh, N.B. 2015. Religion and Conservation: A Review of Use and Protection of Sacred Plants and Animals in Nepal. *Journal of Institute of Science and Technology 20(2):* 61-66.

Robinson R.H. and Johnson, W.L. (1970). *The Buddhist Religion: A Historical Introduction.* California: Dickenson Publishing.

Sarma, J. and Devi, Ashalata. 2015.Study on traditional worshiping plants in Hindu religion from Nalbari and Sonitpur districts of Assam. *International Journal of Scientific and Research Publications*, Volume 5, Issue 5.

Tylor, E.B. 1958. *Religion in Primitive Culture: Part II of Primitive Culture.* New York: Harper & Brothers Publishers.

17

Economic culture, entrepreneurship and women empowerment: Manipur chapter

— *Dr. Th. Binarani Devi*

Introduction

The North East region of India was well known for its food self-sufficiency, traditional culture and its rich natural resources. The natural resources of the region were harnessed sustainably by the indigenous people. All the traditional cultural and ritual activities which are in collaboration with socio economic development of the respective societies are so remarkable while it compare with other parts of the country. Wood gathering, livestock and animal husbandry, handicrafts, handlooms, fishing and agricultural activities such as sowing, weeding, transplanting, harvesting and post harvesting activities like thrashing, husking, grinding etc. were undertaken by our rural women. Women are the backbone of the North East Indian society. As a matter of fact, this is mainly due to relentless contribution of women. After the liberalization of economy and in the new circumstances created by structural adjustment programme for globalization, the traditional role of women is being undermined whereas mechanization and automation is becoming prevalent in the market based economy which has adversely affected the village based traditional economy[1]. Even though there is less figure in the decision making process, no activity is left untouched by women, may be agriculture, industrial production, trade or what else. In North East India, due to patriarchal social structure, women are found to be victims of subordination and oppression as men exercise control over women, and restrict women's freedom of choice, behaviour and action. Women's production are considered complementary to income generation activities, eg, these might include child care or basic services provisions. Many developmental agencies, alternatively, increasing their emphasis on women assisting to secure income through their own efforts. Such approaches are often categorised as income generating activities and cover initiatives as diverse as small business promotion, personal sharing, self-help groups etc. The limits of a welfare oriented response to these growing crises are now well recognized. Hypothetically, we need to find out the strategic needs that derive from the imbalance in gender relationship, women's position in society and what exactly they are. Despite of their major contributions in the socio economic and political life of the state, they are not given due position in society. Thus, there is a mismatch between women's role and status. At the same time, in spite of this, increasing number of women are entering into the business world and starting and operating their own business. Women perform most of the work in the family but they are also taking active part in business, became CEOS, got high ranking government jobs etc. This is a right time to study-why the issue of gender discrimination, violation of women's rights, women emancipation and empowerment are on the rise while they are contributing a great role in the socio-economic and political development. All the secondary literary information in this area are trying to justify with the first-hand information collected through direct flexible interview with the concerned persons in this small paper.

Agriculture and women in Manipur: Agriculture is the main occupation and the largest productive unit of the economy of Manipur. Women involved in the traditional agricultural activities. Their contribution in the agricultural economy of the state is acknowledged or not acknowledged does not mattered to the Manipuri women. Transplantation, reaping, weeding, husking etc are carried out by women. Agriculture in Manipur is depended upon Monsoon, which is occur fairly in June and July. Huge labour forces are required during the month of June and July. Since household family member is the basic unit of production in Manipur in such peak period and almost all the families face acute shortage in labour. To meet this shortfall in labour, women started reaching out for help to each other in the community with promise of repaying with the same service in agricultural work. This kind of interdependence, which has been arranged to meet the need for agricultural labour in large numbers and within a short period of time, is a common feature of the rural agrarian economy of the developing societies. In Manipur, this type of mutual exchange of labour is known as *Khutlang*. This type of economic activities contributed to the rich cultural heritage of Manipur too. *Khulang Eshei* is the type of song sung by the women agricultural worker during the agricultural activities. This is becoming one of the famous folk song of the Manipuries. There has been a great deal of controversy about whether labour standards including the right to organize, can be improved through trade sanctions. Globally enforced labour standards will do little to change the lives and livelihoods of the vast majority of working women in the informal economy where such standards are impossible or impossibly expensive, to enforce. A more inclusive approach would be to institute a universal social floor based on supporting all and supported by all. The opening of markets led to the commercialization of agriculture and new technologies penetrated into our agricultural lands. But in this context too regarding upgradation of agricultural development tools women were neglected. The transmission of knowledge about the new technologies like use of tractors, high quality fertilizers, selection of HYV seeds, pesticides etc. became man-to-man affairs. Men were increasingly drawn into the modernizing agriculture sector while women stayed in subsistence agriculture with no access to credits, training and technologies. The agricultural development has normally and almost entirely been manned by men right from the decision making to implementation[2].

Women and handloom and handicrafts activities in Manipur

The handloom and handicraft- small cottage industries, mostly operated by women are contributing handsomely in the growth of GDP and GNP. As per Manipur State Government record there are 2.12 lakh weavers and 2.11 looms in the state[3]. The artistic design and production of handloom and handicrafts saved an unchallengeable pride for

Manipuri women. Overall, it is seen in that is dearth of enthusiasm and zeal among women of today to compete in the international arena. With the introduction of developmental measures, the production relations have been modified and distribution system is being influenced by the market forces of the liberal global economic structure. Thus, the situation has undergone sea-change since independence with the gradual transformation of the economy from the non-monetized to the market economy and the integration of the indigenous people in the national 'main stream'. All the traditional and ritual contribution of Manipuri handloom and handicraft productions are turning into a gloomy scenario with the adventure and interference of modern technology and business expansion. But the fate and glamour of Manipuri handloom and handicraft productions are trying to protect by newly educated women with advance business knowledge in the name of different entrepreneurs. Support of the government for development of the production and protection of the interest of the weaver are quite necessary. Timely availability of the raw material and market for selling the handloom production is very important. During the lockdown period of COVID19, the Manipur Handloom and Handicraft Development Corporation Ltd initiated for availability of raw materials for the weavers but due to unavailability of market for selling the productions the handloom producers suffer setback. The artistic designs which are mixing with the culture and tradition of the community are imitating by power looms and big industries of other Indian states. And they are trying to get patent of those Manipuri designs in their own way. A very simple example is when Prime Minister of India, Narendra Modi used Manipuri Leirum Lengyan in the public meeting during the COVID 19 period. After that, Textile Manufacturing Unit of Barabanki, UP started to produce the same in the name of Modi Gamsha in their power loom. In this regard, the Directorate of Handloom and Textile submitted objection letter (NoHE-79/H&H1971) to the Development Commissioner for Handloom, Ministry of Textile, Government of India, Udyog Bhavan on 30th May 2020 in the interest of the Manipuri weavers and emotion of the people of the state. Handloom products protector, Chingtam Luwang while talking to Imphal Times said that the previous Chief Minister and the present Chief Minister, N. Biren Singh had directed the Department of Handloom to take GI tag for the Leirum Phi as it is bonded with

Manipur's Culture some years back. However, it is the department of Handloom of the state government neglect the important of the Leirum Phi[4]. Manipuri women weavers are famous for their artistic designs of traditional clothes. These designs are embodied with the traditional culture of different communities of the state which are compulsory to use in different cultural and ritual occasions. Therefore, the handloom designs of Safee Lanfee, Wangkhei Fee, Moirang Phee got GI (Regulation and Protection) 1999[5].

Ima market of Manipur: Manipur, a tiny border state in North East India, is acknowledged for her Ima Market (mother's market) or Khwairamband Bazar, where all the stalls are run by women. This Ima Market gives a colourful example of the entrepreneurial skill, experience and activities of Manipuri Women right from the British period. Women do not stay behind the veil, do all the buying and selling of goods in the market and even dominate the markets in both rural and urban. With the economic activities, even though traditional, they have the idea for producing goods for market and selling goods at the market, which are available from time to time. After of completion of their household activities, women sell the basic items which they produced, may be from kitchen garden, handloom and handicraft production etc. This market gives a good platform for exchange of their views and acknowledgement of all the issues and problems from time to time. The two important social movements during the British Imperialism in Manipur, one in 1904, and the other in 1939 were led by women community of Manipur for the sake of the whole society, in order to maintain economic stability and social harmony. But it is not wrong to say that any spectator became confused when they come to know and see what Manipuri women can do when they are in group[6]. Both the movements in the socio-economic and political history of Manipur were originated/started by the women of Ima Market. The activities that define the making of a nation are seen 'male' activities (thus, war, conquest, ravaging, the others'; taking over territories, making governments, setting up the state) and women, therefore, are inevitably outside of these. There are times when women might choose to stay out of the process of nation making, or their priorities might simply be different. But there are times when they may wish to be involved, and find it difficult to do so[7]. Manipuri Women's Movement 1904 or First

Nupi Lan is an explicit example. This movement was compelled to the Women of Khwairamband Bazar (Ima Market) to prepare for a fight against the injustice of the British. For the Britishers, the issue was quite political, but for the women of Manipur it was a socio economic issue. But one of the most outstanding features of the issue was without women the issue was in a never ending condition[8]. Very simply Ima Market is serving as a good platform for solution of all the social, economic and political issues of the state. And this market has serving for protection of all the life of all corners of the state. Not only the women vendors or traders, all the producers of other far places are also giving a place for selling their productions. Women producers of different parts of the state –agriculture, horticulture, handloom and handicraft, fisheries etc brought all their productions to the Ima Market with the great hardship of transportation. Women traders of this Ima Market collect all these different productions. Those suppliers of the far flung areas known as 'Mangai' of the traders[9]. They share their life in all angles. Due to the emergence of the outside traders in this market, non-availability or not enough availability of local goods, changing patterns of lifestyles, monopolization of the productions etc. the atmosphere has been changed in somewhat sense.

Financial support system for women: As market is dominated by modern financial system and interference of internal and external business groups, local Manipuri women traders are facing acute struggle in their business. But they are not remained in silent. Traditionally, Manipuri women have their own system for running their business as well as maintenance of their family. *Marup* or cooperative financial movement spearheaded by women for generating income. It is a type of Self Help Group with common economic needs who undertake an economic activity by participating directly in decision making and sharing the benefits on an equitable basis. It strengthens the existing income generating activity of members and also helps the members to start a new activity of members. This system not only makes them economically independent but also helps their family's financial contributions and acts as the financial intermediaries.

In 1991, liberalization of the Indian economy had an important bearing on the financial sectors, banks which have turned weak, were confronted with the challenge of making themselves profitable while maintaining their prudential requirements and competing with private and foreign banks in a new liberalized milieu[10]. The ongoing poverty alleviation programmes are expected to address specifically the needs and problems of such women as poverty affects women more than men. In the name of the women centric economic development, the tenth plan proposes to ensure provision of training, employment and income generation activities with both 'Forward' and 'Backward' linkages with the ultimate objectives of making all women economically independent and self-reliant through different programmes. No doubt there are some positive sides of globalization and the NEP which have contributed to bring about welcome changes in the lives of women but the gains are attained by those women who can afford them both economically and socially. But as we all know, about 80 percent of the population of our region stay in the rural areas and are mostly poor and hence the true character of the current globalisation and its negative impacts are borne by the weak, the poor and the backward. There must be equitable distribution of technological progress keeping in view of the fact that the human development must be strengthened in order to achieve social and gender justice[11]. Organizing women into self-help groups under various poverty alleviation programmes-1. Swarnajayenty Gram Swarozgar Yojana; 2. Swarnajayenty Shahari Rojgar Yojana; 3. Rastriya Mahila Kosh; 4. Support for training and employment programmes, 5. Training Cum Production Centers for women etc. and offering them a range of economic options along with necessary support measures to enhance their objective of making them economically independent and self-relevant. Economic empowerment is an approach to enable women to realise this inherent knowledge, skills and competencies for creation of small business enterprises. In India various ministries, institutions and organizations have been working for the up liftmen of women through implementing of various schemes like-SGSY, NORAD, IMY etc.[12]

There are other capacity building schemes for women entrepreneurs like 'Stree Shakti', 'SEWA', 'Swayamsidha' and 'Swadhar', which have been launched with the idea of social and economic empowerment of women by ensuring direct access to and control over resources through a process of mobilization and convergence.[13] Bharatiya Mahila Bank, Annapurna Scheme, Orient Mahila Vikas Yojana Scheme, Dena

Shakti Scheme, Udyogini Scheme, Mahila Udan Midhi Scheme, Mudra Yojana Scheme for Women etc may also be mentioned in this context.

Government also encouraged women entrepreneurs to enter into various small scale industries or entrepreneurs which are reflected in various policies and programmes launched by them e.g, Prime Minister Rojgar Yojna. North Eastern Development Finance Corporation Ltd (NEDFI), established on August 1995, has some special scheme like Women Enterprises Development Schemes (WEDS) for the economic empowerment of women of North East India. Internationally and nationally, we got successful women entrepreneurs in this context. In Manipur, for establishing small scale industries, by encouraging the talent of the local women entrepreneurs, the Institute of Cooperative Management, Imphal is taking a great role.

Enterpreneurship: Women established small enterprises which can provide their means of earning with their own knowledge and skills. This type of activities of women includes almost all the items i.e starting from small daily basic needs of the people to the modern well design artistic goods which can attract the international markets too. In these global liberal societies, women entrepreneurs have set up small scale industries like pickle making, catering, weaving, juice making, jam and jelly making etc. to become economically independent. Their activities started with or without any/little capital as a part of their daily routine activities.

Small business enterprises, run by women, play an important role in the economic development of Manipur. These enterprises, may be in informal economic sectors, are now being proposed as a way to achieve sustainable socio-economic development and eliminate poverty. Women entrepreneurs are individual or group of women who initiate, organize and operate a business enterprise (weaving, embroidery, agriculture, animal husbandry etc). The number of women entrepreneurs in India has been on a rise in general and in the developing and underdeveloped states like Manipur, the number of women entrepreneurs has been increasing with extraordinary productions as well as maintaining their rich cultural traditions. Women entrepreneurs are mostly on their own initiatives to become self-sufficient and to establish their own identity. They are both individual and collective, depending upon the situation, i.e, work or family. They can take decision of their own by creating something on their own efforts and view success by achieving their targets even though they are coming out from the traditional patriarchal power structures and taking up new roles and sustaining even under adverse environmental conditions. Their success stories continue to inspire and motivates millions more. They won international and national awards from time to time.

For justification of my paper, I took up two case studies from different districts with different productions, which can proof about the successful economic activities of women as entrepreneurs.

CASE I. Ranjana Emporium: The artistic design of Ranjana Devi is attracting national and international markets. The main items of this Emporium are mosquito nets, cushion cover, kouna –products and many more. Not only to produce the beautiful items, the centre provide job opportunities and training to the younger generation. This centre gives livelihood of 87 regular employees with different activities. Regular training courses are also there with different batches and courses. Those who got training from this centre have established their own business and enterprises. And, this number has considerably increased in recent times, with women getting better exposure to several opportunities and avenues with different platforms. Ranjana Devi, Imphal West District of Manipur, founder Proprietor, won State Award in Embroidery in 2006, Sabitri National Award for Embroidery in 2007, Dr. Ambedkar Fellowship Award in 2007, First Prize in Handloom and Handicraft Exhibition in 2008, Chief Minister Entrepreneurship of Successful Award, Manipur with Cash Award Rs. 5 lakhs in 2013, International Achiever Award 2017 in Bangkok. The centre has been expanded its business with e-marketing system nowadays. *Giska.com* is their web address and *ranjanaemporiumsagolband* is their instagram addresses. Through these addresses, people order the productions of the centre and the Proprietor gives satisfactions to all the customers by any means. Now they have opened their outlets in other states of India, like Bangalore[14].

CASE II: Meira Food: Meira Food of Imphal East District of Manipur was established with minimum amount for producing daily use food items, especially pickles, candies, salted dry fruit items prepared from the locally available fruits and vegetables. The growth of this centre is so quick and advanced. It was started from her own kitchen by producing some pickles, jam, jelly, mixture etc. Now this centre has a good place in the international market, mainly in South and South East Asian countries. According to Subbra Devi, (M.Sc in Food & Nutrition) Proprietor Meira Food, in 2004-05, turn over was only Rs. 30000, that was increased year after year- in 2005-06- Rs. 100000, then in 2012-13- Rs 7500000/ and now it crossed over two crores per annum and giving employment to 162 women. Not only to earn money and giving employments, Meira Food is recognised as Industrial Partner of State RUSA Vocational Courses under UGC New Delhi[15].

This type of large scale participation by women at the top level in the industries and factories help to improve not only the women's self-employment but also helps to develop the national economy. Even though we can observe the successful activities, acknowledgement and contributions of women entrepreneurs, we need to understand and acknowledge exact position and problems of these entrepreneurs. The hard and talented activities of women entrepreneur are facing acute problems in their production and marketing processes due to-

- Infrastructural factors Band, blockade, lack of water supply, supply of power, good roads, medical facilities, sanitation;
- Non availability of funds, coupled with raw materials, is one of the major problems of the small scale industries;
- Non availability and lack of awareness about welfare schemes and benefits.

Empowerment: Women entrepreneurship development is the instrument of women empowerment. Empowered women contribute to the health, productivity of their families, communities and countries, creating a ripple effect that benefits everyone. Throughout the world, women performed long hours on unpaid domestic works, in some places, women of some communities/sections still lack rights to own land or to inherit property, obtain access to credit, earn income, or to move up in their workplace, free from job discrimination. At all levels, including at home and in the public arena, women are widely underrepresented as decision makers. But, they have the capability to contribute to creating their own reality. Development implies both material and immaterial betterments with the maintenance of human rights and equality by abolishing all forms of discrimination[16]. There is no force more powerful than a woman who is determined to rise. Many a time, the contribution of women is neither given due attention nor marginalized while formulating socio-economic development plans and women occupy a place of subordination to men in many occasions. Given the biological and social construction of gender roles, women tend to concentrate in jobs where they can combine their household duties and 'work'. The additional advantage is of course the fact that such labour is cheap and easily exploitable on various counts. This is true of all the countries across the sub-continent although the exact manner and degree to which this happens varies a great deal. Economic empowerment develops women's capability to impact, transform or form a better nation. Even after seventy years of Independence, India's development is slow due to the lack of women's participation. Women are often invisible in the development scenario. Development process without the participation of women, who formed a significant chunk of the society, will be lopsided. Being influenced by unique physical, racial and socio-cultural diversities quite different from the rest of the country, North East India witnesses a great variation in socio economic conditions of women in both spatial and social terms. It is obvious that discrimination exists.

Women empowerment has various dimensions and only change of law is not enough to bring about change in real condition. Every person in the society and in the family has to be aware of the rights, needs, well and woes, pleasure and pain as well as honour and dignity of the women. When women became the decision makers or at the managerial position, they would be able to break the glass ceiling around them and to create women friendly environment. Women in such position would also help to bring about change in attitude, beliefs and thoughts and in enhancing motivation and self-confidence among them. If the small sector moves into progress rapidly both in modernization and diversification of production efforts should be made to improve the level of technology, by producing sophisticated machines within the country. In the spheres of social and household relations the important task is to raise the social awareness by continuous exhortation.

Conclusion: It is quite cleared that women have a great contribution in the socio-economic development of North East India. Though some benefits do accrue to middle class women in terms of more educational, health, jobs and professional advancements, the majority of rural and uneducated women are being deprived of even their traditional modes of occupations and employment in the wake of development. Therefore, serious attention and a fresh looks are require to reorient our developmental model and policies so that economic development and women's development do not work at cross purposes. A concerted attempt has to be made to evolve strategies for the economic independence and socio-political empowerment of the majority of poor, illiterate women, both in rural and urban areas. In the spheres of social and household relations the important task is to raise the social awareness by continuous exhortation. In the social life the bias against women and girl child has to be fought by social and economic movements and by ensuring freedom to women from the oppressive social codes. Every person in the society and in the family has to be aware of the rights, needs, well and woes, pleasure and pain as well as honour and dignity of the women. With the progress of the socio-political and economic development in this liberal globalised society, the position of women is blurred in their respective societies. Both men and women will have to work together in this direction so that human resources are not wasted or exploited by the brutal forces with traditional, indigenous cultural norms and activities.

Key Words: Business, Development, Economy, Employment, Entrepreneur, Factory, Government, Market, Skill, Trade

Notes

1. Th. Binarani Devi, LPG and Violence Against Women, in Meinam Binota and Sunita Devi (Ed) Women in Science and Social Sciences, 2014.
2. Phukon Dolly, New Economic Policy and Its Impact on Traditional Skills of Women In North East India, in Day B Dutta, Dev Bimal J.(ed) Globalization and North East India, Concept Publishing Company, New Delhi, 2008 p. 349.
3. Poknapham, Manipuri Local Daily, Dt.31.05.2020, p. 1.
4. Imphal Times, Manipur Evening Local Daily, Dt.31.05.2020, p. 1.
5. Poknapham, Manipuri Local Daily, Dt.01.06.2020, p. 1.

6. Th. Binarani Devi, Women's Movement in Manipur, 2011, p. 115.
7. Butalia Urvashi, Gender and Nation: Some Reflections from India, in Ivekovic Rada and Mostov Julie (Ed), From Gender to Nation, 2002, p. 101.
8. Th. Binarani Devi, Of. Cit p. 99.
9. Personally interview with S. Bilasini Devi, Women Vendor, Ima Market, Dt.10.12.2019.
10. Th. Binarani Devi, Women in the Contemporary Society-Issues and Challenges, 2017, Concept Publishing Company, New Delhi, p. 143.
11. Khan Sakiya, The Micro Finance Experience- Accomplishments and Challenges, in Ray. B.Dutta, Deb.B.J and Keya Sengupta (ed), Globalization in North East India, 2008, p. 222.
12. Phukan Dolly, New Economic Policy and Its Impact on Traditional Skills of Women in North East India, in Ray. B.Dutta, Deb.B.J and Keya Sengupta (ed), Globalization in North East India, 2008, pp. 352-53.
13. Bhuyan Dolly, Self Empowerment and Political Position of Women, July 2012, Indian Journal of Social Science and Sciences-A Half Yearly Multi Disciplinary Research Journal, Vol. 2, Issue II.
14. Personal interview with Ranjana Devi, Proprietor of Ranjana Emporium, Dt.10.12.2019.
15. Personal interview with Subbra Devi, Proprietor of Meira Food, Dt.09.12.2019.
16. Anjali Ghose, Women's Work Health and Empowerment, Aakar Books, Delhi, 2006, p. 29.

18

Koratpa : The 'First Death' Ritual of Meitei Kritanias (Kidna) of Tripura

— *Kshetrimayum Premchandra*

A ritual must be enacted, a myth recited, a narrative told, a novel read, a drama performed, for these enactments, recitals, tellings, readings, and performances are what make the text transformative and enable us to reexperience our culture's heritage. — **Edward M. Bruner**

Meitei Kritania (Kidna): a brief introduction

Poirei or Manipur, despite its demographic isolation, linguistic and racial differences, the place, and its people attracted many migrants from all directions and social groups. One such group of people who migrated to Manipur probably in the sixteenth century (or maybe before) was the Meitei Kritanias or Kidna. They are one among the three social groups whose mother-tongue is Manipuri/Meiteilon, the other two being Meiteis[2] and Meitei Pangals. Surprisingly, the exact period of their migration and subsequent settlement is not established but it is a fact that they were from pre-colonial Bengal. Aribam Chitreshwar Sharma maintains that the Meitei Kritanias Migrated to Manipur during the reign of Meitengu Garibnawaz (1709-1748 CE).[3] However, considering the degree of acculturation and integration of Meitei folk belief system in their ethos and worldviews which would require a fair amount of time, and also the Hindu gods that they worship now, I believe that they were a group of Vishnu worshippers with intense Shakta influences who migrated to Manipur during the reign of Meitengu Lam Kiyamba

(1512 to 1523 CE),[4] possibly as Vaishnavite missionaries on proselytising missions. The absence of any written record with respect to this group's migration to Manipur has aggravated the state of confusion. The presence of tantric elements and worship of Vishnu and Mahadev by the present-day Kritanias imply that they are most likely a Vaishnavite cult which existed prior to the emergence of the Vhallabhacharya and the Chaitanya cults in the 16th century.[5] Be it as it may, they were a group of Bangalis who easily adapted to the local mysticism due to prior exposure to *tantric* occultism. Their oral history, however, identifies four earliest settlers (patriarchs) of this group – Yadhava, Madhava, Keshava, and Vaishnav Das. And these four Vaishnavite missionaries first encountered the people of Kakching in Manipur. This view has some validity as there are morphological similarities between the people of Kakching and the Kritanias. They were the earliest known Vaishnavites who introduced *kritan* tradition in the court of Manipur. Their *kritan* tradition is known as Bangadesh *pala* or *ariba pala.* All in all, the group presents a high level of syncretism between the two forms of religion.

After years of living in Manipur and picking up local customs and language, they were displaced from Manipur along with other groups during the horrific period of the Burmese occupation of Manipur (1819-1826 CE). They entered Bangladesh via Silchar, some chose to stay at Barak Valley in Assam, some are scattered in and around Sylhet of Bangladesh. Some entered Tripura from Bangladesh. In Tripura, the Meitei Kritania population is concentrated in the Bamutia Sub-division of Tripura East District. In this Sub-division, there is a collection of small Kritania villages at the Indo-Bangladesh border in the western side of Tripura. The total population of Meitei Kritanias is roughly 2500. The names of the villages are given below with their corresponding Sub-divisions and Districts:

Sl. No.	*Bamutia Sub-division, West Tripura District*		*Settlers*
	Village name (Manipuri)	*Village name (Bangla)*	
1.	Rangamati	Rangatia	Kritani (K)
2.	Borjush	Borjush	K
3.	Kaori	Bhogjur	K
4.	Lairenkabi	Noagaon	K
5.	Unung	Jamirghat	K

(Contd...)

6.	Patita	Pratikshara	K+Meitei (M)
7.	Khunou	Sonatala	K+M
8.	Panijai	Gachhamura	K
9.	Pakha	Lamarbari	K
10.	Borjuri	Berimura	K
11.	Bhandaimura	Bhandarmura	K
12.	Pukhri Leikai	Brahmapushkari	M
13.	Limang Khuman	Taltola	M
14.	Torok Pokpi	Shantipara	M
15.	Shansen Leikai	Sesuria	M
16.	Bhajalghat	Bhajalghat	M
	Mohanpur Sub-division, West Tripura District		
	Village name (Manipuri)	**Village name (Bangla)**	
17.	Jagatpur	Jagatpur	K
	Khwai Sub-division, Khwai District		
	Village name (Manipuri)	**Village name (Bangla)**	
18.	Gouranagar	Gouranagar	K+M
19.	Kalyanpur	Kalyanpur	K+M
	Agartala, West Tripura District		
	Village name (Manipuri)	**Village name (Manipuri)**	
20.	Borjala	Borjala	K+M

Sl. No.	***Surname***		***Occupation/ Services rendered***	***High/low (social hierarchy)***
	Meitei	***Bangla***		
1.	Thangjam	Karmakar	Blacksmiths[1]	High
2.	Laishrabam	Datta	Idol makers	High
3.	Nongrakpam	Datta	Those who can control rain through their *raga*[2]	High
4.	Tokshubam	Datta	Those who worked with wooden pestle and mortar[3]	Low (*mikhun kidna*)
5.	Nungsatakpam/ Chandontakpam	Datta	Those who rubbed *chandan* on a stone[4]	High
6.	Takhenchangbam	Datta	Those who came via *Takhen* (Tripura)	Low (*mikhun kidna*)
7.	Moibungkhongbam	Datta	Those who played conch	High
8.	Seleibam	Sen	Those who played gong	Low (*mikhun kidna*)
9.	Pungyanbam	Ray/Roy	Those who played *khol/pung*	Low (*mikhun kidna*)
10.	Phijaba/Phijabam	Datta	Weavers	Low (*mikhun kidna*)
11.	Dhojaibam	Datta	Those who carried flag[5]	Low (*mikhun kidna*)
12.	Sekombam	Datta	-----	Low, *Chamar* (*mikhun kidna*)
13	Hijam	Datta	Boat makers	Low [Hijam *macha* (*mikhun kidna*)] High (Hijam *achouba*)

1. Said to be Lairikyengbams
2. Descendants of Yadhava
3. Believed to have integrated with one of the hill tribes of Manipur
4. Descendants of Keshava
5. Dhoja in Bangla means flag. Worshippers of Vishnu

Meitei Kritanias have distinct Mongoloid features but sometimes one may encounter individuals with sharp Aryan features. The earliest settlers were given Manipuri wives and fully acculturated as happened with other migrant groups. The fact that they were given surnames/ *sageis* proves that they were granted Manipuri citizenship by the court. Like the *Lairikyengbams* their surnames are based on the profession/ work one individual was skilled at. Here is the list of surnames they were given by the kings of Manipur and their internal social hierarchy[6]:

Rituals of Meitei Kritanias

Meitei Kritanias perform many rituals which are intrinsic to the Meitei community. Sadly, in Tripura, most of these rituals have been abandoned by the majority Meiteis who enjoy the status of *yek-salai.* While there are traces of rituals based on the traditional belief system performed in not so distant past, the declining state of affairs as regards Meitei faith in Tripura is a downright reality. There are reasons for that. For one, Meiteis have positioned themselves as stout Vaishnavites, a non-tribal social status they exhibit with pride. Secondly, the depleting number of persons who know the intricacies of such elaborate Meitei rituals. However, Meitei Kritanias still perform these rituals with much attentiveness and religious zeal. The practitioners of these rituals feel that a collapse has been felt as the support structures have diminished from their society. This apprehension arises from a dying *maiba/maibi* (shamans) tradition and their inconsequential status in a changed socio-cultural setting. Call it a native's practice or some primitive culture arising out of savage minds, Meitei Kritanias still perform these rituals, with whatever they have retained like their forefathers did.

Some important rituals still performed by Meitei Kritanias are enumerated below:

1. *sharoi-khangba*
2. *chaban thaba*
3. *koratpa*
4. *apokpa khurumba*
5. *khunlai latpa*
6. *tinmu-laimu tanthokpa,* etc.

The rituals given above are all pre-Hindu rituals. There is a fair amount of Hindu influence over and above these ritual practices, but the Meitei abstractions run deep at the core of each ritual. Of all the rituals practiced by Meitei Kritania, *koratpa* stands out; firstly, as it acts as a repository of many rituals, and secondly, it exhibits a syncretism of Hinduism and Meitei folk belief system.

Ritual: Manipuri equivalents and tenets

Closest that comes to analysing the former kingdom of Manipur is Clifford Geertz's conception of a 'theatre state'[12]. Like Bali, Manipur is famous for colourful festivals and rituals that take place round the year. One can take a step further and call Manipur a 'ritual state'. The subsequent paragraphs shall corroborate some points to as why such a tall claim is made. The claim is made although what constitutes ritual is an ongoing debate. It is established, however, that faith and ritual are bound by an umbilical cord – complementing each other and dichotomous at times. Manipuri equivalents for the English term 'ritual' are many. The following terms are used alternately to denote 'ritual':

(i) *heikat-leikat tamba* – to offer fruits and flowers

(ii) *mathou-mangamtouba* – to carry out services due for them (spirits)

(iii) *lai-tin khurumba*– to pray to deities and spirits

(iv) *heitha-leitha pangthokpa* – to carry out the task of offering fruits and flowers

(v) *irat-thouniba* – to pray to and ask for blessings

(vi) *laishon-tinshon sonba* – to say the prayers for deities and spirits

(vii) *thouram-thouchat touba*– to carry out

(viii) *thou touba* – to do what needs to be done

All these terms imply offering prayers and feeding certain spirits/ energies for the well being of an individual, or individuals, or the state. Manipuri scholars have come to use *irat thouni* (to pray to and ask for blessings) as a vernacular equivalent for the English term 'ritual'.

Rituals were borne out of the basic human tendency to forge an affective bond with nature and its varied manifestations. Human beings felt the need to propitiate the spirits which made nature angry. They also appeased those which made them sustain. They prayed to the spirits in the sky, spirits on earth, spirits which gave them directions, spirits of those who had passed away. Besides, there is an underlying human propensity to make sense of what they do and legitimise those 'doings' as actions beneficial to an individual or to a group. Ritual is a social action, meaningful and relatable to a particular ritual group, which must correspond to other such similar or associated actions. It is also our way of showing 'group association'. This group association can be anything that puts an individual under a distinct ritual umbrella. It is also a cultural marker having an innate ability to orient and reorient social groups. What is important in a ritual is 'space' and 'occasion' – where and when they are performed. The transmission part can be considered as a convention developed much later.

The ancient civilisation of Manipur was founded on three very basic constituent elements or tenets which enabled Manipuris to sustain and multiply. Those tenets are food, health, and leadership.

Human history is replete without their search for better hunting grounds and fertile soils. Manipuris (various social groups) also set out on such a mission and finally settled at the present-day Manipur. They studied local vegetation and seeds. They studied the seasons and learned which crops were best suited for one particular season. They practiced the seasonal cycle of planting and harvesting. They maintained a calendar based upon crops. But the incalculable behaviour of nature and its unpredictable impulses hampered their confidence in the cyclic sequence of the seasons. This anxietyled to the establishment of two opposing forces of *lai* and *tin* (roughly 'deity' and 'insects' which are above and beneath the ground – which can be regarded as metaphors for benevolent and malevolent forces) in their belief system. They understood the respective roles of the fertility of nature (*lai*) as well as its destructive energies (*tin*). They welcomed seasons for those seasons brought them abundant food while, at the same time, finding ways to ward off the malevolent energies which caused death and destruction to their cattle and crops. Nature was the source of life, giver of food. And, earth which bears them food was considered a female energy. They performed certain rituals to herald new seasons for a bountiful harvest; they repeated those rituals turning them into cyclical rituals.

One of the prime concerns of every social group is both mental and physical health of the individuals who make up the group. Healthy lives pertain to an increased population (abled bodies) which was needed for protection from other social groups in the times of war or calamities as well as for an increased workforce. The efforts to keep individuals free from disease let to the discovery of medicinal plants and their properties. They also believed that certain spirit mediums were responsible for many kinds of illnesses. Those malevolent spirits must be tackled as per the belief system they have developed. Rituals performed in respect of these spirit mediums brought together individuals to celebrate life and ask for blessings from the protective energies. These rituals which are celebrations of the interrelatedness of villages and individuals underscored group development and advancement, a form of mystical communion in which they sing and dance together for common prosperity.

Leadership in Manipuri sense are those founding fathers of various communities or ancestors from whom different clans or lineages came forth. These founding fathers provided an institutional base for the groups concerned by formulating various rules of social and economic engagements, taboos, and rites. Later on, the leaders who led each group were glorified by worshipping them and also by giving them images that correlated with their faith and spirituality. They were and are still revered and worshipped. It is believed that their ancestors performed the basic social function of creating and maintaining groups which ultimately merged with other groups to form a congruent community having different clans and sub-clans. These groups merged with the *Ningthouja* clan which had its 'exemplary centre'[13] at Kangla in present-day Imphal. Various clans worship and pay their homage to their 'ancestors' and deities in a number of rituals. After the consolidation of all the clans and their principalities were complete, the narrative of 'leadership' changed.

From Tenets to Doctrines: Existential Equilibrium

Ritual action is, in fact, a system of connecting and reconnecting the performers with the 'ones' who/which are believed to have the ability to change the natural order and all those constituent elements in that order. To put it simply, one cannot take the belief tag away from ritual.

Rituals, in the Manipuri sense, are their earnest efforts to appease the spirit mediums so that they are protected from death and misfortune. The transition from the basic key ingredients of wellbeing and expansion to that of a 'decree' came about when kings institutionalised various support structures of governance such as *Luwang nonghum shang* (the house of the shamans – later bifurcated into *pandit loishang* and *maiba/maibi loishang*), and as a matter of politico-ritual principle encouraged to incorporate three slogans which had been the 'values' that kept the Manipuris together –

(i) *khun-jao lei-chaoba* – bigger villages, bigger state,

(ii) *chak-hong nga-hongba* – abundant rice and fish, and

(iii) *ningthou punsi nong-shangba* – long life for the king.

Each and every Manipuri ritual will correspond to one or all of the 'values' mentioned above. Hence, it can be fairly concluded that the Manipur is incorporated in their rituals what they believed were the key ingredients for a peaceful and meaningful existence. I call these three core values 'existential equilibrium' for they maintain and perpetuate stability in the ritual state. Much of Manipuri ethos and worldviews come from these three value systems.

Where belief is abstract, ritual is concrete. However, it is these concrete, verifiable acts that unify groups, organise societies, organise knowledge systems, build a 'shared emotional focus'[14], legitimise power structures, open up channels for symbolic communication with the spirits, etc. It is, I believe, our efforts to establish a form of communication with the higher spirits which gave us our rituals. Its beginning could have been in shaping relationships between an individual and nature. It got its extension in the establishment and organisation of families. Our first prayers were offered to nature and many of its marvels. We sang and danced for hills, rivers, trees, birds, flowers, etc. We prayed to the forces of nature for the right amount of rain, cool and calm wind, and enough sunshine to dry our crops, meat, and fish. We began to understand seasons so we welcomed them with songs and dance. We understood the importance of directions so we appeased them with appropriate rituals. We remembered how we lived with nature in our ancestral environment so we offered them our produce. We understood the energy of the sky. We also understood the energy of the earth. So we started believing that we came from them. We formed our knowledge, we developed rules, and we developed taboos. Our ethos and worldviews developed and ultimately got expanded. Songs and dances performed at the green fields and jungles started finding an audience at courts and enclosures. They became our cultural expressions, our heritage.

Koratpa: similar rituals

It is difficult to establish the exact meaning of *koratpa.* However, it could have been derived from *kumlak lamtaiaba* ritual which was performed to appease the spirits which control seasons and also directions that protect the realm. In a later period, after Bangla and Sanskrit were introduced to the Manipuris, a phonological change took place and the ritual came to be known as *kurak lamtaiba.* It is a cyclical ritual performed every year in March-April, just before the beginning of the tilling activities. The two-prong focal purpose of this ritual is to ward off possible diseases that afflicted cattle and also for pests and disease-free crops. I am told that the people of Kakching used to refer to this ritual as *koratpa* but the manner and mode of performing the ritual are quite different from that of the Meitei Kritanias.

There was another ritual which shares some affinities with *koratpa* in spirit and approach. It was known as *khunthong latpa* or *leikai lamtaiba* which was a very important ritual for the four *leikais* of *Kanglei*[15] but no longer in vogue. This ritual was performed at the four *lamtai-pungs*[16] or mounds where the spaces/lands of the different localities merge. *Lamtaiba* is a conflation of two words –*lam*=place/spot, *taiba*=to merge/to stitch together. The idea is that by symbolically merging the spaces between two areas, the malevolent spirits are stopped from entering the space. This ritual was performed by seven shamans sent to each of the four spots from the palace and the ritual symbolically erected a divine boundary by joining together the four cosmic mounds. The ritual reassured that the Kangla, the seat of Meitei power, as the centre of the world. The ritual sanctified the space covered by these four mounds, and it was perceived that the realm was protected especially from death and destruction.

Koratpa of Meitei Kritania works on similar principles. *Koratpa,* in this way, is not just about faith but also entails a moral sense, a signification of replicating a ritual centre. The ritual also conforms to the three doctrines of existential equilibrium mentioned earlier. The primal focus of *Koratpa* is appeasement of the first death in the village after finally setting up living spaces in Tripura after a long and treacherous wandering. Giving an exact year of settlement in Tripura would be difficult. However, considering the time taken by this ritual group which got displaced from Manipur due to the seven-year-long Burmese atrocities in Manipur, I would consider the early part of the 1830s when they started their villages in Tripura. The ritual enacts the feeding of spirits, offering them flowers, also a certain rite called *mang thong thingba*[17] or 'closing the door of the dead' which Meiteis practice in their death rituals (rites of passage).

Koratpa: sacred spaces and their tutelary spirits

Wherever Meiteis settle, they make the place sacred. The place must be sanctified and measures for the protection of the living and non-living beings must be put together in the ways they had done at their place of origin. These measures derive from their earnest efforts to communicate with the cosmic powers which they believe are resided in directions, natural objects, and 'spaces'. They held the belief that the ancestral environment must be consecrated for they contend that human beings must devise ways to relate to the ancestral environment for that is one way of maintaining 'order'. This maintenance involves appeasement rituals. The tradition of purifying a settlement area in other cultures has been reported by Mircea Eliade. Contesting that settlement in the territory is 'equivalent to consecrating it', he wrote in *The Sacred and Profane: The Nature of Religion:*

> When settlement is not temporary, among the nomads, but permanent, as among sedentary peoples, it implies a vital decision that involves the existence of the entire community. Establishment in a particular place, organising it, inhabiting it, are acts that presuppose an existential choice – the choice of the universe that one is prepared to assume by "creating" it. Now, this universe is always the replica of the paradigmatic universe created and inhabited by the gods; hence it shares in the sanctity of the god's work.[18]

The hills, rivers, lakes, villages, open spaces, etc. in Manipur are sacred spaces that signify much of Meitei theogony and cosmogony. Meitei Kritanias felt the need to replicate the idea of 'sacred spaces' in tune with Meitei cosmogony in Tripura. The ritual of consecrating a specific area in the Meitei sense is the exploitation of the idea of repelling possible evil spirits that previously inhabited the area. Those spirits are offered fruits and flowers, a peace making gesture with the spirits. After the peace offering is made, the new occupants identify a spot to place their protective spirits. Meitei Kritanias choose a grove or an old tree to be such a sacred spot.

Where *koratpa* is not performed in a Kritania village, *Nityai puja* at the *mandapa* is performed in place of this ritual. But, the very socio-psychological and philosophical connotations intrinsically attached to *koratpa* ritual cannot be transmitted by *Nityai puja.* I have collected and observed how this ritual is performed in three different villages. There are differences in their method and approach but the central idea is retained and expressed in all the three performances. The *koratpa* ritual I am reporting here was performed at Rangamati, Bamutia Sub-division, Tripura in 2016 and the persons performing the ritual are Nongrakpam Rohinikumar Datta as *maiba,* and two other male helpers. The spirits/gods worshipped/appeased in this ritual are:

(i) Nongsatakpam/Chandontakpam Tabet (female) as *lamsenbi* or the presiding spirit of the realm/area
(ii) *Hanubi Lai*as *khunkonbi lai* or caretaker of the village
(iii) *Umanglai* – ancestral/tutelary deities/spirits
(iv) Vishnu, the Hindu god
(v) Narottam or god of the village *mandapa* – the 15th-century Vaishnavite who preached Gaudiya Vaishnavism
(vi) *Saroi-ngaroi* – malevolent spirits/spirit mediums

The principal spirit, or rather, the main purpose of this ritual is to appease the spirit of Nongsatakpam Tabet who died first from among the settlers after they have established their village at Rangamati. The ritual was conceptualised and performed, on the lines of *lamtaiba* rituals which they were party to in Manipur, to seek blessings for a death and disease-free village. *Hanubi lai* or *khunkonbi lai* which they propitiate as the caretaker of the village is interesting because the first settlers and subsequent generations claim that such a spirit in the form of an old woman was spotted in and around the village. This could be their interpretation of the previous presiding spirit of the realm/area. There is certainly an aspect of peace offering ritual to *koratpa* in which the performers cleanse and merge the two realms and also the past and the present. This deed of giving the spirit a place in this ritual is well received and social solidarity is achieved through compensating her of any misfortune which she can cast upon the village or the community.

The third God that the Meitei Kritanias make their offerings in this ritual is Vishnu, one of the major gods in the Hindu pantheon. In *koratpa* there is always one Hindu god among other spirit mediums and He is most likely either Shiva or Vishnu. This is because Meitei Kritanias, though they were Hindus initially, were drawn into the dual religion system of Manipur. It is a legacy that they are still living with. The fourth god they must appease is Narottam who features in many of their beliefs and oral history. Narottam is the god of the village *mandapa.* Meitei Kritania *mandapa* is different from Meitei *mandapa* as their *mandapa* has no *bamon* (Brahmin). Since Narottam is the *mandapa lai,* He does not occupy a place at the ritual site. The fifth and final spirits are known as *saroi-ngarois* who are 'mischievous' spirits who are said to be the cause of misfortunes.

Offerings (*potchang-cheijang*) made to the spirits and Gods vary as they are from two different faith systems. For the *lamshenbi lai* (Nongrakpam Tabet) one portion of each of fruits, flowers, betel nut, and leaf placed on three plantain leaves of the same size are offered. *Hanubi lai* is offered one egg, fruits, flowers, betel nut, and leaf. Nine portions of flowers, fruits, *brati,* and betel nut and leaf are offered to the *umanglai.* The offerings made to Vishnu are silk thread, one nail, *brati,* fruits, flowers, betel nut and leaf, and *fola* (mashed puffed rice, milk, banana, and sweeteners). Narottam is offered fruits, flowers, betel nut and leaf, and lentil and rice cooked together (*khichadi*). Seven portions each of flowers, fruits, *brati,* and betel nut and leaf for *saroi-ngarois.*[19] Even though Manipuris follow a dual religion system they never mix gods from these two different faiths in their rituals. This secular aspect of gods from two diverse faiths being worshipped at the same spot with the same ritual is possible because both the systems are polytheistic. Offerings, especially food and flowers, are generously made to Hindu gods and the same can be said about Manipuri gods as well. The food offered to the deities/spirits is brought back and shared by the community members. The members ostensibly perceive that the food offered was accepted by the gods and by eating it (what is left by the gods) they have been blessed with their wishes. It's not just food that they share; flowers offered to the gods are also received with much devotion. They feel that they have shared what they can offer to their gods. This psychic satisfaction is obtained through the ritual in which the worldly things in the form of offerings are symbolically transported to the spirit realm and a return of the offerings is perceived. Catherine Bell contends that 'the system of offerings communicates messages about the relative status of the invisible recipient' with those who are making the offerings and this system establishes 'different relationships with the living' with the spirits concerned.[20]

Koratpa: performing the ritual

Commenting on the regenerative nature and also to liberate history from the cosmic cycles, Mircea Eliade wrote:

> It is above all an attempt to give value to history on the cosmic plane; that is, to regard historical events and catastrophes as genuine cosmic combustions or dissolutions that must periodically put an end to the universe in order to permit its regeneration. The wars, the destruction, the sufferings of history are no longer the premonitory signs of the transition from one age to another, but themselves constitute a transition.[21]

Kritanias were forced to flee Manipur along with other social groups during the Burmese invasion. Unparallelled Burmese atrocities were unleashed upon the people of Manipur, putting the realm in retrogressive chaos. Kritanias etched the trauma of war, devastation, and migration in their collective memories when they were displaced from their own homes in Manipur. *Koratpa* is one such consecrating ritual which could have been conceptualised as a ritual to defend their space from enemies and possible catastrophes brought about by war and other misfortunes and calamities. It marked a new beginning; the triumph of the protective spirits over the evil spirits. The tree where *koratpa* is performed is an old tree on the outskirt of the village. There are many nails on the tree. Each year a nail will be hammered only three times onto the trunk of the tree and a silk thread of some length would be tied to the nail. Nails correspond to the number of years since their first settlement and the silk thread formulate the image of the entire village being encircled by a sacred thread, a way of homologising the village to the sacred space that they have carried all through their journey, and also as a protection from death, disease, and misfortune.[22] The nail can also signify a ritual of construction; village, house, or community.

The day of *koratpa* is fixed on the day of *Kanglen* which normally falls in July. *Kanglen* marks the end of Rath-yatra festivities in Manipur. In the recent past, villagers participated in this ritual with much fervour and enthusiasm. They would gather at the village *mandapa* and prepare fruits, flowers, and other items to be offered to the spirits. *Wari-lairikhaiba/thiba* used to be performed before going to the spot for the *koratpa ritual.*

A small area is dug up in front of the tree where the ritual takes place. The small ditch is the space occupied by *hanubi lai.* Fruits and flowers prepared for the spirit are offered in it. The person who acts as *maiba* sits in the middle facing the tree, while his helpers are on the left and right. The *dao* used in digging up the small ditch is an important prop for the whole proceeding. After the prayers are said and offerings made to *hanubi lai,* the *dao* will draw seven semi-circle lines vertically in an upward movement. This is known as *mang thong thingba* or closing the door of the death. The seven lines represent seven days. The first line drawn is Saturday (beginning with *han*) and more lines are added up in an upward movement which finally stops on Sunday (ending with *sah*). *Hansah* could be a shortened form of *Om harim hansah* which is a Hindu mantra to prevent diseases. This mantra is on the lips of the *maiba* while drawing the lines. It would be noteworthy to mention here that one of the greatest achievements of Hinduism in Manipur is the replacement of traditional rituals by Hindu rituals in the affairs of the rites of passage.

The second *lai* to be fed is *lamsenbi lai.* The same actions of offering and closing of the death door are repeated here again. The spirit is placed at the north side of the tree as well as the performers who sit facing east. The southeast side is for the *umanglai* and offerings are made to the spirit after *lamsenbi lai*. *Saroi-ngarois* are placed at the southern side of the tree right below the space occupied by *umanglai.* Much is not said while making their offerings to *hanubi lai, lamshenbi lai* and *umanglai,* the following lines are said to appease the spirits of *saroi-ngarois* so that they do not cause any trouble to the realm:

Lamaba tumaba, lamshenba tusenba
Saroi humfumathoi, lai koti kunthrahumdoi
Nakhoi pumnamaki nafamda
Oja gurusingna piramba chakthadu
Eina gurugi tungda leiduna pirabani
Masina penbiyu
Gurugi yathangni.

[spirits of the realms, meadows and crevices, sixty-one *sarois* and all the thirty-three crore gods and goddesses, the offering made to you by my ancestors has been made by me today again, be content with this, it is the order of the *Guru*]

After saying this, the *maiba* changes his role from a shaman to that of a Hindu priest and makes his offerings to Lord Vishnu. The place for Vishnu is in between *hanubi lai* and the tree. He is last to be fed and worshipped. Except for Vishnu, all the other spirits receive the 'closing of the death door' ritual. There is no image or idol of Vishnu, His presence is only perceived. A few leaves of *tulasi* is used to sprinkle water at the spot where the presence of Vishnu is imagined. All the items prepared for Vishnu shall be placed and the *priest* places three big plantain leaves of equal size and put *fola* on it. He, then, chants the *mantra* out loud, *'Klim Krishnaya Govindaya Gopijanavallabhaya Swaha'*.[22] After this *mantra* is chanted, the priest would say the following in Manipuri:

Hey Vishnu deva
Khunsina khundarakpa matamdagee
Kalen hourakpada, oja gurusingna
Irat puja touramba matung inna

Nanai eina gurugi tungda leiduna
Puja katcharibani
Matam pumnamakta prabhuna
*Khunsi ngak*pi senbiyu
Awa anang tahanbiganu.

[Hey Vishnu deva, since the days of the first settlement, at the commencement of summer, in the way the elders have performed this ritual, I am offering you prayers, may You guard the village, and grant good health and prosperity.]

Each portion of *fola* must be eaten up by the three performers of the ritual. The two helpers now carry all the items brought from the village and leave the *maiba/*priest alone at the spot. The *maiba/*priest follows the other two towards the southern side of the tree and for once closes the door of the death by drawing seven similar lines vertically. This is the last activity at the spot. The death has been tasked to remain at the spot and never infiltrate the village. It marks the end of the ritual. *Fola* that they have kept shall be distributed and shared by the villagers with the hope that their deities have been generous and they have granted the villagers with good health, prosperity, and a peaceful realm.

Conclusion: Syncretic Prototype

The place where this ritual takes place is a prototype *umang* or *laipung* where they witnessed *lai haraoba* in Manipur – a replica of the sacred space in which existential dimensions get magnified. The presence of nature in the cosmic vision of Meiteis can be witnessed here. The tree that acts as the tree of knowledge, the tree which has witnessed the ups and downs of the village is the tree that represents immortality. The tree holds the secrets of life, life's degeneration and regeneration, its many experiences. The presence of Hindu God Vishnu in an otherwise Meitei ritual tells so much about the syncretism of the two faiths and *koratpa* could be a prime example for Hindu influences over provincial faiths and vice-versa. Interestingly, it throws some light on the assimilation of Hindu traditions in the local faith system since *koratpa* has been performing every year since the early 1830s with no or little change. Tantric, Shivite, and Vaishnavite traditions that we have been acculturated over the centuries can be found in this ritual. *Koratpa* can well be considered as a syncretic prototype – a marriage between the original (traditional) faith system and branches of Hinduism that entered Manipur right from the 15th century.

Elsewhere in the academic circles, rituals have been dissected with a new vigour from various perspectives, not as some accessory to myth but as an independent field, by anthropologists, theologians, and culturalists right from the mid-1970s. This ever-expanding field is multidisciplinary and is spread across theology, psychology, sociology, and social and cultural anthropology. Rituals are said to be a social drama, the origin of theatre, and some others see ritual as a separate entity which should be studied minus the faith system. Rituals can forge people's social identities only to be recast in less functionalist terms. They are symbolic activities which enable people to appropriate, modify, or reshape cultural values and ideals. Ritual, for the western mind, is the action, or rather 'memories encoded into actions'. The emergence of ritual as a tool to analyse cultures and certain acts as a 'universal category of human experience' began in the nineteenth century. As an independent discipline, ritual studies has been applied, as a tool, to performance studies as the primal source of present-day performances, as a tool to draw comparisons between cultures, to describe religions, and ultimately, to analyse societies and the nature of social phenomena.

For a Manipuri, a ritual is a human action that acknowledges the presence of the eternal forces of good and evil and involves subsequent appeasement of those spirits. It also signals a sense of continuity, the past merging with the present or the present trying to make sense of the past. *Koratpa* ritual still exhibits a charm, a mystery, and an interaction with the Meitei Kritanias. When the three performers return from the sacred spot, villagers would be found waiting for them so that they could share the *fola* which is one of the main offerings in the ritual. The simple joy of sharing, the joy that the spirits have been appeased, and the belief that there shall be good health and prosperity in their families all contribute to the making of this ritual more meaningful to the community. *Koratpa* is a ritual that is etched in their collective consciousness, a driving force which enabled them to move on with life in the times of trouble and displacement. With so little a population and superior language and cultures trying to swallow vulnerable cultures, I am not sure how long can the Meitei Kritanias protect their sacred space and spirit mediums. I do not know how long they can safeguard their religious and cultural heritage! In the given circumstances, I can only wish them good luck and pray to their protective spirits to protect them from misfortunes and degradation.

Notes and References

1 Edward M. Bruner. "Experience and Expression" in *The Anthropology of Experience*. Victor Turner and Edward M. Bruner (eds.). Chicago: University of Illinois, 1986, 7. Print.

2 Subsuming other groups which integrated into the Meitei-fold such as Bamons or Brahmins, Lairikyengbams and all the other small groups.

3 Aribam Chitreshwar Sharma's book *Manipur Nat Sankritan Bichar* quoted by Smt. Sorojini in Mayanglambam Gourachandra Singh's book *Lamitlon: The Manipuri Toponomy*. Kakching: Peoples' Museum, 2004, xxii. Print.

4 *Lairikyengbams* migrated to Manipur during his period. See. *Lairikyengbam lon* in ms.

5 There were three sects in this school prior to the emergence of Chaitanya. They were Madhavacharya, Nimbarka, Vishnuswami all of 13th century Bengal. See. Melville T. Kennedy. *The Chaitanya Movement: A Study of Vaishnavism in Bengal*. Calcutta: Munshiram Manoharlal Publishers Pvt Ltd, 1993. Print.

6 This stratification is based on cleansing ritual pertaining to Hindus after birth and death. High status groups do their cleansing ritual on the 11th day after a birth in the family. Surnames falling in the low status group also known as *Mikhun Kidna* do their cleansing activity on the 16th day of the same events.

7 Geertz. *NEGARA*.

8 A term borrowed from Clifford Geertz. See, Clifford Geertz. *NEGARA: Theatre State in Nineteenth Century Bali*. Princeton: Princeton University Press, 1980.

9 RandallCollins. *Interaction Ritual Chains*. Princeton: Princeton University Press, 2005, 112. Print.

10 Kanglei is a name given to the present day Imphal. It had four principal *leikais* or locality, viz. Khurai, Khwai, Yaiskul, and Wangkhei.

11 They were Khurai *ahongpung*, Wangkhei *kongba soudongpung*, Khwai *tera wangthonbi pung*, and Yaishkul *kakwa lamdaipung*.

12 *Mang thong thingba* is not an original Meitei tradition. Meiteis buried dead and this tradition was introduced by the Hindu missionaries.

13 Mircea Eliade. *The Sacred and Profane: The Nature of Religion.* Willard R. Trask (trns.). New York: A Harvest Book, ____ , 34. Print.

14 The English word portion used here is to convey the Manipuri word *tangkhra* which is a group of different items placed together on a plantain leaf neatly cut or made into a bowl

15 Catherine Bell. *Ritual: Perspectives and Dimensions.* Oxford: Oxford University Press, 1997, 68. Print.

16 Mircea Eliade. *Cosmos and History: The Myth of the Eternal return.* New York: herper Torchbooks, 1959, 136. Print.

17 It was a common practice in Burma and Manipur to guard a village or encircle the village by a sacred thread in the times of epidemic, especially cholera.

18 For better understanding of the *mantra* look up, https://gnosticteachings.org/faqs/prayers/836-klim-krishnaya-govindaya-gopijanavallabhaya-swaha.html. Accessed on 25 July, 2017.

19 Richard Schechner. *Performance Studies: An Introduction.* London: Routledge, 2013, 52. Print.

20 Catherine Bell. *Ritual Theory, Ritual Practice.* Oxford: OUP, 2009, 13. Print.

19

Challenges associated with the Adoption of E-Learning in the Educational Institutions of Arunachal Pradesh in the context of Covid-19 pandemic

— *Mr. Benny Sebastian, Dr. K. Sotechand*

Introduction

The Coronavirus pandemic, christened Covid-19, and the ensuing lockdown has forced all educational institutions across India to temporarily shut and this unprecedented move has created a breach in the education system despite the central and state government doing their best to provide support for e-learning and online education. As the lockdown associated with the persistence of 'Corona Virus' in the country continues to affect daily lives of the residents in the north eastern states, schools have been struggling to provide education and related materials to students. Needless to say, the pandemic has transformed the centuries old, chalk–talk teaching model prevalent in India, to one driven by technology and hence, there is an urgent need to address some of the basic challenges. Schools meanwhile have been gearing up with an increasingly difficult task of making learning possible among students through online networking applications like virtual class, Whatsapp and Zoom. In keeping with these national phenomena, the northeastern state of Arunachal Pradesh too has geared up for a similar initiative.

A great number of studies have been done as to whether computer-mediated education in the form of e-learning is better than traditional face-to-face teaching in relation to, for instance, learning outcome and student satisfaction. Researchers, educators and educational decision makers alike are eager to find out which format leads to the best results for their students and the educational institutions. However, as we shall see, our concern is not to debate on the advantages of one system over the other, but to examine how this new mechanism of education-distance learning tools - can be best utilized in the State of Arunachal Pradesh in the present context of the lockdown.

Keeping with the global phenomenon, in India, the ongoing technological changes have made education to transform itself from traditional Gurukul system to modern learning. When the education system undergoes major reform, the educational processes will surely pass through the same. It is the need of the hour for the educationists to introduce some innovation in the education system (Rizwana and Singh, 2016).

In this challenging process of transition from a traditional to modern perspectives of education, North East Region was seen as falling behind in quality training and absence of valuable higher instructive institutions when contrasted with different locales of India. In spite of the fact that there are a number of colleges and universities, the nature of education imparted is far from being modern. The region has been witnessing fast development of higher instructive foundations; however because of absence of consideration in methodical instructive progress, it disparaged the incentive in quality advanced education.

The study of Educational Development Index (EDI) for the whole North East shows poor to average instructive improvement with some positive signals given when some extraordinary mediation were made; however the outcomes have not generally corresponded with the endeavors put in. All things considered, however, Sarva Shiksha Abhiyan (SSA) guaranteed a great deal of expectation and assurance to many unprivileged children in the nation, North Eastern states specifically. The numerous components contributing to the region's composite EDI isn't palatable whenever contrasted with that of many other states. In order to keep in pace with the rest of the country, there is a great need to approach the entire issue of education from a technological perspective as opposed to the traditional face to face interactive learning.

Concerning approach point of view, it is to be noted that ICT (information communication technology) activities are not all that significant, yet the significant thing is how we use it. It is important that educators and partners figure out how to connect with them with suitable innovation. With ICT activities, our states can improve access, procedure and yield of our school instruction framework through meticulous execution with a base up approach. Generally, ICT has truly improved the instructive framework over the globe and more must be investigated.

The Education Technology additionally empowers instructors to incorporate venture based learning. With direction from dynamic educators, students at various levels can utilize these devices to build information and create aptitudes required in present day society. In the present time, the educator's job is that of a facilitator. The educator needs to facilitate and encourage learning by giving prominence to creative learning with access to technology. Using these learning tools the educators can discover the way to connect with the students all the more rapidly taking into consideration the requirements of each of them.

With the restrictions imposed on class room learning, it is difficult for a student to visit the institution every day to get support as available in a conventional system and at same time, it is even difficult to the institution itself to provide various services to the learners at different stages of a student learning life cycle, due to limited human resource available. Information and Communication Technology (ICT) is a prime resource to overcome such barriers. Information and communication technology is group of technologies by which various support services shall be provided at different phases of student learning life cycle using distance learning tools or online learning. Online learning is commonly defined in contradistinction to Face to Face (F2F) learning. Its most prominent feature is the absence of the physical classroom, which is replaced by the use of web-based technologies offering opportunities for out-of-class learning independent of time, place and pace (Bernard et.al., 2014)

Covid-19 has become instrumental in the adoption of this mechanism or mainstreaming of it in Arunachal Pradesh. Arunachal Pradesh education department is trying its best to deliver education to the students during this lockdown period. Speaking to All India Radio, State Education Secretary, Niharika Rai said that the department will telecast TV based online classes for classes 6 to 8 daily on DD Arunprabha Channel during the days of restrictions. She reiterated that materials for the same are being prepared in association with the teachers of Kendra Vidyalaya.

The government has recently announced that online classes have been started for classes 1-12 free of cost on the channel 'SWAYAM Prabha'. The channel offers to tutor all school-going children and cover the syllabus prescribed by NCERT through TV programmes telecast on a regular basis. The sessions have commenced from May 18, as the Chief Minister, Pema Khandu had informed. Classes are held on channel 27 Panini for secondary classes and channel 28 Sharda for senior secondary classes. The Panini channel has live programmes from 2:30 pm to 4 pm on the prescribed days while at Sharda channel, the timing is from 4 pm to 5:30 pm and another class from 5:30 pm to 7 pm.

Facilitating teaching and learning in an online environment poses a number of challenges to educators, who often struggle with adapting the practices they have found effective in F2F classes to an online environment. (Mills, 2015). However, as far as the situation in our state is concerned this is currently the best alternative as keeping schools open poses a safety risk for students. Globally, many countries have adopted this approach- online learning.

Research methodology

1. Problem statement

The impact of the spread of Corona pandemic on education sector has been significant with the disruption of academic schedules at education institutions due to suspension of classes over a prolonged period. This unplanned closure has severely affected the scheduled plans for completing courses within the academic year. The disruption in the delivery of education has obligated education institutions in the state to implement novel ways to impart knowledge to the students.

2. Objectives

2.1.: Primary Objective: The primary objective of the study is:

To examine the challenges associated with the adoption of e-learning/distance learning tools in the educational institutions of Arunachal Pradesh in the context of Covid-19.

2.2: Secondary Objectives:

(i) To study the level of the adoption of e-learning/distance learning tools in the educational institutions of Arunachal Pradesh.

(ii) To assess the attitude of students as well as teachers towards the adoption of e-learning/distance learning tools in the educational institutions of the state.

3. Scope of the study

The study aims to examine academics' perspectives and perceptions with regard to the challenges associated with the implementation of distance learning initiatives in the educational institutions of Arunachal Pradesh in the context of the lockdown compelled by the corona pandemic.

Challenges

No doubt, the transition to online learning due to COVID-19 was sudden and hasty. The disruptive decision to introduce online learning in schools during lockdown might have come as a shock to many. Therefore, the teachers as well as students had to gear up to adapt themselves to a new pattern of learning process. We will now examine the key constraints and challenges for education institutions, students and teachers in implementing this initiative.

1. **Connectivity:** For holding online classes, the teacher as well as participating students need internet connectivity at their homes. The report, titled "Covid-19: A wake up call for telecom service providers", pointed out that connectivity and signal issues are the prevailing problems students face while attending online classes. In many places, even regular supply of electricity is not available. Moreover, most Indians can't afford

a basic gadget to access online education. Some are of the opinion that online education can only be provided at the advanced level in certain research subjects for students in universities. India has a long way to go before e-learning becomes viable for all.

The quality of connectivity in terms of broadband/ Wi-Fi strength is important in the case of online services to be used. In the midst of the current disruptive situation, it has become difficult for most education institutions to leverage the offerings of education technology companies and implement remote and virtual learning given that students may have accessibility challenges in terms of devices, connectivity, etc. "We wanted to conduct regular online classes but most of our students are from marginal families and they don't have internet connections," said Sr. Shalini Greta, Headmistress of St. Mary's School, Namsai.

2. **Affordability:** Making virtual learning or distance learning work for all students is challenging. You can have all the best tools in place, but without equitable access at home for all your students it's tough to replicate a traditional, in-person learning experience. To access online classes, both teachers and students need to have devices like laptops/ desktops, smart phones or tablets. Access to devices, especially for children is dependent on the economic status of their families.

   Only a handful of private schools could adopt online teaching methods. Their low-income private and government school counterparts, on the other hand, have been compelled to choose alternatives for having access to e-learning solutions. When contacted a government teacher, this is what she had to say: "I teach in a college where many are first-generation learners, coming from low-income households, who don't have devices with advanced storage capacity. Now, I hear some teachers are holding Zoom classes and that sounds lovely in elite institutions. But my realities are different considering the students I teach."

3. **Lack of Adequate training:** Online teaching requires distinct skill sets that are not part of teacher training curriculum.

Teachers conducting on-line classes need to have the requisite training as it goes beyond replicating classroom teaching in a virtual medium. In the classroom, the teacher has visibility of all students and through their body language can assess their level of concentration and understanding, which enables course correction during lesson delivery itself. In conducting classes online, such visibility is not there and it is likely that only some proactive students will benefit from participating as compared to the reserved and not so bright students. In conducting on-line classes, teachers will be required to re-orient their lesson delivery techniques by introducing frequent assessments to understand the pace of learning of all students. The truth is that many of our teachers are not adequately trained to operate the related gadgets or to utilize this mechanism properly without the assistance of a third person.

4. **Language barriers:** There are bigger problems to solve. Adapting to online education is easier for English medium students and teachers due to ready availability of tools or content. The situation is grim when it comes to schools which employ local dialects or vernaculars. However, the state is in no position to deploy different modes of learning in vernacular as it cannot claim to have a common vernacular that could be used as a medium of instruction among all the communities that inhabit the land. Over and above, English has not penetrated the interior villages as a common medium of communication or instruction.
5. **Exertion on Parents:** The schools provide the students with worksheets, study routine, appropriate lessons and crafts ideas on line. In order to support this distance learning method particularly in the case of kids of lower classes, parents are required to be equally active and enthusiastic on the other side to help teachers track their progress. Children require the help of their parents or elders to help them operate these learning tools. "It might be a new experience and fun way for the kids to learn in a different environment in a different way," stated Yami Juja, teacher of a private school in Miao. But how are those parents who have not earned a qualification to assist their children in need.

6. **Multiple board system:** In the absence of a comprehensive action plan, for our complex school education system — divided by multiple boards of unequal standards — the benefits of technology will profit only a section of teachers and students that adapts to technology and can afford it. The government mechanism is now in no way equipped d to coordinate all the various education boards to draw up an ample alternative to resolve the present crisis.
7. **Heavy Schedule:** Many students acknowledged that weak persistence in online learning seriously restricted their learning effectiveness. Students reported the home-learning program to be even more stressful than regular classrooms. Some of the common reasons for this went along the lines of: "Normal classes may have been difficult, but having friends makes it so much more manageable and less stressful. Online classes take out the benefits of having friends to socialize with and being stuck alone with nothing but assignments."

   Many students participating in home-learning programs also say that the workload of online classes is larger than that of regular classes. The general consensus is that home-learning programs — although highly beneficial and a good alternative to school as schools are closed — still require some getting used to by students, as it is a novel concept and not many are experienced with them.

Findings

The challenges mentioned above would be true of many states across the country holding exception of a few. The northeastern states and Arunachal Pradesh in particular has a long way to go in this process of tech-mediated teaching and learning.

1. A major problem of concern for students and parents in the state is the lack of network coverage in some remote areas of all the districts. With a tough typography of the Himalayan state, some regions have minimum connectivity with rest of the state —roadways or internet. Besides, interior village schools are yet to get regular supply of electricity without

which many of these gadgets and systems would simply be useless.

2. It has been observed that this mechanism of shifting classes to virtual platforms is largely being adopted by institutions in urban areas catering to affluent sections of society and sometimes additional fees are being charged to cover the subscription and set up costs.
3. In addition, based on an analysis of students' responses as well that of a few teachers the author was able to contact over phone, the challenges for students did not come from technical operational obstacles. Instead, they have difficulties due to the lack of a good learning attitude. Students often have problems such as lack of self-discipline, suitable learning materials, or good learning environments when they are self-isolated at home.
4. As of now, the online education sector currently is not guided by any standard norms or regulations by the government. Further, the definition and framework of online education is lacking and in some cases online education even includes teachers sharing worksheets and study material on WhatsApp and training sessions on Skype. Students are confused as to which learning tool would best suit them.
5. The initiative introduced by the state government is yet to yield the expected results as many of the teachers in our schools express reluctance to operate the related gadgets as they have not been adequately trained to handle them.
6. As we appreciate the initiative taken by Arunachal Pradesh education department in trying to deliver education to the students during this lockdown period offering free classes to cover NCERT syllabus through Swayam Prabha TV, one wonders if the teachers and students in the interior schools are in the knowhow of it. An evident lack of active academic involvement on the part of both the school authorities as well as students has been witnessed.

Suggestions

1. For students without access to technology or connectivity, the

television and radio programming initiated can be supplemented a mobile library where books of the prescribed syllabus and other books can be provided/exchanged/donated to the students in respective areas like ration system.

2. For wider acceptance of such online courses across the state, content has to be developed in Hindi or other vernacular languages.
3. Since all the courses were switched to online education mode, the computer servers may not be able to host such a large scale of new users; the online education platform may often shut down because of overload. In order to solve all kinds of unexpected issues, teachers can prepare alternative plans before classes start and inform students in advance.
4. In order to ensure that students concentrate on online study, faculty should reasonably break down the content into different topics and adopt a modular teaching method. In other words, on the basis of ensuring a clear knowledge structure in the curriculum, faculty divide the teaching content into several small modules with each lasting approximately 20–25min.
5. It is suggested that the government provide the students free internet services or recharge their phones with data during online interaction classes.
6. It is an urgent priority for the government to regularize the online education sector and define standards and regulations for it. There is a need for monitoring the online mechanism as many companies take advantage of the situation and demand exorbitant amount for providing these services.
7. This is definitely a time when there must emerge a sense of solidarity among various schools in each locality. The schools that have proper infrastructure and related facilities for online learning must accommodate students of other needy schools in the locality and provide them with opportunities to be benefited by the same.
8. One of the major concerns observed was the lack of adequate training for teachers. A course on techniques of networking or training that enhances practical knowledge to handle distance

learning tools ought to be integrated into the curriculum of the teacher training program.

To add on to this, however, the government should still have more offline options for students without internet access, such as the distribution of books and learning materials.

Conclusion

The sudden, forced immersion of learners into virtual learning or distance learning during this period of Covid-19 has proved that the education industry is disrupted. The undeniable truth is that a crisis has occurred in education sector all over the world. The implementation of well designed alternative learning methodology seems to be an option before every country. The aligned anxiety among parents and students needs to be relieved by ensuring that students actively and effectively engage in continued learning. Education is going to be digital in the foreseeable future and with the right infrastructure and policies in place, we would be better prepared to handle it. Laxity in timely intervention in adopting alternatives to impart knowledge might find the state wanting. In view of the extraordinarily large scale of online education, it is necessary to make contingency plans in advance for addressing possible problems associated with the issue of the online education platform.

The challenge before our government is to overcome the learning crisis we are already living with and respond to the pandemic we are all facing. As we cope with this situation think of creative ways to reduce as much as possible the negative impact this pandemic will have on learning and schooling and build on this experience to get back on a path of faster improvement in learning. This catastrophe is to be seen as opportunity to recover stronger, with a renewed sense of responsibility and a better understanding of the situation. However, only time will tell whether online classes will be a good substitute for normal classes.

References

Bernard, M. B., Borokhovski, E., Schmid, R. F., Tamim, R. M. and Abrami, Ph. C., 2014. A meta-analysis of blended learning and technology use in higher education: from the general to the applied. Journal of Computing in Higher Education, 26(1), pp. 87-122.

Mills, J., 2015. A Conceptual Framework for Teaching Statistics from a Distance. The Journal of Effective Teaching. Vol. 15(1), pp. 59-68.

M., Dr. Rizwana and Singh, Padmilini (2016). Students' Attitude towards E-learning: A study with reference to pg students. International Journal of Multidisciplinary Research and Development. 3(3).

Websites:

1. https://www.researchgate.net/publication/274925552_Higher_Education_ Scenario of the North-Eastern India
2. https://www.ijmra.us/project%20doc/2019/IJRSS_MAY2019/IJMRA-15532.pdf
3. https://www.ncert.nic.in/publication/journals/pdf_files/ijet/jan19/ijet_jan19.pdf
4. https://www.ipedr.com/vol79/002-IC4E2014-1-003.pdf
5. https://indianexpress.com/.../education/arunachal-pradesh-offers-free-classes-to-cover-ncert-syllabus-through-swayam-prabha-tv-6412666/

20

Human Security amid COVID-19: Chain of events in Northeast

— *Dr Ingudam Yaipharemba Singh*

Introduction

The COVID-19 outbreak creates tremendous critical situations among the people who work for a living and the concern of human security become more important at this time of crisis. Northeast India contributes a large number of casual workers to metropolitan cities such as Bangalore, Delhi, Kolkata, Hyderabad and from states such as Tamil Nadu, Gujarat etc. Every aspect of the mass movement leads to a delicate situation of human crisis and security aspect economically and socially of the northeastern people. The exodus facilitated by the government brings relief for the natives but losing their earning is a big burden which always looms ahead and the uncertainty whether they will regain the employment after how much period is a major concerned. The double blow of pandemic and financial insecurity is very much for the workers. Everything translates to the approaches of the human security paradigm and solving it will be a big issue both for the respective state governments and the individual's altogether.

Amid the nationwide lockdown, many northeastern people are requesting the respective state governments to arrange some sort of transport to bring them back from other cities of India. When Shramik train started students, workers, and others started to return including some medical staffs such as nurses are coming back due to the work pressure, ineffective incentive and lack of protective gear for them in addition to racial discrimination. Every problem leads to a negative side of human relations and connectivity amid the outbreak in the workplace and living space also. The very nature of the outbreak reveals the basic importance of individuals and human safeguard is of prime significance. In an aspect of containing individuals, the security of human from the invisible fatal enemy is emerging as a challenge due to various dilemmas of human needs and wants.

Human security is about the physical and emotional needs. The very concept of Human security focuses on three fundamental ideas; *first*, it focuses on traumatic areas such as mental, physical or social dimensions of individuals; *second*, beneficiary focused aid and *third* is evidence-informed policymaking through a human security lens. The different impact of the pandemic, government, international organisations, civil society organisations, private sector and the public continues to respond to the challenge applying comprehensive and multidimensional human security-centric approaches remains crucial to lessen the spread of the coronavirus and to reduce death rates. Government need to collaborate responsibly and take necessary precautions need to avoid fear, panic, fake news and overreaction mindful of the most vulnerable populations of the country who cannot take safety measures without the assistance of the government. Various sectors involved to avoid contributing to spreading any misinformation or encouraging non-compliance with legitimate public health directives during the critical time of the outbreak. Human security approaches is a promising way forward at a national and regional scale. It is the basic understanding the human security paradigm can contribute to face the pandemic. It is the high time for unity nationally and regionally avoiding misunderstanding and directing all available resources to fight and contain the virus to protect every individual. The containment of the virus is in two fronts; one is to take measure to stop the spread of the virus within the population resulting into a series of the governmental lockdown and another to contain any human carrier of the virus after the government allowed migrant carrying vehicles to enter respective states passing another region. Both the fronts are massive and required extensive human resources in large scale due to the numbers of native people returning to the respective state. Northeast states face the challenge of bringing back the native people from other states including red zone declared region and when everything becomes limited, students, and workers like everyone else face the heat. Thousands of northeast students are studying in different colleges and universities all over India and the respective state government facilitate their return. The government felt the responsibility and cater to available resources to bring back the individuals whoever want to come back. Therefore, the process started keeping in view the significance of human security. Protection of individual is the basis of the bringing back mission amid the challenges. The Government is doing whatever necessary from arranging special trains for the returnees to providing an essential quota of rations including monetary subsidies to the neediest. The efforts of the government and related authorities to ease the plights of the people are astonishing. Governmental will in containing the outbreak through every aspects are very positive and worthy.

Looming factors

The COVID -19 outbreak did bring out a fundamental factor of protecting the individual from disaster whether natural or manmade that claims thousands of lives. A human being is so much vulnerable at this pandemic that maintaining social distance is very much necessary to beat the virus. When the outbreak happens even the mightiest fall and the effect are felt every nook and corner without caste, creed and colour. A host of issues are emerging. Northeast region got consumed in the outbreak with hundreds being treated with the coronavirus. The outbreak exposes the nature of vulnerability and the shadow-effect of it. The exodus from other parts of the country proves the criticality of human security in terms of economic, social, mental and physical. The pandemic is a public health emergency, but it is far more than that. It is an economic crisis, a social crisis and a humanitarian crisis that is fast becoming a human rights crisis.[1]

The economic and social impacts of the pandemic are and would be of an unprecedented scale and only a few short months into the crisis the impact is already staggering in the country. Primarily necessary lockdown measures are affecting worker's livelihood and businesses are facing a loss of revenues resulting in income losses. All societies who are marginalised and faced difficulties, many of the people are most severely impacted by the crisis and other challenges in a daily struggle to survive. The impact on the poorest population level the pandemic has been most devastating for the health and well being of the people with medical conditions such as disabilities, pregnant women, terminal ailments, old aged and with lower socio-economic status.

Thousands of workers of northeast origin are working in different sectors across India. Establishments such as gyms, spas, restaurants, shopping malls and textile and garment industries were the main employers and also the worst-hit sectors due to the lockdown. Shopping malls employed north-easterners as security guards and for other security purposes. Private hospitals employed nurses and other medical attendants from this part of the country. South Indian textile and garment units employed people from the northeast in large scale. Altogether, many people are working in different organised and unorganised sectors. But, many of the establishment closed down since Lockdown 1.0 and do not hurry to resume its business as major metropolitan cities are in red zone category and high risk of contamination. The migrants work in insecure conditions and are dependent on their employers, who provide necessary lodging and food supply. The workers live in accommodation either owned or rented by the employers in groups. Shortly, the migrants are solely dependent on their employers for every necessity. At the time of total lockdown, not getting of essential food items is a huge problem leading to more problems. During normal times the casual workers can send some amount of money to their family back home; this luxury is also get deleted due to the stoppage of work and non-getting of salary.

Due to the pandemic and lockdowns, the workers including families are left with little access to money and food and struggled to go home. They are in dilemma that returning to their homes means fewer job opportunities, but also confident that they can expect some form of earning. The demand for a job will be much higher so do the unemployment rate. This will create a cross crisis of livelihood and lost income generation impacting majorly on human security perspective. The concerned about future employment opportunities is a looming issue, thus, leading to financial loss and poverty. Most of the workers cannot work remotely and there are businesses which have to operate physically and the customers cannot come for purchasing also. For the time being, they are out of jobs and incredibly important to provide some kind of unemployment aid to the marginal workers to keep them afloat during the pandemic. Similarly, providing aid to the businesses establishment to keep them afloat when everything dies down the workers can come back and resumed its active duty.

The Ministry of Statistics and Programme Implementation's Report on Periodic Labour Force Survey for 2017-2018, Government of India concluded that the unemployment rate crossed 5 percent in six northeastern states. Different states show varying magnitude, Nagaland with 21.4 percent unemployment is highest, Manipur with 11.5 percent, 10.1 percent in Mizoram, 7.9 percent in Assam, 6.8 percent in Tripura and 5.8 percent in Arunachal Pradesh. The unemployment rates most likely rise after the lockdown was announced. According to a report by the Centre for Monitoring Indian Economy, as of April 2020, 122 million people had lost their jobs the last year. While the nationwide unemployment rate was 23.5 percent in April 2020, by 3 May, it had risen to 27.1 per cent. The rates are bound to increase in the northeast plagued by numerous critical issues. The report also further argued that small traders, wage labourers, unorganised sectors are the worst-hit area.[2] The returnee will be staying at the respective state for some time as the pandemic is in its peak and as no question of the workplace and other sectors resuming its function, the worker will not be returning soon. It will be a big challenge for the state government to provide continuous financial aid until everything comes to normal otherwise may lead to social unrest. And if the worker didn't go back it will create a labour vacuum in the host state also. Therefore, it is a double dilemma of the unemployment crisis in native states and the creation of labour vacuum in host states.

Amid the pandemic, one situation makes news in Kolkata related to health care when more than 300 plus Manipuri nurses came back[3] abruptly citing various reasons ranging from personnel safety owing to non-availability of PPE, N95 masks, unregulated working schedule plus quarantine procedure, lack of essential commodities, non-getting of salary and instances of racial discrimination at both at work and lodging places. Rent owners denied rooms; the localities are harassing and abusing the nurses by calling names as they work at ground zero. It is a big pressure mentally and physically during the pandemic being a frontline worker. The event is a clear cut case of both clinical and non-clinical discrimination. This is a critical matter in stabilising the returnee for job losses, the uncertainty of joining back while balancing with professional ethics. The receiving state will not be in a position to compensate them, thus creating a niche in the financial insecurity and self-dignity.

Conclusion

It is common knowledge that the hardest hit is the informal workers. The pandemic consumed the livelihood of many without immediate solutions and for some time it will continue to do so. Workers from Northeast are returning to the native state amid the pandemic empty hand. Many of them are not sure when the workplace will open again and resumed their duty.

By and large, the human security approach is a tool to help us understand and tackle today's multi-dimensional challenges in an integrated manner. The government recognised the right of people to live free from fear, want and indignity with equal opportunities to develop their potential. It is only when these rights are met that people begin to feel safe in all aspects of their lives and enjoy human security. During this pandemic, insecurities have multiple dimensions especially food, health, economic and personal, community and political each presents its own set of challenges in the northeast as well as anywhere else in the country, but for people in crisis acting on a single issue is not enough. Insecurities such as job loss, financial loss etc must be tackled together comprehensively. It is better to understand multiple factors are interconnected and mutually reinforcing. The outbreak exposed many people to vulnerability and worsening poverty, short of food and exposed to health crisis leading to personal safety. By viewing these complex challenges, the human security approach is the solutions that are people-centred comprehensive context-specific and prevention-oriented. This strengthens the protection and empowerment of people, communities and addresses the root causes of insecurities helping in minimizing the discrepancies in peace development and personal safety in this part of the region. Achieving human security amid COVID-19 starts with the needs and challenges of the common people. Any approach must engage closely with individuals to investigate vulnerabilities and set priorities during this pandemic and develop effective strategies to tackle insecurity.

The key impact on societies is primarily the pandemic which put a heavy burden to the marginalised section. The burden will be much heavier among the vulnerable section of the society and it is a serious concern on the human security front. The humanitarian system has to find a way to be responding and it is very difficult due to the prevailing situation, but, has to make way to ramp up the humanitarian efforts in a lot of ways. In longer-term looking at this crisis, what has the pandemic told us about ourselves and it is, unfortunately, our societies are not very resilient. We have to well set up for handling the kind of pressure and while the pressure from a pandemic is very particular.

The good words of Antonio Guterres, Secretary-General of the United Nations will be perfect in understanding the response to the pandemic. *"The best response is one that responds proportionately to immediate threats while protecting human rights and the rule of law. Looking ahead, we need to build back better. Strengthening economic and social rights bolsters resilience for the long haul. We are all in this together. The virus threatens everyone. Human rights uplift everyone. By respecting human rights in this time of crisis, we will build more effective and inclusive solutions for the emergency of today and the recovery for tomorrow"*.[4]

References

1. António Guterres. 23 April 2022. We are all in this Together: Human Rights and COVID-19 Response and Recovery. *United Nations Covid-19 Response*. Retrieved from https://www.un.org
2. Kimi Colney. May 19, 2020. Migrants from the northeast are stuck between hostile employers and unemployment at home. *The Caravan*. Retrieved from https://caravanmagazine.in
3. Atri Mitra. 20 May 2020. No pay, heckling: 300 nurses leave Kolkata hospitals, go back to Manipur. *The Indian Express*. Retrieved from https://indianexpress.com
4. António Guterres. 23 April 2022. *We are all in this Together: Human Rights and COVID-19 Response and Recovery. op.cit*. p. 1.

21

New media and the changing dynamics of media education: De-generalisation of the pedagogy

— *Sunil Koijam, Gautam Huidrom*

Introduction

The so called media capital of the country, New Delhi alone houses more than 70% of the headquarters of various media organisations. These lead to the natural choice of many media institutions establishing their centre in the capital. Apart from a few government run universities and colleges, almost at every nook and corner of the state, we find a media institute promising high end jobs in media industry. The industry is lately becoming so glamorous in nature that it also naturally attracting young talents. Who doesn't want to come on the screen with good make up and control over the subject?

With the medium changing, the dissemination of ideas too changes. The audience changes, it calls to the need of the changes in the content too. We can see that through the history. In the eighteenth century, the British popular press was obsessed with blood and sex, low life, mass slaughter and the scandalous activities of the elite' (Jackie Harrison : 206:55). The level of journalism has a swing every time the tide changes. It will not wrong to say that "journalism has been treated as "an engine for turning everything into a cliché." (Minogue 1997:7). Especially the younger generation is not interested in the political administration and politics of the country. Their detestation for the political class has been responsible for a paradigm shift in the attitude of the press—from the obsession of politics to the Page 3 syndrome (Nagaraj, K V: 2010).

The integration of new media in the medium is redefining the world of human communication in general and mass communication in particular. It is giving us new opportunities to learn and live life all together in a newer environment. The click of a mouse or a touch in your smart screen of your mobile is taking us in a whole new level of interactive understanding of things. It is changing us in every aspect. If we look into the youth's participation in electoral politics, a study done by Dalton, found out that the rapid growth of Internet use and the alleged declining levels of political involvement of younger people have made the relationship between these two a popular and much debated issue. New media may well challenge the role or fill some of the gap left by traditionally strong socializers such as family, church, and school. Especially, the role played by parents for their children as key socializers with regard to politics is changing. In the past decades, trends of increasing individualization and volatile electoral behaviour are observed (Dalton, 2002).

At the same time, it is also empowering every individual to take their own decision. Decisions which are playing a major role in shaping up the present social system. Irrespective of the various changes in the social and political landscape on both international and national levels during the last decades, the significance of participatory behaviour of citizens is at the core in several key works on democracy (e.g., Held, 2006). The very nuances of social responsibility is increasingly been redefined as all of them are given the opportunity to speak out their mind at the right time and right platform. India's new government initiatives like the "Swatch Bharat Abhiyan", digital and financial inclusion like the "Jan Dhan Account" and "Digital India: Start Up India" are some the path defining ideas. But India being a pluralistic country, with diverse languages and culture, with various belief system and practices, the messenger and the one training the messenger has to be very careful. The Northeast of India constitutes more than 140 tribes with their unique culture and identity. Each community has its own social setups which is the backbone of its survival also. Many of the tribes do have their special way of community communication which is exceptional in itself. So the system cannot be just painted on a single large canvas with a single colour; rather the need is to re-contextualise it with their respective ethos. Deconstruct and construct to suits to its ever growing demands and understandings.

The premises

Media institutions were set up to bridge the gap of demand of professionals who can work to strengthen the fourth pillar. The classical debate of whether media person has inborn qualities to be a professional or whether the requisite skills has to be acquired by a proper training is still out there large and open. Yet, the coming up of such institutions which has a place for proper skill training only add up only to believe that it has some role to play. The design of the syllabus become important in not only sustaining its credibility but also in enhancing the academic and the research related to the subject. With the fast changing environment, it only adds up in bringing more challenges. The changing technology vis-à-vis new media demands for alternative learning avenues apart from the classical classroom scenario. Peer learning, group dynamics and other experimentation are very familiar exercises that many uses nowadays. The challenges are to understand the genuineness of an event and its associated story. The existing knowledge system has to be constantly upgraded or the question of its survival is in question. This ultimately creates disconnect in the field which may leads to many uncertainties. These uncertainties are to be addressed well on time. A shift in the way the pedagogies are designed has to be given due emphasis. Classroom teaching is more or less redundant in today's context and it has to be upgraded. Smart teaching atmosphere with modern teaching aids are in the market nowadays. This has to be supplemented with systematic up gradation of the skills requirements.

Understanding of the various social media platform which is more playing an important role in media culture is very necessary. The rise of many Youtube channels and other online media platform which are dedicated to only news and current affairs is an important area of study in this context. The running costs of such channels are very cheap compared to the satellite channels but catering the news at the local and to the ground level; it is giving a run for money to those established media houses. Most of the small towns in the region have more or less than 4-5 such digital media houses that cover at the state level. In this era of breaking news and who gives you the first hand information, the crazy race for covering exclusives is making all hell loose. These in turn makes the contents of their theoretical studies of news a new meaning.

Commodification of media education

As its true in all business, the success of a product depends on its design and its appeals, media education in present context, is also successfully being branded. People are looking more on the glamour side of the profession. Taking advantage of it, some institutes charges heavy sum of money per course. Admission to such seats sells like hot cakes. The infrastructure and the required resources may not be there but there is mad rush to such institutes. The placement ratio is always in question. If placed also, how much is the retention ratio by those media organisation and how many left mid-way in the career is also a big question. It is also interesting to know that most of the media houses also run a media institute which only helps in attracting raw talents. With the kind of pay check one gets in such industry, and the kind of networking one's enjoys; students also shell out huge amount in taking admission. The credibility of such institutions is always in question, but all went well as it goes well. The mad rush for admission is never ending.

Mainstream media and new media

The theoretical understanding of the subject should be coupled with proper uses of the newer medium. The challenges for this are fast changing, so should our education be. The structure should be made such that it's encouraging. Orientation and workshop of the subject concerned should be deliberated more often. Media studies requires great amount of specialization in the area in which one is venturing into. Talk about politics, enough macro specialization is there, it may be one party reporting, parliament reporting, election reporting, sports, business, lifestyle etc etc. There is enough for everyone. The need is the calibration of the professional involved with the right kind of skills and the right kind of media. For any mainstream media, it's to somewhat manageable; but for the newer media, anything can be blown out of proposition. The kind of credibility one has to possess is always questionable. Objectivity as we all calls, loose in the chaos. The intended message may not be always the received message.

The undercurrent media, as they call it is also making it presence felt. This alternative form of media is creating waves in the new media platform. Social networking sites, blogs and video blogs offers such media a space to speak out their mind. It's more of understanding the digital media literacy and the time to rethink its education in the current internet age. (Buckingham, 2007). The content in these sites sometimes clears off the doubt we always have in the presentation by the mainstream media. The general notion is changing regarding the authenticity of information. The challenging part is to read between the lines. In this scenario, not only the training for the messenger is required but also the literacy of the media for the general mass is vital. The two side of the coin need to be equally polished.

Understanding the context

As changes happen in all walks of life, so do the participation and practice of media education should also change. Right now, it's too much in the plate. The media institute should identify and start categorising the priorities. It's not always a packed deal as it was from the beginning, but the space for creative output should be kept. The various medium has its own importance. The folk media and the traditional media which was put into the cold storage are significantly being used in the present context. The contemporary media like the TV and Radio is becoming old fashion, the newer media like the internet and social media is happening. It's not that everything is hunky-dory, it's important to understand thing in their context. The most popular consumer auction site eBay (Lucking-Reiley, 2000) has localized Web sites with the same rules, regulations, and structural features in more than 20 countries. These standardized Web sites present an excellent world laboratory (Danowski, 2001) to test cross cultural differences. The multiple specialisations in various layers of understanding the context to which the targeted audience wants are the norm of the day. In this, the board of studies are in constant look out for creating new niche markets and also categories the newer understandings. This makes the area of studies ever expanding and ever evolving. There is an important link of understanding between the media education and media literacy. (Fedorov, 2015). This calls for how media education and literacy corresponds to the socio-cultural aspects of different countries.

Glocal and the ethics of reality

The world has converged into one global village, and no one can escape from the reality. Everyone has to think global but your local content should not be compromised. We are all living in a world of connected networks, anything that happens in one corner is easily been pick up by another. This is also an opportunity as well as a challenge especially to a developing nation like India. With the diverse background, the ethical issue is always been in the limelight. The media scape keeps on changing. More pressure are amounted to the media persons, more responsibility is garnered to the institutions that are fulfilling those requirements. There should be complete blend of time proof traditional practice and modern experimental outlook. The content, the technology which is converged should be seamlessly catered to the mass with the right amount of ethicality. The syllabus content of the institutes in the last few decades has changed dramatically. One unique pattern that we can see is the constant up gradation of the practical oriented paper which includes television, radio and their production. There is a quantum changes in the areas of new media and digital media studies. The concept of de-westernisation can be felt, with the growing numbers of papers on development for change as a core paper and specialised exercise. The rise can be seen from a simple journalism course to multi masters' programme not only in journalism but also in all other form of media. The board of studies are strengthened with the entry of media professional working in the field to bride that divide and it's a good beginning.

Summary

Media education and the educators are here to stay. It's on to the stakeholders that the stream of study is categorically well defined and updated. As the study is so interdisciplinary in nature, the outlook has to be larger. It is affecting every individual including the one in the last mile. The change is evident of the fact that the growth is there. It is with these growing changes, the institutes have to be prepared for. It calls for a proper research and training with proper guidance. The Northeast part of India has to really push themselves up with the understanding that it's not a race to finish rather it's creating a level playing field for everyone who is making up the society. With a credible and efficient media, the society is bound to grow.

References

Angela Cora Garcia & Alecea I. Standlee & Jennifer Bechkoff & Yan Cui, (2009), "*Ethnographic Approaches to the Internet and Computer-mediated Communication*" SAGE Publications Ltd.

Buckingham, D. (2007). Digital Media Literacies/: rethinking. *Research in Comparative and International Education*, *2*(1), 43–55. https://doi.org/10.2304/rcie.2007.2.1.43

Creeber, G., & Martin, R. (2008). *Digital Culture: Understanding New Media: Understanding New Media*. McGraw-Hill Education (UK).

Cohen, J. and Young, S. (eds) (1973), *The Manufacture of the News,* London: Constable.

Conlin, M. and Park, A. (2004), *"Blogging with the Boss's Blessing*," Business Week, (June 28), pp. 96-98.

Fedorov, A. (2015). Media Education and Media Literacy: Expertss Opinions. *SSRN Electronic Journal*, *2003* (March), 1–18. https://doi.org/10.2139/ssrn.2626372

Gillmor, D. (2004), We the Media: Grassroots Journalism by the People For the People. O'Reilly Media.

Harrison, J (2006), *News,* London: Routledge.Mc Manus, J H (1994), *Market-driven Journalism: Let the Citizen Beware?* Thousand Oaks, C A: Sage.

Philipsen, G. (1992). *Speaking culturally: Explorations in social communication*. Albany: State University of New York Press.

22

An Understanding towards Reconstructing Iron and Brass Metal Technologies of the Early Konyak and Khiamniungan Nagas

— *Tiatemjen Tzudir*

Introduction

Planet earth has endowed mankind with diverse minerals which they discovered in rock forms particularly identified more so for its uniquely classified physical structures, diaphaneis, luster and colors. Metals are usually found in mineral state. Procurement of metals from such minerals require extractive methods which allows varied oxides content to get eliminate so as to receive its original pure metallic state. Such metallic practices were initially applied mainly to non-ferrous metals before their discovery to ferrous metal in the form of iron. Iron as an elemental substance is basically brittle and hard and in its purest state can rapidly corrode when exposed to moist air and temperature. Claimants of historians on Iron Age probably began between 1400/ 1500 B.C and 1000 B.C according to certain parts of the world with reference made to the Hittites of Anatolia (Turkey) from Mesopotamia who seemed to have first harvested/hunted iron in the form of meteorites and used it for making weapons and ornaments around the late Bronze Age (Hummel 1998:123) up till the Chalcolithic. In India the discovery

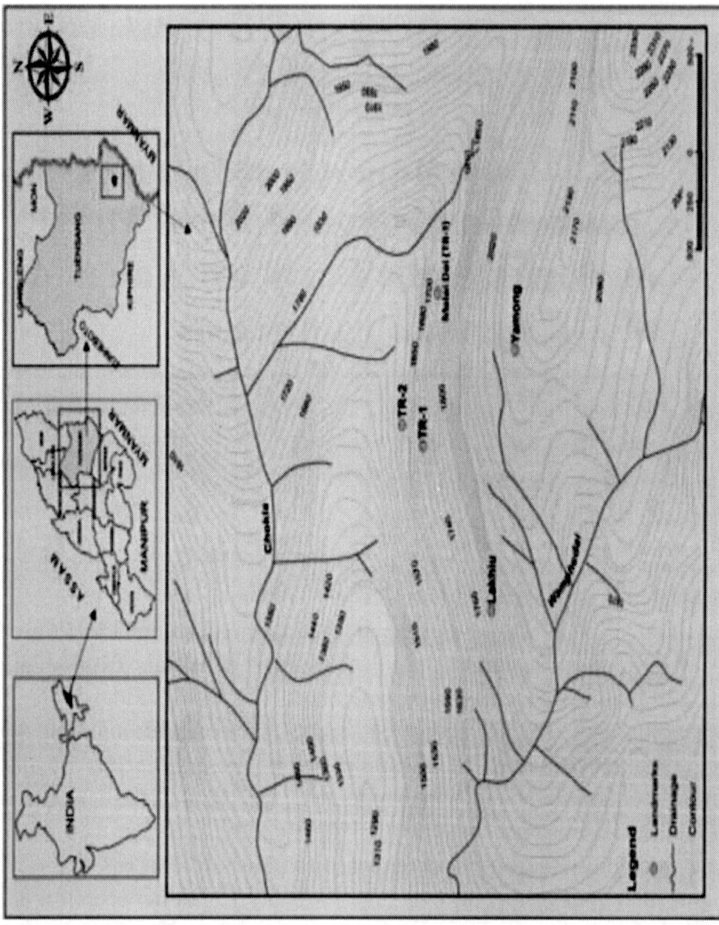
INDIA
ASSAM
MANIPUR
TR-2
TR-1
Yamong
Legend

and use of iron started around 1200 B.C. that indigenously and independently in at least three nuclear zones namely Karnataka in the south, U.P.- Rajasthgan in the north, and West Bengal-Bihar area in the north-east (Prakash and Tripathi 1986: 568-579). According to scientists when in reference to Myanmar their Bronze Age appeared around 1500 BC with the arrival of iron around 500BC. However around Myanmar, old iron furnaces at Konzin, east of Sriksetra are said to be found with remains of clay tuyere surrounded by lumps of hematite reddish brown clays. In fact Furnace excavated at Zi-o village was dated around between 1500 and 1800 AD. Only 800 or so furnaces at Myanmar has been dated so far where furnaces found outside Sriksetra were of simpler shape that likely suggests to be much older model in comparison to Zi-o. There has been history of iron in North east India that has an influence from neighboring areas with the techno-cultural progress in upper Burma mainly associated to the Singphos and the Khamptis who migrated and settled in the eastern part of Arunachal Pradesh are known for the use of metal including iron in the area (Leach 1970). Also through the radiocarbon datingof charcoal on iron slag reveals evidence on continuous iron smelting in the Khasi Hills, Meghalaya, spanning the last two millennia dated to 2040 ± 80 years BP (353 BC–AD 128) (Suliga & Prokop, 2013). There are natural availability of iron mixed clay *(lao-mati)* and iron (*lo*) in Doiyang Dhansiri valley and the existence of process of smelting of iron at Bassapathar, Doiyang, Dhekial, Kamargaon, Komarbandha, Hamdai and at some other places support the view about the growth of native production and trade in iron since early Christian era in Assam (Dutta 2012: 22, 23, 25, 122, 125 and 127). While these findings confirmed the use of iron in few areas of Northeast India in the prehistoric period, scientific studies on such materials remains greatly wanting.

Nagaland in comparison to other crafts, no demonstrable evidence on the technology of iron smelting is reported by the early explorers and ethnographers to the Naga Hills. Other notable ethnographers like J.P. Mills (1922, 1926 and 1937) and the renowned Austrian ethnologist Fürer-Haimendorf (1939, 1969 and 1976) who worked extensively among the Konyak Nagas failed to make any notes on the practice of iron smelting among the Naga tribes. Howeve rearly Konyak and Khiamiunagans Nagas and their relations with both iron and brass likely began with their gain of knowledge and understanding towards pyrotechnology which considerably helped them to be skilled in technology requiring processes concerning metals that cannot but undoubtedly be proceed under the Ellingham diagram equation of “*G=”H-T’S* (Seetharaman, Seshadri 2005:1) Despite absence of early accounts; a Khiamniunagan Naga village located on the eastern corner close to the Myanmar border called Wui is said to have early practices on iron smelting whose early ancestors used to smelt from an elongated strip like iron which they received from a bog site situated which could be observed even today just right above the village known as ‘Malai Dai’. The surrounding village site when explored led collections to numerous iron smelting slag and identification over its geological mineral formation that consists mainly of greenstone with pelagic sediments of ophiolite and metamorphic with iron, chromite and limestone. Similar surveys on site exploration were made to another such belonging to the Konyak Nagas called Tizit, Namsa located particularly at a residential site with its geological landscape filled mostly with sandy soils where heaps of iron smelted slag formed from magnetite ores were found.

Figure 22.1: Map of Nagaland showing location of Wui and excavated trenches

The surveyed sites at Wui Khaimniungan were archeologically excavated. Archeologically excavations were made at *Malai Dai* (MLD) for procuring the available iron ore that was situated on an elevation of 1721m within coordinates N 26° 0’ 02.9"; E 095° 04’ 28.3". Simultaneously two trenches (Tr-1 of size 2x2m and Tr-2 of size 1x2m) were also archeologically excavated from two different habitation locality of the area (See Fig. 22.1).

Fig. 22.2.a.

Fig 22.2.b.

Fig. 22.3

Fig. 22.2. a&b: Archaeologically excavated Irons Smelting Slags from Wui, Khaimniungan, Nagaland; **Fig. 22.3:** Iron ore sample, *Malie Dai, 2016.*

Table: 22.1

MALAI DAI (MLD)- IRON ORE		
Mineral Group	D=λ/2sinθ	MineralIdentification
Kaolins	7.0379	Kaolinite
Micas	5.0561	Muscovite
Oxides,Hydroxides	4.2475	Quartz
Mica	3.3785	Biotite
Amphiboles	3.1370	Tremolite
Oxides,Hydroxides	2.4535	Goethite
Oxides,Hydroxides	2.2839	Quartz
Oxides,Hydroxides	2.1764	Quartz
Mica	2.0367	Biotite
Kaolins	1.8208	Kaolinite
Kaolins	1.7182	Kaolinite
Kaolin	1.6628	Kaolinite
Kaolin	1.6251	Kaolinite
Oxides,Hydroxides	1.54117	Quartz
Oxides,Hydroxides	1.1069	Hematite
Oxides,Hydroxides	1.2881	Hematite
Oxides,Hydroxides	1.2532	Hematite
Oxides,Hydroxides	1.1863	Hematite
Oxides,Hydroxides	1.1527	Hematite

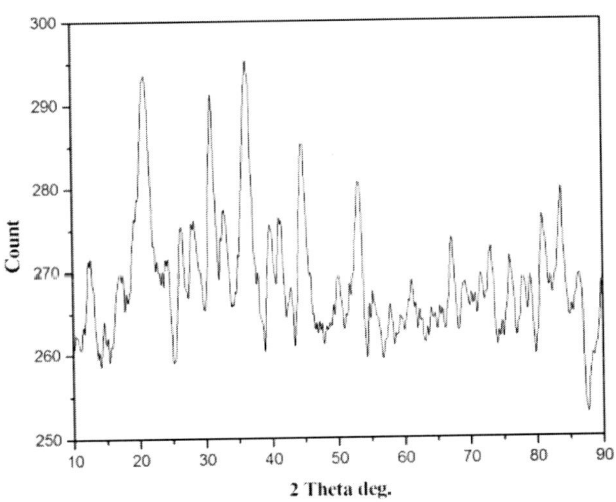

Figure 22.4: XRD Graph on the Malai Dai iron ore

Trench-1 altogether revealed six cultural layers and was excavated to a depth of 216cm yielding cord-mark potteries, animal bones, glass beads, slags(See Fig. 22.2 a&b) (See Fig. 22.3) and lumps of charcoal. Tr-2 also revealing six layers, evidence from this trench includes both plain and cord mark potteries, perforated roof tiles of slates, glass beads and lots of charcoals. Charcoals from both test pits provided C14 dates that extends to cal BC 800 to 753 (Tr-1, Layer 6, *Beta-409506*) and cal AD 980 to 1035 respectively (Tr-2, Layer-6, *Beta-411106*) (Tzudir, T et.al, 2019). Available slag and ore samples from the excavations were further studied under the X-Ray Powdered Diffraction (XRD)(See Table 22.1; also see Fig. 22.4) (See Fig. 22.5), Electrical furnace (see Fig. 22.6) and Field Emission Scanning Electron Microscope (FESEM) (See Fig. 22.7) as both from the treches1 and 2. The XRD confirms considerable amount of iron content marked with hematite followed by rutile, llmentite, dolmite, clinochlore, tremolite and goethite with other quartz minerals such as muscolite, clinchlore et al; all as clearly identifying the usual characteristic one could identify in relations to a bog iron ore as well as from an iron smelting slag.

Fig. 22.5

Fig. 22.6

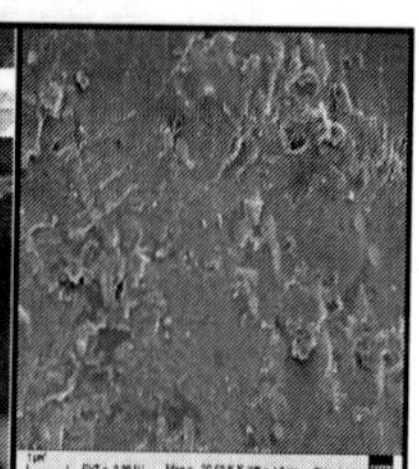

Fig. 22.7

Fig. 22.5: Methods related to iron slag preparation for analysis2016; **Fig. 22.6:** Elelctriacl furnace teston the iron ore from *Malie Dai*2017*;* **Fig. 22.7:** Iron slag sample from T-2 under the Mg-30.53KX, 2017

With the laboratorial chemical analysis results availed on the slag and ore and electrical furnace tests made ways for further experiment to conduct through the traditional means which finally was made following the iron bloom smelting at Wui (See figure). Iron ore from *Malie Dai* were collected at the depth of 5 feet=152.40cm and got smelted under a law shaft cylindrical furnace constructed from surrounding mineral clay soils that are mainly composed of sandy

Fig. 22.8.a. *Fig. 22.8.b.* *Fig. 22.8.c.*

Fig. 22.8:a. Iron bloom smelting at Wui; **b**. The smelted iron sample received from the experiment; **c**.Iron inclusion visible through the available iron bloom, 2019.

lime stones. The iron ores were initially processed by eradicating excessive clay minerals from it followed by roasting. The hematite (FeO) ores were thus smelted between 1078°c to 1090°c where the iron blooms were received which were hammered by giving very low compression where few small iron pieces were successfully smelted (See Fig. 22.8.a,b & c). Among the early Wui settlers used to collect such pieces of smelted iron and further welded by applying a particular clay solution extracted from terminate nest called *lawam* that has considerable amount of minerals and iron content as per the results received from the XRD. The applied lawam on such pieces of smelted iron were further annealed with carbon making the ferrite to austenite before the pieces becomes a lump of considerable size for forging a tool.

Similarly archeological excavations were also made at Tizit, Namsa on two trenches that within coordinates N26°56'.2"; E95°03'11.7". The excavated trenches were both located adjacent to each other. From the trenches extremely fair amount of smiting slag were collected and has identified to have formed from magnetite (FeO) smelting ores. The collected slag and its structures clearly too indicate that it's from tapping as clearly defined by their nodular shapes including visible pores as creations of gaseous traps (See Fig. 22.9.a, and b). However, from the Trench 2, lot-6, on its western side remains of a smelting furnace was recovered with considerable amount of thin sized charcoals, ashy grey soil and small bits of slag inclusions at the depth of 21cm. Charcoals from the located furnace test pit provided through Carbon-

14 confirms with the dates that extends to AD 1426 - 1516 (Tr-2, Layer-2, Beta-524671).Further scientific laboratorial tests were conducted from the collected slag sample analyzed under the Field Emission Scanning Electron (FESEM) (See Fig. 22.10) and Energy Dispersive X-Ray Spectroscopy (EDX) which clearly reveals considerable amount of iron content of about 27.40% in weight with atomic percentage of about 11.27% along with inclusions of other elements. Also looking at the size, depth and area site from where the furnace being recovered also has remains of sewages located at both sides undoubtedly meant for slag exclusion which probably must have been temporarily closed during the smelting operation. Such indications from the available findings clearly reveals the type of low mounted furnace of low shaft (See Fig. 22.11, also see Fig. 22.12).

Fig. 22.9.a.

Fig. 22.9.b.

Fig. 22.10.

Fig. 22.9: a&b: Smelting Slag samples excavated archeologically from Tizit, Namsa, Nagaland; **Fig. 22.10:** FESEMonthe smelting slag from Tizit, Namsa under 10,000 magnification 2019.

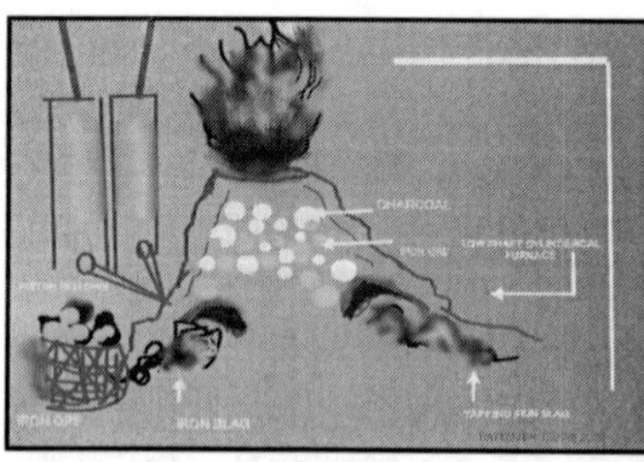

Fig. 22.11

Fig. 22.12

Fig. 22.11: A layout Sketchmade on the Early Naga Iron Smelting Furnace and procures, Tizit Namsa 2020; **Fig. 22.12:** Trench 2 with sketch reconstruction on the smelting furnace on the recovered site, Tizit Namsa 2019.

Observing the evidence from the present findings and whereas also looking at the early Naga iron forging seemed to have lack of reports from the early ethnographers whose records based on absence on smelting led many to presume that blacksmithy among the Naga tribes was relatively a recent craft and iron obtained in scraps was an import from Assam, Manipur and Burma. Similarly devoid of proper understanding on the historical context of the region, there are also passing references to Naga metallurgy that erroneously reports its context from the Neolithic and Chalcolithic stages to Iron Age, as in southwestern part of eastern India (Chattopadhyay and Sengupta 2011: 61-63).

Also besides ethnographic records it becomes deemed necessity as to have a clear understanding over the knowledge related to early iron forging technology. Early Konyak and Khaimniungan forging job seemed to be of more than annealing and shaping them with hammer blows. It expects a forgeron to be competent enough to identify and understand types and stages of an iron metal when at the time of forging including other tasking force visa-a-vie quenching, tempering, polishing and edging. It needs a forgeron to be scientifically knowledgeable enough to observe situations of the processing metal so as to be able to intelligently deduct the arousing connected facts which undoubtedly has been prevalent within early Naga iron forging technology. Intuitions over such innate processes connected to early Naga iron forging allowed for an attempt to be made on a traditional iron forging under experiment confining to one of the ancient Naga dao (See Fig. 22.13; also see Fig. 22.14).

Fig. 22.13

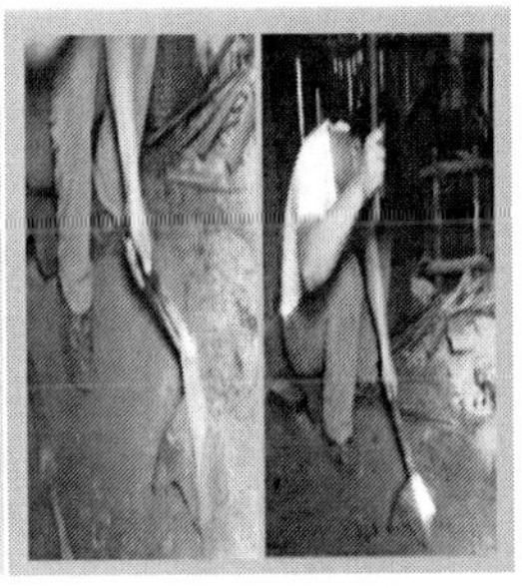

Fig. 22.14

Fig. 22.13: Expeimental iron forging technology on the Naga Machate 2019;
Fig. 22.14: Handson activity on Wui Khainmniungan Machete forging at Wui, 2018.

The experimental forging method was followed by annealing the metal to malliate which thereafter was applied with compressive hammering technique. Such a method is applied for a considerable period of time starting again by putting the iron metal into the hearth which is repeated made whenever it goes out of heat till it gets the desired shape of a *dao* (machete).Reasons behind the constant contact of iron metal to hot charcoal inside the heart is a way of significant means of hardening the state of iron metal transforming it into iron carbon alloy through cooling and heating cycles. The carbon drastically affects the crystalline structure of an iron transforming its metallic atomic structures to austenite (Face-centered cubic). It allows the metallic body centered cubic which is the ferrite is made to transform into face centric cubic (austenite) whose body's packing pattern is led to open up with spaces for the crystal structure intercession of atoms to take place which are smaller than iron but still can be fit in thereby allowing the austenite to have higher solubility of carbon over the ferrite. Such a process is similarly applied among the early Konyak and Khiamniungan Naga iron forging method (See Fig. 22.15). The hands-on experiment also allows one to learn the correct techniques on handling a hammer during forging. Actual technique in handling an early Naga stone hammer according to Khoatsu; a Wui forgenor is to hold right below between the tip sections of its handle by not giving too hard but a considerable amount of grip supplied through the palm sections of thenar *adductor*, *pollicus* and *hypothenar* muscles. This allows balance in weight for a hammer to utilize its potential to maximum by maintaining the rhythmic motion between the user and the tool which would otherwise led to injury one's wrist by rapturing the *palamaris longus tendon* (See Fig. 22.16). Once the iron is shaped and made into a considerable amount to hardness it is further heated to a much higher degree which is than swiftly followed by immersing into the cold water. The water over the surface of hot iron is slightly made to immerse for two to three times till it gets quenched which is another means to harden the metal allowing a drastic change in the micro crystal structure to martensite concentrating more on the edging side section of the *dao* to be more toughen (See Fig. 22.17).

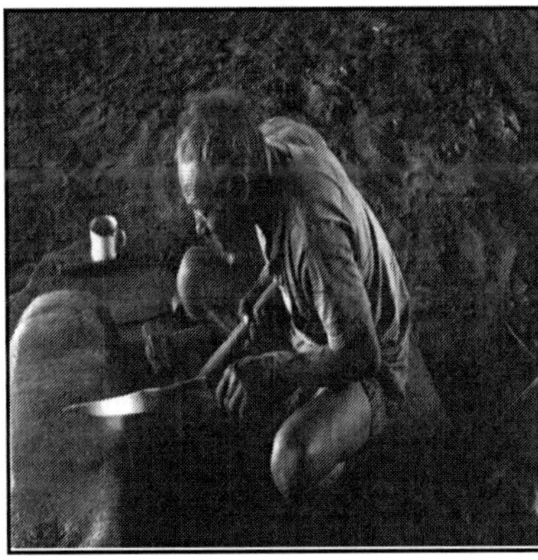

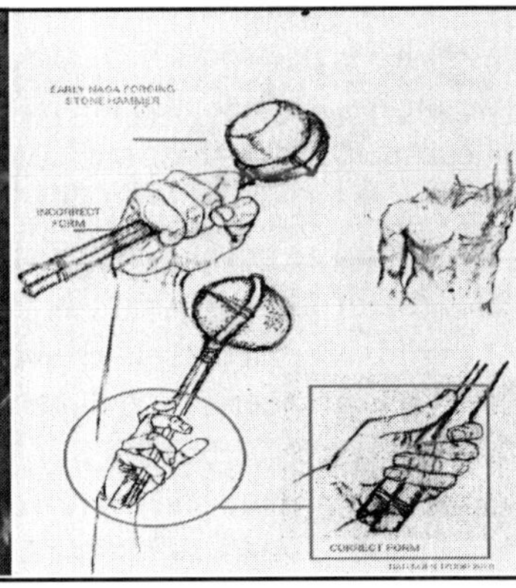

Fig. 22.15 *Fig. 22.16*

Fig. 22.15: The Konyak Monyakshiu Smith, 2018; **Fig. 22.16:** Layout Sketch made on the handling technique of early Naga Stone Forging Hammer, 2020.

Among the early Wui Khaimniungan forgerons their method after quenching is further followed by polishing the edging section which is partially edged. Thereafter the metal is given the heat treatment and this is where the edged section is finely shaped through hammering transforming its crystal structures to slightly cementite as towards completion of tempering method. Such a stage is considered to be most delicate part that has the tendency to get brittle and cracks over the surface metal (See Fig. 22.18) if accurate procedures are not applied which comes only with experience.

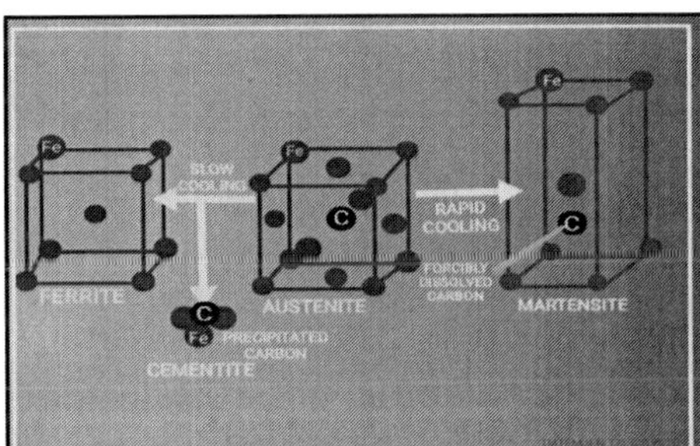

Fig. 22.17 *Fig. 22.18*

Fig. 22.17: Graph on the changes in atomic microstructure associated to iron forging technology, 2020; **Fig. 22.18:** The crack and brittle marks on the Wui iron machete sample, 2019.

Another earliest metal technologies especially associated with the early Konyaks would be referred to bronze/ brass casting technology. Casting usually adopted among the ancient worlds involved three basic metal methods vis-à-vis sand casting, investment casting and permanent casting. Methods similar to such ancient forms especially adopted among early Konyak Nagas were the sun baked clay mold practiced in the form of stone clay mold brass casting. Amongst such early Konyak metallic cast practices, the stone clay mold has become a lost tradition at a very early period. Methods involved in such early stone clay mold include pieces of brasses that were melted down and poured into a stone or clay mold and is greased with pig fats as one ways of making ornaments (Jacobs 1990, Tzudir 2017).

One should know that metallic alloys are by far the most complex compound of chemical arrangements where brasses amongst such metallic character are readily and popularly recognized but equally difficult to define with accuracy. Absence of scientific knowledge in relations to any form of metal or alloy would led remain an inconceivable task to describe such metallic state (Pranab & Sengupta 2011:1). With due such valid queries under considerations an experimental research was made over the present 'extinct' indigenous stone clay mold brass casting (See Fig. 22.19). It thus required the need to construct an efficient furnace which was made into an enclosed rounded shape ran to be run by a hand crank air bellower (See Fig. 22.20). Here the pieces of brass were melted under 838°C followed by pouring it from a metal container into the clay dough impression made

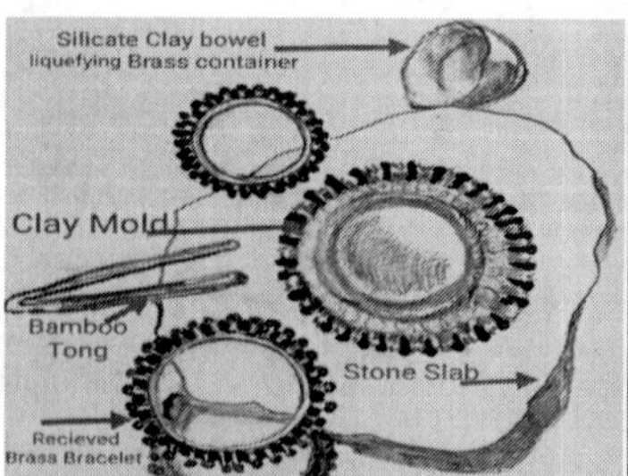

Fig. 22.19

Fig. 22.20

Fig. 22.19: a sketch layout on the extinct stone clay mold casting, 2019;
Fig. 22.20: Brass Casting furnace, 2019.

from a miniature Christ figure. Once the metal figure is cooled and solid from the impression, it is further polished thereby creating it into a wonderful piece of art work.

Such hands-on brass casting however helps one to differentiate between varied casting tools, metals and correct heat temperature. It is a type of technological procedure that also equally helps one to indentify technical failures associated to casting which were in fact considered to be Fig. 22.21.abc the works of certain creative forces that had the

Fig. 22.21.a *Fig. 22.21.b* *Fig. 22.21.c*

Fig. 22.21.a,b & c: A Site of Procedures undertaken in another Early Naga Casting Method called the Lost Wax Brass Casting, Wangti Konayk, Nagaland 2018.

capacity of availing both good and evil consequences as according to the early Konyaks and Khiamniungans which they believed must be controlled for which early Naga brassmith attached several social and spiritual restrictions. Casting is an intricate job that requires concentrations and inspiration which the early Naga brassmith probably knew about the difficulties and as cannot be possible in a distractive atmosphere where a technology based on pyrotechniques and elemental substances always have the tendency technical failures if prior precautionary measures are not made (See Fig. 22.21).

Answers to such technical failures received is due to contacts with particles such as charcoal, dust, ash and stone along with scientific reasons being due to higher percentage in zinc as in comparison to amount of copper with also due to the nature of zinc led the cause for brittle marks and cracks on the finished brass metal item (Merica and Woodward 1917: 17) (See Fig. 22.22,a,b,&c)

Fig. 22.22.a *Fig. 22.22.b* *Fig. 22.22.c*

Fig. 22.22.a,b&c: The technical failures associated with Brass Casting, 2015 & 2018.

The experiment thus helps one to learn the art of communicating with varied senses involving heat, smell, sound and color as part of early Konyak metal casting (See Fig. 22.23). Early Konyaks treasured brass for its gold like color, workability, hardness and corrosion resistance. Besides casting there were also cold works and warm forging significantly applied to brass in creating ornamental jewelry practiced among both early Konyak and Khaimniunagn Nagas.

Conclusion

Nagas in relation to early metal technologies are endowed with varied insights requiring to be explored. Iron metal in particular was of significant means that greatly allowed the community to survive for them to exist as settled community. It helped in molding their identity that made them what they are today as a unique race. Metal being considered a valuable item and even more scarce in an era when the Nagas first made their early settlements probably made the lives of those few who knew and carried the technology were in a state that even they could not continue to sustain such practices. Reasons associated to varied restrictions being imposed upon spiritual beliefs in connection to metal practices also seemed quite deliberate in certain case as though probably meant to control and bring orders to such works so as to confine their trait within the few specific working group only who actually possessed knowledge related beyond forging that rather fairly made them kryptonite and compelled others to be solely dependent upon them. And besides other reasons this could be one of central cause for the extinctions of certain significant early metal practices as in likely to smelting. Cultural trait to such stealth could

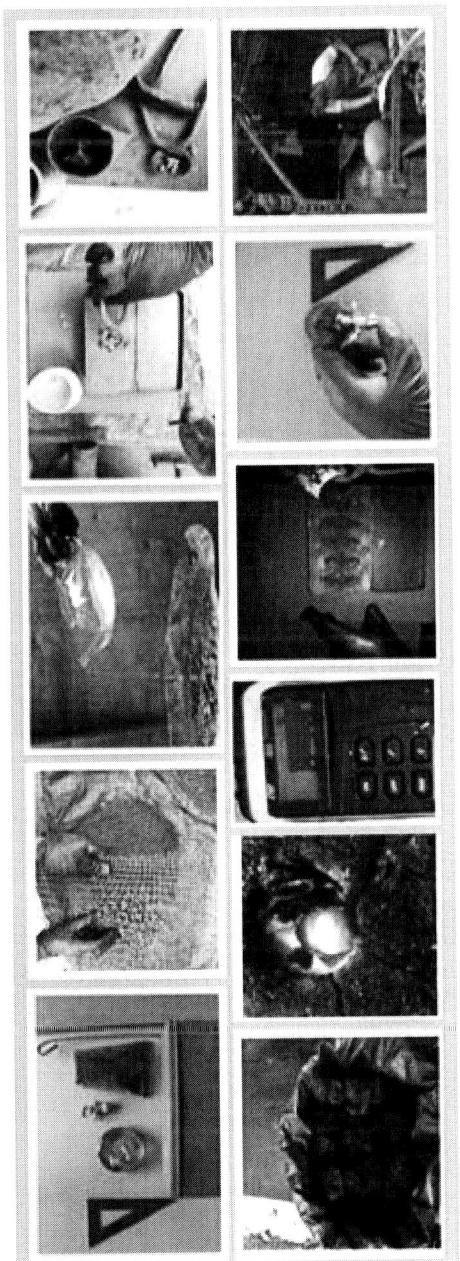

Fig. 22.23: *Experimental technology conducted on the Extinct Traditional Stone Clay Mold Brass Casting, 2019.*

clearly be observed even today besides reasons associated long lost memories accountable to oral tradition. The only way to understand the indebt knowledge on early forging and casting metal technologies of the Nagas is to learn the technology possibly by means of doing. Also present challenges could thus be secured only through collective efforts made through interdisciplinary approach. Available data from the recent studies thus shed some lights especially on the early Naga iron smelting tradition though it thus too require more systematic researches that would possibility identify and connect to even other potential early sites beyond the present Konyak and Khiamniungan regions of Nagaland.

References

Chattopadhya, Pranab K and Sengupta, G.2011. *History of Metals in Eastern and Bangladesh*, Pentagon Press, New Delhi: 1.

Craddock (1978) 'The composition of copper alloys used by the Greek, Etruscan and Roman civilisations', *Journal of Archaeological Science,* 5, 1-16.

Craddock (1995) Early Metal Mining and Production, Edinburg University Press.

Dutta, H.N. 2012. History, Art and Archaeology of Doiyang Dhansiri Valley. Assam, Guwahati: EBH.

Haimendorf, C.F. von. 1936-37. Tour Diary of Fürer-Haimendorf (26.6.1936-11.7.1937) (834/1872) (translated from German by Dr. Ruth Barnes), SOAS Library: London (http://himalaya.socanth.cam.ac.uk/collections//anag/record/r68438.htmal).

Haimendorf, C.F. von 1939. The Naked Nagas. London: Methuen & Co.

Haimendorf, C.F. von 1969. The Konyak Nagas: An Indian Frontier Tribe. New York: Rinehart and Winston.

Haimendorf, C.F. von 1976. Return to the Naked Nagas: An Anthropologist's view of Nagaland 1936-1970. Delhi: Vikas Publishing House.

Hudson, Bob.2006. 'Iron in Myanmar', *Enchanting Myanmar,* Vol. 5:6 9n. p. (Https://www.researchgate.net/publication/285136314)

Hummel, R.H.1998.Understanding material Science, New York.

Jacobs, J. (1990). The Nagas- Society, Culture, and the Colonial Encounter. London: Thames and Hudson Ltd. Thames and Hudson Ltd, London.

Leach, E.R. 1970. Political Sytems of Highland Burmese- a Study of Kachin Social Structure, the Athlone press, London

Merica, Paul D. and Woodward. 1917. Failure of Brass. Washington Government printing, USA: 3.

Mills, J.P. 1922. The Lhota Naga. London: Macmillan & Co.

Mills, J.P. 1926. The Ao Nagas. London: Macmillan & Co. Mills, J.P. 1937. The Rengma Nagas. London: Macmillan & Co.

Prakash, B and Tripathi, V 1986. Iron technology in Ancient, Historical Metallurgy. n.p.

Seetharaman, Seshadri 2005. Fundamentals of Metallurgy, Woodhead Publishing Limited and CRC press, n.p.

Suliga, I. and Prokop, P. March 2013. Two Thousand Years of Iron smelting in The Khasi Hills Megahalaya, North East India, *Current Science* Vol. 104: 761-768.

Tzudir, T. 2017. 'Brass Metallic art of the early Konyak Naga', *History Today* 18: 116.

Tzudir, T., Jamir, and Sharma. (2019). Analayisis of Iron ore, iron slag and soils of termite nest from wui village, Nagaland, India. *Current science,* 116, 312-313.

Index

B

C

E

F

J

K

L

M